LAWYERS, NETWORKS AND PROGRESSIVE SOCIAL CHANGE

Written by a lawyer who works at the intersection between legal education and practice in access to justice and human rights, this book locates, describes and defines a collective identity for social justice lawyering in the UK.

Underpinned by theories of cause lawyering and legal mobilisation, the book argues that it is vital to understand the positions that progressive lawyers collectively take in order to frame the connections they make between their personal and professional lives, the tools they use to achieve social change, as well as ethical tensions presented by their work.

The book takes a reflexive ethnographic approach to capture the stories of 35 lawyers working to positively transform law and policy in the UK over the last 50 years. It also draws on a wealth of primary sources including case reports, historic campaign materials and media analysis alongside wider ethnographic interviews with academics, students and lawyers, and participant observation at social justice conferences, workshops and events.

The book explains the way in which lawyers' networks facilitate their collective positioning and influence their strategic decision making, which in turn shapes their interactions with social activists, with other lawyers and with the state itself.

Lawyers, Networks and Progressive Social Change

Lawyers Changing Lives

Jacqueline Kinghan

•HART•

OXFORD • LONDON • NEW YORK • NEW DELHI • SYDNEY

HART PUBLISHING
Bloomsbury Publishing Plc
Kemp House, Chawley Park, Cumnor Hill, Oxford, OX2 9PH, UK
1385 Broadway, New York, NY 10018, USA
29 Earlsfort Terrace, Dublin 2, Ireland

HART PUBLISHING, the Hart/Stag logo, BLOOMSBURY and the Diana logo are trademarks of Bloomsbury Publishing Plc

First published in Great Britain 2021

A catalogue record for this book is available from the British Library.

Library of Congress Cataloging-in-Publication data

Names: Kinghan, Jacqueline, author.

Title: Lawyers, networks and progressive social change : lawyers changing lives / Jacqueline Kinghan.

Description: Oxford, UK ; New York, NY : Hart Publishing, an imprint of Bloomsbury Publishing, 2021. | Based on author's thesis (doctoral - Goldsmiths, University of London, 2019) issued under title: Lawyers changing lives : a narrative study of progressive lawyering (1968–2018). | Includes bibliographical references and index.

Identifiers: LCCN 2021008440 (print) | LCCN 2021008441 (ebook) | ISBN 9781509938094 (hardback) | ISBN 9781509950089 (paperback) | ISBN 9781509938117 (pdf) | ISBN 9781509938100 (Epub)

Subjects: LCSH: Public interest law—Great Britain. | Cause lawyers—Great Britain. | Social change—Great Britain.

Classification: LCC KD667.P83 K56 2021 (print) | LCC KD667.P83 (ebook) | DDC 344.41—dc23

LC record available at https://lccn.loc.gov/2021008440

LC ebook record available at https://lccn.loc.gov/2021008441

ISBN: HB: 978-1-50993-809-4
ePDF: 978-1-50993-811-7
ePub: 978-1-50993-810-0

Typeset by Compuscript Ltd, Shannon

Preface: A Legal Past and Present

> [S]tories of the actual experiences of clients and lawyers in concrete legal contexts remain few and far between … [yet] only such stories can convey how law is used and experienced by people enmeshed in its workings.[1]

LIKE MANY LAWYERS in this book, I clearly recall the time I decided to become a lawyer. I wasn't very good at Maths or Science and preferred literature and languages. My best friend announced when we were 12 that she wanted to be a doctor and I remember wanting something 'to become'. We were sitting in our car one weekend on a rainy Saturday afternoon in Belfast, Northern Ireland, and my Mum suggested becoming a lawyer and it stuck. At 17, my Dad helped arrange work experience with a lawyer from our church in the small community where I grew up. In her early 30s, Claire had been a barrister and was now teaching at Queens University in Belfast. I went along to her office and one of the first things she asked me was what I thought about the Bloody Sunday Inquiry, which at the time proposed to investigate the unlawful deaths of civilians killed by British soldiers during the Troubles.

I remember not being very sure what it was at first but when she told me, and probed me, I realised – perhaps for the first time – that I had opinions about matters outside of the relatively closed sphere of my school and church upbringing. I relished the opportunity to deal in principle and objectivity but also to inject, simply by someone asking me what I thought, my own reasoning and perspective. She asked me whether I thought we should investigate deaths at the hands of the state? Why? Who has an interest in the investigation and does it matter? I realised that I cared about the answers to these questions. Claire was – and is – an intelligent and compassionate lawyer with a heart for equality and fairness. I am in danger of sounding trite I know, but she inspired me. I began to see that law might have a valuable role to play in society and that it might have the potential to lessen the impact of injustice on peoples' lives. I wondered then who the lawyers doing this sort of work were and where I could find them.

While my family was relatively apolitical, I look back and see that growing up in a small church community instilled a strong sense of altruism and fairness. I was also attracted to people who were passionate and engaged in what they did. Throughout my studies, I gravitated towards role models who provided an example of what it was to be a social justice lawyer or simply a new way of thinking about law's role in society. I found my early years of study at Edinburgh

[1] Martha Minow and Gary Bellow, *Law Stories* (University of Michigan Press, 1998) 1. Reproduced with permission from University of Michigan Press.

University a little dry but was immersed, in my third year on exchange in Montreal, in critical legal studies with particularly quirky and intriguing professors. I ended up working in rural First Nations Reserves at the end of my year of study where I participated in a sentencing circle, visited courts and prisons, flew in an airplane with a local judge across the beautiful Canadian expanse and thought about the possibilities of the law in achieving social change because of the commitment and dedication of another lawyer who inspired me. When I left he gave me a beautifully worn copy of Moby Dick and inside it he had written 'To Jacqui, the best student I've ever had, no matter how difficult the circumstances we must always strive to do the right thing'.

I can look at this inscription now with a smile. As law students and lawyers we seek approval. We are driven by doing a job that matters, but also by doing it well. I'm not sure how much Pat realised that by writing to me in this way he was giving me the courage and impetus I needed to move onto work that I valued. That was a Masters in the US and it was there that I focused on human rights and child law clinical programmes,[2] providing the interest and experience to return to the UK and set up similar projects some years down the line. To get there, I experienced a turning point. In fact, when I look back I see it as a wrong turn, but one that planted a seed of interest in the culture and values of legal practice that lie at the heart of this study.

The path I took next was to train as a barrister in a set of Chambers that didn't represent my own values. They did excellent work, and I was attracted to that, but I spent my training period never quite feeling at home and not being able to put my finger on why. The barristers I worked with spoke with an accent I didn't recognise and moved in social circles I didn't understand. Coming from Northern Ireland this was to be expected, but the network never felt like one in which I could belong. Few barristers there saw the law, or the transformative potential of the law, the way I did and it felt isolating. Unlike some other sets of Chambers, I looked around and couldn't find anyone in this particular environment to inspire me. I realise now I was looking in the wrong place.

Rather than making an application to stay in Chambers I secured a role at the House of Lords (as it then was, now the UK Supreme Court) to work for an appellate judge. While it was an elite institution of course, it was an incredible experience and the judge I mainly worked for, Lord Rodger, was an encouraging, kind man of huge intellect but with an affable sense of humour that seemed to temper its intimidating weight. Perhaps precisely because of my earlier experiences I wanted to feel 'at home' and this became an important determining factor in the places I would pursue employment.

I took up a post at UCL Faculty of Laws coordinating pro bono projects and later establishing the UCL Centre for Access to Justice, concentrating on

[2] Law school clinics provide free legal advice to members of the community or otherwise work in partnership with charities and NGOs on projects predominantly, although not exclusively, in pursuit of social justice ends.

teaching and facilitating free legal advice projects in the community. I was, and still am, driven by a desire to expose students to the operation of law in the real world and to allow them to make decisions about their future careers based on context and experience. Day to day, I immersed myself in working together with lawyers in charities engaged in strategic litigation and challenging legal aid cuts but found that I wanted to explore and write about what we were doing and why. I always felt there was comparatively little sociological research in the UK on lawyers working in the public interest. I would teach studies on equivalent lawyers in the US, their movements and what motivates and sustains them. While there are some illuminating studies of discrete corners of practice in the UK, I could find nothing comprehensive across practice sites or periods of time leaving me to wonder what connections exist between the different types of work that progressive lawyers do.

I felt strongly that the enthusiasm, passion and engagement of my students should not rest in a theoretical vacuum. Many of the leading lights of the law centre movement in the late 1970s and early 1980s were retiring and amidst increasing cuts to legal aid and shifts in the work of charities, NGOs and legal aid firms I found myself asking, *what will sustain this work in future?* For the students in my classroom, the next generation of lawyers, surely this was the critical point. If people, relationships, and the culture of progressive practice played as important a role as I suspected it did then: *how do we collectively define ourselves? How has that changed over time? How can we better align legal education to the work we do? What challenges do we face? What ethical frameworks do we adopt?* I was therefore drawn to exploring the rich history of progressive legal practice as it seemed important to look to the past in order to situate the present and future, especially so at a time of cuts to social welfare, legal aid, proposed abolition of the Human Rights Act and Brexit. Amidst pressure, uncertainty and change it seems an important time to look for common threads in our stories.

Acknowledgements

I OWE A great debt to the lawyers who participated in this study without whom it would not have been possible. I thank you for your willingness and openness in sharing your stories and hope my own interpretation and critical analysis have given voice to the pursuit of social justice that your stories represent. I am indebted to Professor Kate Nash who believed in this project from its early conception and supported me throughout by giving thoughtful guidance, encouragement and inspiration at every stage of the doctoral thesis from which it grew. Thank you also to Dr Brian Alleyne for guidance on narrative research methods and to my thesis examiners, Professor Andrew Francis and Dr Kiran Grewal, for such an engaging and thought-provoking viva voce examination. I am grateful to Peter Kandler, Sue James, The Boar Newspaper (University of Warwick) and Fiona Bawdon for permission to use images. Thank you also to Michigan University Press, Oxford University Press, Thomson Reuters and the Hamlyn Foundation for permission to use epigraph quotations (in the preface, chapters two, six and nine) and to the AHRC for financial support. I am grateful to Sasha Aristotle for her excellent research assistance.

I wish to thank my colleagues and friends for sustenance, humour, intellectual challenge and, at times, a roof over my head during my travels. A special thank you to Professor Lisa Vanhala, Professor Kathryn Hollingsworth, Dr Anna Donovan, Rachel Knowles, Shiva Riahi, Fiona McFarlane and Jemma Neville. My thanks extend to Lisa Vanhala and the anonymous reviewers for taking the time to read and providing invaluable comments on the draft manuscript. Responsibility for remaining errors is my own. To my wider family, I'm indebted to you for love, support and encouragement. To Rob, Alfred and Edith, thanks always for laughter at the end of long days and for the sense of perspective you bring. It is to them that this book is dedicated.

Table of Contents

1

Introduction

USING NARRATIVE RESEARCH methodology, the central aim of this book is to investigate whether a network-based progressive lawyering movement exists in the UK. In view of this aim, and informed by the theoretical framework outlined in chapter two, the wider research questions underpinning this study are as follows:

1. What stories do lawyers tell about how they pursue social change?
2. How do they construct and negotiate their identity as progressive lawyers?
3. How do they describe the tools they use to achieve social change?
4. How do they perceive professional ethical tensions in their work?
5. How do they think of and construct the challenges to sustaining progressive lawyering in future?

This is not a study of the success or failure of the tools that lawyers use, but of the processes by which lawyers construct and negotiate how and why they use them across their networks. I am especially concerned with the difference that a collective progressive lawyering identity might make to both legal education and practice in the UK. As I will explore, the professional lives of lawyers have been subject to considerable change over time but the values and motivations underpinning their work remain constant. These values are strongly held and form an important link between personal and professional life, such that they are often described in emotional terms. While scholars have traditionally viewed progressive lawyers, and cause lawyers, as being on the 'fringe' or 'edge' of the legal profession,[1] I am interested in where *lawyers* perceive themselves to be situated in relation to one another, the rest of the profession and the state itself. I therefore analyse participants' experiences of unique periods in legal and social history, weaving both personal and professional narratives and providing contemporary analysis of their accounts.[2] The book documents lawyers' perspectives across a spectrum of both strategic[3] and high-volume day-to-day

[1] Richard Abel, 'Lawyers and the Power to Change' (1985) 7 *Law and Policy* 5. See also Andrew Francis, *The Edge of Law: Emergent and Divergent Models of Legal Professionalism* (Routledge, 2011).

[2] Michael Kelly, *Lives of Lawyers Revisited* (University of Michigan Press, 2007).

[3] I refer here to strategic litigation, which seeks to impact a wider group of people than those directly involved in the case itself. See further discussion in ch 2.

casework in areas of law that we now understand as social welfare and human rights (although this is not necessarily how they were understood in the early decades of the study).

Throughout the book I explore in depth the lives of 35 progressive lawyers on the left of the political spectrum who seek to transform both law and policy through the causes they pursue and the clients they represent. In my wider ethnography I draw on interviews and field notes from many other encounters with progressive law students, lawyers and campaigners through my role teaching and working in partnership with charities and NGOs at the UCL Centre for Access to Justice.[4] I use the term 'progressive' in order to capture a diffuse group of lawyers all on the left working to advance social change.[5] Importantly, the term has the potential to embrace a broad range of legal activity across a variety of subject areas[6] and practice-sites in the UK (see chapter three for full discussion of the identification of progressive lawyers). While the terms 'social justice', 'human rights' or 'activist' lawyer might adequately describe some participants in the study, the term 'progressive' conveys participants' collective focus on ensuring that institutions are held to account and that governments have a role to play in addressing unfairness in society.[7] It also reflects the shared desire to shift resources and power from the top of social hierarchies to those experiencing exclusion and disadvantage at the bottom.[8] The term also captures lawyers working as both radicals and reformers,[9] and further connects the research to critical legal studies thus encapsulating the rejection of an idealised version of the law that is separate from politics.[10]

Chapter two sets out the theoretical and historical foundations of the study. Drawing upon cause lawyering literature, against the backdrop of broader theories of public interest lawyering and legal mobilisation, it considers the different tools that lawyers use to achieve change. In view of the unique relationship between lawyers and the state by the UK's legal aid model, the chapter sets out its historical development in order to understand the changing context of progressive legal practice. I argue that in view of the current context of

[4] Between 2015 and 2017 in addition to 35 in-depth semi-structured narrative interviews I conducted 18 further formal interviews in my wider ethnographic fieldwork. I also gathered field notes from ethnographic research encounters with lawyers, academics and law students throughout and drew upon participant observation at nine social justice events as part of the study (conferences, workshops, panel discussions).

[5] Abel (n 1) 5.

[6] These subject areas are human rights as well as related social and economic rights. In practice this might include, but is not limited to, equality rights and freedom from discrimination, right to benefit entitlements, right to housing, right to education, environmental rights, freedom of expression, privacy rights and rights associated with dignity and the right to a fair trial.

[7] Jonathan Rowson, '*What is a progressive*?' (Open Democracy, 11 June 2015), available at www.opendemocracy.net/en/opendemocracyuk/what-is-progressive/.

[8] Scott Cummings, 'Movement Lawyering' (2017) *University of Illinois Law Review* 1645, 1648.

[9] Kate Nash, *The Political Sociology of Human Rights* (Cambridge University Press, 2015) 172.

[10] David Kairys, *The Politics of Law: A Progressive Critique* (Basic Books, 1998).

constrained resource and wider pressure on the justice system, the 'conservative' and 'radical' spectrum of lawyering traditionally outlined in the literature has become more nuanced for progressive lawyers in the UK.[11] Chapter two also introduces the central theme of identity and considers collective identity and social movements as a basis for delineating the work of progressive legal practitioners and the personal and social interactions that lie at the heart of their casework, policy advocacy and campaigns. I outline in this context the value of a network-based approach as a basis for identifying a social movement of progressive lawyers in the UK.[12] As I argue in this chapter, theoretical insights can be derived from the controversies within cause lawyering theory and I set out the relevance of these controversies with a focus on ethical and professional critiques.[13] The chapter explores whether progressive lawyers transcend traditional ethical boundaries by striving to achieve social change and the extent to which their values and beliefs might inform, for example, their case selection or involvement in wider campaigns.[14] By drawing together the literature on cause lawyering, legal mobilisation and social movements I shift the focus to lawyer *motivation* within and across progressive legal networks; and interrogate the difference collective identity might make to lawyer's strategies to pursue social change. Finally, the chapter considers the extent to which alternative visions of lawyering might assist in overcoming these controversies and their relationship to legal education.[15]

Chapter three explains the research process and outlines how participants were identified for the study. Many are considered elite in their field: they hold senior positions in private practice or in charities and NGOs working across the policy and practice of human rights. Others are highly esteemed within the progressive legal movement for their work at grassroots level daily representing vulnerable clients in law centres and legal aid law firms. Five subsets of progressive legal practice are delineated: Barrister-Campaigner, Legal Aid Lawyer, Charity/NGO Lawyer, Law Centre Lawyer and Law Clinic Lawyer. There is of course much overlap between these types of progressive lawyering, and movement between them, but I demonstrate how participants in the study, irrespective of labelling, tend to recognise lawyers within and across these subsets as forming part of a movement of lawyers 'like us'. The chapter explains how the subsets of

[11] Thomas Hilbink, 'You Know the Type: Categories of Cause Lawyering' (2004) 19 *Law & Social Inquiry* 657; Austin Sarat and Stuart Scheingold (eds), *Cause Lawyering: Political Commitments and Professional Responsibilities* (Oxford University Press, 1998).

[12] Mario Diani, 'The Concept of a Social Movement' (1992) 40(1) *Sociological Review* 1; Mario Diani and Douglas McAdam, *Social Movements and Networks: Relational Approaches to Collective Action* (Oxford University Press, 2003).

[13] Andrew Boon, 'Cause Lawyers and the Alternate Ethical Paradigm' (2004) 7 *Legal Ethics* 250; Robert Rosen, 'On the Social Significance of Cause Lawyering' (2000) 3(2) *Legal Ethics* 169.

[14] These activities are explained and delineated further in ch 2.

[15] Gary Bellow, 'Steady Work: A Practitioner's Reflections on Political Lawyering' (1996) *Harvard Civil Rights-Civil Liberties Review* 297; Gerald Lopez, *Rebellious Lawyering: One Chicano's Vision of Progressive Law Practice* (Westview Press, 1992).

practice might also be thought of as 'network nodes', which facilitate interactive processes and a shared sense of belonging that is central to the concept of a social movement.[16]

Drawing on narratives from the study chapter four explores whether progressive lawyers share a collective identity. I interrogate the ways in which lawyers describe their own backgrounds and values as both a motivating and sustaining feature in the work they do and set out the relevance of social class, which is a prevalent narrative theme, and widening access to the profession. My aim is to delineate how lawyers in the study collectively frame who they are and their motivations for what they do. The chapter recognises how progressive lawyers engage in processes of social identification from early on in their careers in order to frame a personally meaningful but collectively experienced turning point away from corporate legal practice. A key finding is the relevance of social class to constructions of narratives around pathways to practice and the connections made between personal experience – often expressed in emotional terms as anger at the experience of injustice – and a desire to make a difference in one's professional life for others. Across class backgrounds, and despite divergent approaches, I explain that a collective identity exists for progressive lawyers as illustrated by their shared constructions of turning points, values and motivations within and across their networks.

Chapter five addresses the ways in which lawyers construct the tools they use to achieve social change and identifies the relationship between those tools and state funded legal aid. As explored in chapter two, the relationship between progressive lawyers and the state is salient in view of changes to legal aid, challenges by way of judicial review and continuing activism by lawyers on access to justice and human rights issues. Building on this discussion, I seek to explore narratives that describe the changing perceptions and constructions of tools for change over the five decades of the study. I describe lawyers' perceptions of their relationship with the state in their roles as campaigners and how those campaigns relate to strategic litigation. The chapter outlines the historic divide between the pursuit of strategic litigation and high volume casework and considers lawyers' narratives in relation to both. My focus is on the strategies that lawyers pursue and what they *believe* they are accomplishing.[17] I argue that networks are an important factor in understanding lawyers' collective beliefs about the strategies they adopt and outline how narrative analysis reveals a deeper understanding of the relationship between the different tactics lawyers use and the collaborations that exist to support them. As such, I illustrate how the distinctions between different types of cause lawyering activities have become more nuanced in recent

[16] Mario Diani, 'Social Movements and Networks' in the *Blackwell Encyclopaedia of Sociology* (Wiley and Sons, 2015).

[17] Ann Southworth, 'Lawyers and the Myth of Rights in Civil Rights and Poverty Practice' (1991) 8 *Boston University Public Interest Law Journal* 469.

years by virtue of the access to justice crisis as a result of, for example, cuts to legal aid and wider austerity reforms.

In chapter six the exploration of collective identity is developed by analysing the ways in which progressive values are instilled in legal education. I analyse narratives in the study that draw on participants' own experiences of legal education across different contexts and periods of time. The theme of social class is prevalent again and experiences of exclusion and their recurrent relevance in later professional life are examined. Throughout the chapter, I explore several contrasting narratives and highlight how experiences studying in the US leads to personally meaningful constructions of law and social change and networks of interaction.[18] One outlying participant in the study is identified whose educational experience in a UK context conveys a similar experience of learning to those who have studied in the US, and this narrative is explored in depth by way of comparison. I seek here to begin to outline the ways in which a renewed cultural, experiential and critical approach to legal education[19] might develop lawyers' consciousness of law and social change. The chapter begins to highlight the ways in which such collective consciousness might better sustain the future of progressive lawyering despite pressures in the contemporary context, which are discussed further in chapter eight.

In chapter seven I explore how participants in the study construct and negotiate ethical tensions in their work in order to contribute to the body of knowledge in relation to professional and ethical controversies outlined in chapter one. My focus rests on the ways in which the representation of the progressive social self serves to embed professional ethical controversy. As this chapter shows, drawing out and confronting tension in legal ethical decision making can be uncomfortable but I argue that the silence, and discomfort, is in itself a resource to be drawn upon in order to better understand lawyers' engagement with ethical rules. In my analysis, I outline three distinct approaches to the challenge of maintaining neutrality, considering in particular controversy around the cab rank rule for barristers and the (separate but related) ethical requirements of independence for solicitors. I describe these approaches to ethical decision making for progressive lawyers as: *resolute*, *constrained* and *conflicted*. I intend these terms to have multiple meanings to reflect the interplay between the constructions of ethical choices and the political values that lawyers hold. My aim in this chapter is to place ethical rules in a relevant social and cultural context and, as such, my concern is not here with participants' understanding of the ethical rules themselves but how progressive lawyers differentiate themselves in the stories they tell about their ethical decision making. A key finding in this chapter is the

[18] While I did not factor study in the US into my snowballing or sampling I was surprised to discover that 12 of 35 participants had spent formative time there.

[19] Jerome Frank, 'Why Not a Clinical Lawyer School?' (1933) 81(8) *University of Pennsylvania Law Review* 907; Duncan Kennedy, 'Legal Education and the Reproduction of Hierarchy' (1982) 32 *Journal of Legal Education* 591.

explicit way in which participants negotiate their ethical decisions in relation to one another and the extent to which their collective identity might impact upon constructions of their ethicality.

Chapters eight and nine turn to the future of progressive lawyering. I set out what participants perceive to be the challenges to sustaining progressive lawyering in order to explore the ways in which collective identity might make a difference to sustaining it in future. The focus of chapter eight rests on the resource needed to maintain the movement articulated by participants as *funding, passion, perseverance* and *knowledge*. The sociology of emotion features as it relates to issues of emotion management and burnout, as well as to understanding of the group efficacy of social movements.[20] Throughout the chapter I consider how the identity of progressive lawyers is interwoven with the four conceptions of resource articulated by participants and highlight how they are mutually reinforced as values and characteristics perceived to be important to the future of progressive practice and also to collective identity.

The final chapter weaves together the findings of the study in order to develop existing theories of cause lawyering in a UK context. I describe how narrative analysis informs both ethical and professional cause lawyering controversies and contributes to a new understanding of the identity of the progressive legal practitioner by outlining a 'collective legal conscience' in the context of a network based social movement identity.[21] Here, the study findings are analysed together in order to propose a progressive lawyering movement in the UK based on Diani's conception comprising: (i) networks of interaction; (ii) shared beliefs and solidarity; and (iii) collective action on conflictual issues. This chapter also reflects upon the importance of enhancing our understanding of the culture of progressive lawyering in the UK in order to connect theory to practice; and sustain the movement into the future.

[20] Arlie Hochschild, *The Managed Heart: Commercialization of Human Feeling* (University of California Press, 1983).

[21] Kieran McEvoy and Rachel Rebouche, 'Mobilizing the Professions: Lawyers, Politics and the Collective Legal Conscience' in John Morison et al (eds), *Judges, Transition and Human Rights* (Oxford University Press, 2007).

2

The Context and Controversies of Progressive Lawyering

'Lawyers are not simply carriers of a cause but are at the same time its producers: those who shape it, name it and voice it.'[1]

IN THIS CHAPTER I draw on relevant socio-legal literature, as well as historical background, to contextually situate the lawyers in the study and interrogate the sites of resistance and controversy in their work.[2] The literature on cause lawyering[3] and the closely related field of legal mobilisation will be explored. I outline the most relevant ethical and professional critiques within the field, focussing in particular on the UK legal aid context. Finally, this chapter sets out a network-based theory of social movements and collective identity that I argue is pertinent to the identification of progressive legal activity and the interactions that lie at the heart of progressive legal practice.

Cause lawyering literature has traditionally exposed two extreme ends of a spectrum between 'grassroots' at one end and either 'elite'[4] or 'grasstops' at the other,[5] also characterised as 'conservative' and 'radical' cause lawyering.[6] The former refers to, for example, facilitating access to justice through individual advice and representation, while the latter is characterised by human rights

[1] Ronen Shamir and Sara Chinsky, 'Destruction of House and Construction of a Cause: Lawyers and Bedouins in the Israeli Courts' in Austin Sarat and Stuart Scheingold (eds), *Cause Lawyering: Political Commitments and Professional Responsibilities* (Oxford University Press, 1998) 227. Reproduced by permission of Oxford University Press.

[2] Stuart Scheingold, *The Politics of Rights: Lawyers, Public Policy and Political Change* (University of Michigan Press, 2004).

[3] This terminology was first developed in a series of essay volumes edited by Austin Sarat and Stuart Scheingold over two decades from the early 1990s. See, eg, *Something to Believe In: Politics, Professionalism and Cause Lawyering* (Stanford University Press, 2004); *Cause Lawyers and Social Movements* (Stanford University Press, 2006).

[4] Thomas Hilbink, 'You Know the Type: Categories of Cause Lawyering' (2004) 19 *Law & Social Inquiry* 657.

[5] Effie Fokas, 'Directions in Religious Pluralism in Europe: Mobilizations in the Shadow of the European Court of Human Rights Religious Freedoms Jurisprudence' (2015) 4 *Oxford Journal of Law and Religion* 54.

[6] David Luban, 'The Moral Complexity of Cause Lawyers Within the State' (2012) 81 *Fordham Law Review* 705.

(often strategic) casework, policy work or campaigning. These distinctions have also been referred to as different cause lawyering 'models' comprising 'service', 'law reform' and 'organising'.[7] They have been arguably brought into sharp focus in view of increasingly prevalent narratives critical of 'activist lawyers' in the UK public sphere.[8] I argue that the overlap and interplay between different types of progressive lawyering tools has in recent times become more nuanced. Consistent with US literature describing how lawyers' conduct is shaped by norms within their communities of practice[9] and across their networks,[10] I begin to investigate the ways in which my research questions can explore this changing continuum and illuminate our understanding of progressive lawyers and their pursuit of social change.

THE CONTEXT OF PROGRESSIVE LAWYERING

The Development of Legal Aid

There has been a long tradition in the UK of lawyers helping those who cannot otherwise achieve access to justice. This might be due to lack of funds, lack of knowledge or because of a simple lack of faith in the justice system. For centuries, lawyers have spoken a language and upheld a professional norm that enables them to move within legal, administrative and judicial spaces on behalf of others. Today, their practice sites are diverse: some work in charities, NGOs or law centres while others are in private practice committing time to pro bono. Still others work in private law firms dominated by legal aid work. The context of access to justice legal practice has changed considerably over time yet has a deeply embedded history. In order to understand the subsets of progressive activity at the heart of this study, and the links between voluntary and state funded legal service provision, it is useful to set out some of this historical background.

Pro bono legal advice in England and Wales from the turn of the century was extensive compared to some other jurisdictions but the inadequacy of provision after World War II raised early awareness of particular areas of legal need. That identification of need led to the opening of the first Free Legal Advice Centre in South London staffed by volunteers and supported by lawyers.[11] An increase

[7] Gary Bellow, 'Lawyers for a Political Movement: California Rural Legal Assistance'. In Philip Heymann and Lance Liebman (eds), *The Social Responsibilities of Lawyers: Case Studies* (NY Foundation Press, 1988) 22, 23–26.

[8] See, eg, Adam Wagner, 'It's not "activist lawyers" this government hates but the laws themselves' (*New Statesman*, 28 August 2020).

[9] Lynn Mather et al, *Divorce Lawyers at Work: Varieties of Professionalism in Practice* (Oxford University Press, 2001).

[10] John Heinz et al, 'Lawyers of the Right: Networks and Organization' (2007) 32(4) *Law and Social Inquiry* 883.

[11] Robert Egerton, *Legal Aid, The International Library of Sociology* (Oxford University Press, 1945) 29.

in divorce, road accidents, the aftermath of bombings and bad housing led to legal disputes requiring resolution.[12] Thereafter, amidst post war upheaval the welfare state emerged but required a system to fairly administer the allocation of recently instituted welfare entitlements. The Legal Advice and Assistance Act 1949 provided this framework and facilitated a comprehensive package of welfare provision by the state underpinned by principles of fair allocation. Separate systems of legal aid were established in Scotland and Northern Ireland, although some provisions of the 1949 Act could also be applied to those jurisdictions, and the development of each related to the post war welfare state. The intention was therefore that legal aid would rest *alongside* healthcare, education and housing and that it would be widely available and not simply limited to those 'normally classed as poor'.[13] Importantly, those who couldn't afford to pay would receive help for free, while others would pay a scale of contributions depending on their means. The legal profession was to be responsible for administering the scheme and the cost of doing so was borne by the state, with barristers and solicitors receiving 'adequate remuneration' for their services.[14] The allocation of civil legal aid funding eventually rested on two underlying principles: first, whether a legal problem was within *scope* for legal aid and; secondly, whether a person is *eligible* for funding. Scope concerns the type of legal problem and is considered alongside whether the merits of the case justify funding the case. The eligibility test comprises an assessment of both the income and capital of the applicant, supported by relevant evidence.[15] This two-pronged test continues to be one of the most important aspects of legal aid entitlement and a considerable part of the work of legal aid lawyers as they navigate the relevant complex forms and procedures governing its application.

The legal aid system is important in the context of this study because it rests upon notions of social citizenship[16] and led to the emergence of a new legal professional identity 'imbued with a public sector ideology'.[17] It is worth noting that both solicitors and barristers in the UK can pursue government funded legal aid work with the latter tending to represent clients in court, as I explore further in chapter three. The establishment of legal aid and welfare provision were deeply intertwined such that attitudes to legal aid still remain closely linked to attitudes about welfare benefits provision, with changes to the system reflecting the political will of respective governments over time.[18] Against the backdrop of welfare provision, the transition from a pro bono scheme to comprehensive government

[12] ibid.

[13] His Majesty's Government, Report of the Committee on Legal Aid and Legal Advice in England and Wales (HMSO, 1945).

[14] Michael Cross, 'Legal Aid's Founding Text Turns 70' (*The Law Society Gazette*, 28 May 2015).

[15] Michael Zander QC, *The Hamlyn Lectures: The State of Justice* (Sweet and Maxwell, 1999) 7.

[16] Hilary Sommerlad, 'I've Lost The Plot: An Everyday Story of the Political Legal Aid Lawyer' (2001) 28(3) *Journal of Law and Society* 335, 337.

[17] Ole Hansen, 'A Future for Legal Aid?' (1992) 19 *Journal of Law and Society* 85, 93.

[18] I acknowledge here the interconnectedness of welfare rights and other social rights, especially at times of economic crisis that is relevant to the austerity related legal challenges that lawyers in the study pursue: Jeff King, *Judging Social Rights* (Cambridge University Press, 2014).

provision of legal aid is important for two reasons. First, it illustrated well how *voluntary* legal service provision demonstrated a need that should arguably have been borne by the state.[19] Secondly, it provided a framework for state funded legal service provision and helped identify predominant areas of legal advice that should feature within it. That said, not all of the proposals in the 1949 Act came into force: most significantly, the sections concerning state-funded legal centres staffed by salaried lawyers. Historically, state provision did not wholly replace pro bono activities but legal aid provided an important guaranteed safety net for the most disadvantaged in society. At its early inception, some 80 per cent of the population were said to be eligible for means tested legal aid.[20] Although it was never strictly codified, an important legal professional principle also developed that has been adopted by many practitioners in the study to this day: if a potential client is eligible for legal aid a lawyer should not act in a pro bono capacity, but rather let the state fund a specialist lawyer with relevant expertise and experience to deal with the matter. In this basic principle one might arguably detect a hint of the long-standing criticism of legal aid lawyers, and indeed lawyers widely, which is that they hold a strong and impenetrable professional monopoly over the system.[21] Complicating this preferred division between voluntary and state funded advice and representation lie two further developing factors of importance to the study: the allocation of legal aid funding to not-for-profit organisations and the development of strategic litigation within them.

Legal Aid and Strategic Legal Casework

The Law Society of England and Wales persuaded the government that legal aid payments should be made directly to solicitors and barristers.[22] However, there was growing concern in the late 1960s that the legal aid system was not working as intended and was failing to meet the needs of the poorest in society.[23] Influenced by the 'war on poverty' and the civil rights movement in

[19] There is a longstanding tension about the extent to which pro bono should 'plug the gap' left by cuts to legal aid and the extent to which access to justice needs should be met by the government rather than voluntary service provision. See, eg, Richard Abel, 'The Paradoxes of Pro Bono' (2010) 78 *Fordham Law Review* 2443.

[20] Steve Hynes and Jon Robins, *The Justice Gap* (Legal Action Group, 2009).

[21] See, eg, Hilary Sommerlad, 'Managerialism and the Legal Profession: A New Professional Paradigm' (1995) 2 *International Journal of the Legal Profession* 2; Richard Moorhead et al, 'Contesting Professionalism: Legal Aid and Non Lawyers in England and Wales' (2003) 37 *Law & Society Review* 765; Richard Abel, *English Lawyers: Between Market and State* (Oxford University Press, 2003).

[22] This is known as the *judicare* model, a term coined in the US given its similarities to the 'medicare' model of national health provision. See, Tamara Goriely, 'Law for the Poor, The Relationship Between Advice Agencies and Solicitors in the Development of Poverty Law' (1996) 3 *International Journal of the Legal Profession* 215.

[23] Committee of the Society of Labour Lawyers, *Justice for All: Society of Labour Lawyers Report* (Fabian Research Series, 1968).

the US, law centres developed with the aim of using the law as a means of redistributing economic, social and educational advantage.[24] The success of the US neighbourhood law offices demonstrated well the possibilities for community based legal advice that combined individual casework, test case litigation and lobbying for legislative reform.[25] In 1970, the first law centre was established in North Kensington and embedded in the local community. The interplay between legal service provision and community action can be seen in the poster in the image in Figure 1 below ('please come and sign our petition'). Standing in the background of the picture (wearing glasses) is Peter Kandler, a co-founder of North Kensington and a key figure in the law centre movement more widely.[26] He described at the time moving into this area of work because he was 'fed up with rich, obnoxious clients' and wanted to 'help people who were deprived in many ways'.[27] Lawyers at the law centre were clear that they offered a 'different type of legal service … more flexible, informal, more activist, proactive and a more enterprising way of providing legal services'.[28] By 1974 some 15 other law centres were established with a combination of funding from the Home Office's Urban Aid Community Development Programme, local authority funding and charitable grants. A key funder in the early years was the Nuffield Foundation, which funded 'experimental' models such as the Newham Rights Centre and the Adamson Community Law and Advice Centre in Wales, as well as the establishment of Legal Action Group in 1971.[29] These models 'avoided local funding and instead developed from national social reform programs' however, as Garth notes, law centre community action became 'political action or ineffective action' with the former creating 'numerous difficulties with local authorities and national sponsors'.[30] Over time, law centres needed to undertake a substantial amount of legal aid work in order to survive financially.[31] After a successful pilot project the government began to award legal aid work to not-for-profit agencies and not simply those lawyers working in private practice.[32] By the

[24] ibid 37.

[25] Daniel Lowenstein and Michael Waggoner, 'Neighborhood Law Offices: The New Wave in Legal Services for the Poor' (1967) 80(4) *Harvard Law Review* 805.

[26] Sue James, *At the Bar: Be Suspicious of People in Authority (an interview with Peter Kandler)* (*Legal Action Group*, June 2020), available at www.lag.org.uk/article/208445/at-the-bar---be-suspicious-of-people-in-authority-.

[27] British Film Institute Archive, *North Kensington Law Centre Documentary* (BBC, 1973), available at https://player.bfi.org.uk/free/film/watch-north-kensington-law-centre-1973-online.

[28] Oliver Lewis (quoting Michael Zander QC), *Radical Lawyers, Law Centres and an Uncertain Future* (*The Justice Gap*, 28 March 2013), available at www.thejusticegap.com/radical-lawyers-law-centres-and-an-uncertain-future/.

[29] Bryant Garth, *Neighbourhood Law Firms for the Poor: A Comparative Study of Recent Developments in Legal Aid and the Legal Profession* (Sijthoff and Noordhoff, 1980) 61.

[30] ibid 66.

[31] Philip Leask, 'Law Centres in England and Wales' (1985) 7(1) *Law and Policy* 61, 62.

[32] These changes were enacted by the Legal Aid Act 1988 and were part of a wider cost reduction scheme. See, eg, Hilary Sommerlad, 'Some Reflections on Citizenship, Access to Justice and the Reform of Legal Aid' (2004) 31(3) *Journal of Law and Society* 345.

mid-1990s legal aid franchises were awarded to not-for-profit providers, a development described by Smith as 'radical in the sense of promising root and branch reform of legal aid' but 'hardly radical in the sense of progressive'.[33] While for some law centres a focus on high volume individual casework meant a move away from more strategic social change activities;[34] for others, legal aid funding tended to keep them afloat in order to free them to pursue high impact work over and above their day-to-day casework.[35] Historically, legal aid funding did not come without tensions between law centres and the profession at large, which perceived them as 'stirring up political and quasi-political confrontation'.[36] A delicate accommodation had to be reached in the early years so that law centres did not impinge on private legal aid work.[37] The practice of strategic litigation as a tool for change however became possible, in part, through the provision of legal aid funding and the costs protection it afforded.[38]

Figure 1 Kensington Law Centre Image (circa 1973)

[33] Roger Smith, 'Legal Aid on an Ebbing Tide' (1996) 23(4) *Journal of Law and Society* 570, 578.

[34] Mike Stephens, *Community Law Centres: A Critical Appraisal* (Avebury, 1990).

[35] Richard Abel, 'Lawyers and the Power to Change' (1985) 7 *Law and Policy* 5. See also Andrew Francis, *The Edge of Law: Emergent and Divergent Models of Legal Professionalism* (Routledge, 2011) 9. Note however that it was not the original intention that law centres would be predominantly sustained by legal aid income given both the inherent bureaucratic constraints and the risk of competition with the private sector: Committee of the Society of Labour Lawyers (n 23) 41.

[36] The Law Society of England and Wales, *Annual Report* (The Law Society, 1973). See, Roger Smith, 'Clinics in a Cold Climate: Community Law Centres in England and Wales' (1997) 35 *Osgoode Hall Law Journal* 895.

[37] Geoffrey Bindman, 'What made me a legal aid lawyer' (2002) 29(3) *Journal of Law and Society* 510.

[38] For discussion on costs protection see, Ravi Low Beer et al, *Public Law in Clinical Legal Environments* (The Public Law Project, 2018) 10, available at https://publiclawproject.org.uk/wp-content/uploads/2018/04/Public-Law-and-Legal-Advice-Clinics-Final.pdf.

High impact, or strategic, litigation in the public interest describes casework that looks beyond securing a result for an individual client and is aimed at changing wider law, policies or practices.[39] Broadly, it aims to ensure that individuals have access to the courts and the ability to seek redress for what are perceived, or argued to be, unlawful or unreasonable administrative decisions. Therefore, the victims or claimants in a strategic case have usually suffered an abuse or infringement that is suffered by many other people; thus, in the event of a 'win' for a particular client, or group of clients, it can mean success for a much broader group, however, it is worth nothing this is also true of a 'loss'. Organisations might choose to become involved in strategic litigation either by: (i) directly representing a client or group of clients; (ii) taking a case in their own right; or (iii) 'intervening' in a case as a third party to proceedings.[40] Third party interventions are common in (although not limited to) judicial review proceedings and have increased in number in the UK in recent years.[41] They are frequently conducted in appellate courts by charities and NGOs.[42] The intervention is usually made by a barrister, sometimes acting in a pro bono capacity, on behalf of an organisation and rests on either specialist legal expertise in the subject area or unique knowledge of how the decision might impact individuals or particular groups of people through impact evidence.[43] By whichever mechanism chosen the interplay between strategic litigation and progressive lawyering is important. Drawing on Hilbink's typology[44] one might assume strategic litigation rests neatly within elite/vanguard lawyering. However, this book interrogates how it is also perceived valuable by grassroots lawyers and other practitioner subsets, identified and delineated further in chapter three, and its relationship to wider social justice goals. In chapter five I consider how lawyers describe, to themselves and each other, their decision to pursue strategic casework and explore the ways in which strategic decisions are underpinned by socio-political values. This is especially important when analysing the relationship between those values and the prevalent narrative of cuts to legal aid funding.

There has been some contestation as to the role of legal aid funding in constraining cause lawyering in the UK. Boon argued that in the early years of legal aid cause lawyering 'blossomed'[45] but predicted a significant decline

[39] Michael Ramsden and Chris Gledhill, 'Defining Strategic Litigation' (2019) 38(4) *Civil Justice Quarterly* 407.

[40] Justice, *To Assist the Court: Third Party Interventions in the Public Interest* (Justice/Freshfields, 2016).

[41] Harriet Samuels, 'Feminist Activism, Third Party Interventions and the Courts' (2005) 13 *Feminist Legal Studies* 15.

[42] Some common interveners include, for example, the Equality and Human Rights Commission (by virtue of statutory powers under s.30 The Equality Act 2006), Liberty, MIND, Shelter, Just for Kids Law, JUSTICE, The Howard League for Penal Reform, Friends of the Earth and Reprieve.

[43] Samuels (n 41).

[44] Hilbink (n 4).

[45] Andrew Boon, 'Cause Lawyers in a Cold Climate: The Impact of Globalization in the United Kingdom' in Austin Sarat and Stuart Scheingold (eds), *Cause Lawyering and the State in a Global Era* (Oxford University Press, 2001) 143.

after the introduction of new contracting arrangements enacted by the Access to Justice Act 1999. Boon surmised that the reforms in the early 2000s would lead to cause lawyering becoming more prevalent in the newly emerging pro bono departments of corporate law firms[46] however, except for limited exceptions,[47] this does not appear to have been the case.[48] Boon and others have traditionally focussed on the historic dependence of lawyers on the state by virtue of legal aid funding as a constraining factor for progressive practice.[49] The Labour government's failed Community Legal Service model in the 2000s provides a further example of the different phases of development of legal aid and lawyer's relationship to them. Moorhead described the constraints of new public managements controls as a means of top down partnership building, which he further described as regulation through 'culture management' where 'approval and participation are used as a means of governmental control'.[50] I argue that across many progressive practice sites new resource streams from progressive grant making bodies that encourage the use of law for social change, as well as crowdfunding,[51] frees lawyers from at least some of these historic constraints. The collaboration between and across different practice sites, and also with frontline organisations, reveals a desire to achieve more with the limited legal aid funding still available; and arguably serves to incentivise some lawyers to pursue strategic casework.

In many organisations therefore, while day-to-day individual client casework continues to be community orientated, lawyers turn to high impact work in an attempt to achieve broader goals.[52] From the 1970s, high impact litigation facilitated diverse choice for lawyers who wanted to work in the public interest while giving new (albeit somewhat contested) meaning to what it meant to be a legal aid lawyer. Outside of the law centres high impact work began to develop in other practice sites during the 1970s and 80s such as within pressure groups,

[46] ibid 175.

[47] Freshfields have acted in 19 interventions to date in the UK Supreme Court and often do so in partnership with UK charities. See Paul Yates, *Excellence in Pro Bono: Freshfields' Work for Third-Party Interventions Picked up by Law Society Excellence Award* (*Law Society Gazette*, 4 November 2020).

[48] See, eg, Stephen Vaughan et al, 'Symbolism over Substance? Large law firms and Corporate Social Responsibility' (2015) 18(2) *Legal Ethics* 138.

[49] Francis (n 35) 90; Goriely (n 22).

[50] Richard Moorhead, 'Third Way Regulation? Community Legal Service Partnerships' (2001) *Modern Law Review* 543, 559.

[51] Joe Tomlinson, 'Crowdfunding Public Interest Judicial Reviews: A Risky New Resource and the Case for a Practical Ethics' (2019) *Public Law* 166.

[52] Tony Prosser, *Test Cases for the Poor: Legal Techniques in the Politics of Social Welfare* (Child Poverty Action Group, 1983). Organisations often publish guides to encourage and promote the impact of strategic litigation. See, eg Child Rights International Network, *Children's Rights: A Guide to Strategic Litigation* (CRIN, 2014), available at https://archive.crin.org/en/guides/legal/guide-strategic-litigation.html; Richard Wilson and Jennifer Rasmusen, *Promoting Justice: A Practical Guide to Strategic Human Rights Lawyering*, (International Human Rights Law Group, 2001), available at http://pdf.usaid.gov/pdf_docs/Pnadf477.pdf.

charities and NGOs.[53] Children's charities historically took the lead by exploring the possibilities of public interest strategic litigation and from as early as the 1970s, Child Poverty Action Group had already established a test case strategy.[54] For many of these organisations, legal aid provided a basic income to allow them to pursue broader types of social activism using legal tools. This interplay with legal aid and therefore ultimately with the state as its provider but *against* the state by way of judicial review is important. In order to understand this practice this book considers how lawyers perceive their relationships with state actors in chapter seven, as well as why some lawyers in progressive practice choose *not* to pursue strategic casework or related campaigning in chapter five.

Sommerlad's 2001 study of lawyers whom she terms 'political legal aid lawyers' is relevant in this context.[55] Sommerlad describes lawyers who have entered the legal aid sector precisely because of a commitment to using the law to fulfil 'the promise of expanded citizenship'[56] but as a result of (the earlier wave) of legal aid reforms and a poor perception of their work promulgated in the public sphere they experience significant low morale and reduced commitment to the value of legal aid work. In contrast to Abel[57] and Francis,[58] Sommerlad describes a group of lawyers who feel beaten, rather than galvanised, by wider pressures. While the study was conducted more than a decade ago, the background context of cuts to legal aid and increased bureaucracy is indicative of how government imposed changes impact upon lawyers' views of themselves and their own work. The study findings also illustrate, in part, collective features for legal aid lawyers including different attitudes to earnings (being perceived as less valuable), a 'client empowerment' discourse and a holistic notion of service and emphasis on continuity of care.[59] The importance of Sommerlad's study

[53] High impact public interest casework can of course be traced much further back to the cases of *Somerset v Stewart in England* (1772) 98 ER 499 and *Joseph Knight, a Negro of Africa v. John Wedderburn of Ballindean* (unreported, 1778) in Scotland. In the latter case interested persons made 'memorials' that resembled what we now know to be third-party interventions: Roger Smith, *Experience in England and Wales: Test Case Strategies, Public Interest Litigation, The Human Rights Act and Legal NGOs* (Essex Human Rights Centre, 2013). The abolition movement itself may well be the first influential social movement in Britain both in terms of law reform and movement tactics: 'The men who successfully abolished slavery invented many of the techniques we now associate with campaigns: national organisations with local chapters, campaigns writing to political representatives, report cards on how those representatives have voted, investigative reporting, petitions, marches, badges, boycotts, logos, fliers, books of evidence with readings in book stores, newsletters, use of the media': Richard Smith, 'Learning from the Abolitionists, The First Social Movement' (2012) *British Medical Journal* 345.

[54] Smith, ibid.

[55] While Sommerlad uses a different label, the group of lawyers in her study forms one of the subsets of practice in this book that I refer to as 'legal aid lawyers' within the progressive lawyering typologies set out in ch 3.

[56] Sommerlad (n 16) 342.

[57] Abel (n 35).

[58] Francis (n 35).

[59] Sommerlad (n 16) 345–48.

rests in the juxtaposition of lawyers' own perceptions of the work they do with how they are perceived by others, and how they collectively experience change. A further overarching question can be distilled from Sommerlad's study and relates to whether the controversy and criticism in the public sphere influence lawyers' perceptions of themselves such that it might impact upon their casework decisions. I explore these issues in chapter five and eight and address other related types of legal work (with a particular focus on strategic litigation) across different locations and the interactions between them.

Contemporary Issues and Campaigns

There has been a preoccupation and anxious concern in recent years about changes adversely impacting access to justice from those working across the profession in charities, law centres, legal aid law firms and the independent Bar. The contemporary context is most notably dominated by what I identify as the 'austerity narrative' woven throughout the book and concerned especially with the cuts to legal aid enacted by the Legal Aid, Sentencing and Punishment of Offenders Act 2012 (LASPO 2012) in England and Wales, as well a lack of investment in the justice system more widely.[60] The LASPO 2012 cuts took effect at the same time as large scale welfare reforms creating a 'perfect storm' for the advice sector.[61] Related restrictions on judicial review challenges and the proposed abolition of the Human Rights Act 1998 represent further concerns raised by participants in the study, which I explore in more detail below.

With respect to legal aid, lawyers have long been anxious about the curbing of legal aid and more senior lawyers in the study have lived through many rounds of incremental cuts. These changes have been most prevalent in England and Wales, however, lawyers in Scotland and Northern Ireland also express concerns about the availability of resource.[62] In England and Wales, LASPO 2012 dramatically altered the depth and breadth of legal aid provision to an unprecedented degree. An estimated £320m was removed from the annual legal aid budget, with another £220m cut back each year until 2018.[63] Changes to

[60] The Fabian Society, *The Right to Justice: The Final Report of the Bach Commission* (Fabian Society, 2017) 10–11. This accords with the view that in the UK and elsewhere 'progressive policies on some human rights issues co-exist with the dismantling of collectivist welfare policies': Hilary Sommerlad and Ole Hammerslev, 'Lawyers in a New Geopolitical Conjuncture: Continuity and Change' in *Lawyers in 21st-Century Societies: Volume 1 National Reports* (Hart, 2020) 15.

[61] James Organ and Jennifer Sigafoos, 'What if There is Nowhere to Get Advice?' in Asher Flynn and Jacqueline Hodgson, *Access to Justice and Legal Aid: Comparative Perspectives on Unmet Legal Need* (Hart, 2017) 161.

[62] See, eg, The Law Society of Northern Ireland, *Legal Aid Lobbying Pack* (Law Society NI, 2015), available at www.lawsoc-ni.org/DataEditorUploads/Legal%20Aid%20Lobbying%20Pack%20March%202015.pdf.

[63] Owen Bowcott, 'Cash Strapped Law Centre Turn Clients Away as Legal Aid Cuts Bite', (*The Guardian*, 18 September 2013). Using the original baseline figures the scope cuts reduced expenditure

scope and to the type of legal advice and/or representation to which those who are eligible are entitled were restricted. Family law cases no longer receive legal aid, unless there is evidence of domestic violence, and most housing, debt, social welfare, prison law and immigration cases (subject to some limited exceptions) are also no longer in scope.[64] There have been widespread studies of the impact of these reforms, which highlight in particular the disadvantage experienced by children, disabled people, migrants and other vulnerable groups.[65] An Equality and Human Rights Commission (EHRC) study has shown that while individuals try to resolve their legal problems in other ways, such as trying to access free advice, almost all participants struggled to resolve their legal issues without legal aid. Consistent with other longstanding empirical studies on access to justice,[66] unresolved legal problems have had knock on impacts such as unemployment, family breakdown, emotional and mental health problems.[67] The legal aid reforms were subject to a number of reviews during the course of this study[68] and several inquiries are ongoing at the time of writing.[69]

The second factor is that of restrictions to judicial review under the Criminal Justice and Courts Act 2015 and the Government's independent review of administrative law led by Lord Faulks QC in 2020.[70] Judicial review is the mechanism by which individuals can challenge the decision making of public bodies. An arguably crucial pillar of democracy, it serves to facilitate access to justice by enabling those subjected to unlawful decisions to seek redress through a formal court process. Importantly, the process is not concerned with the particular merits of a decision but whether that decision has been lawfully made. By way of example, consider a decision of a local council not to provide housing for a prospectively homeless young person. A public authority may be held to

by an estimated £400m: Steve Hynes, *LASPO Review: Revealing the Damage* (Legal Action Group, February 2019), available at www.lag.org.uk/article/206068/laspo-review--revealing-the-damage.

[64] Legal Aid, Sentencing and Punishment of Offenders Act 2012, Sch 1. See, eg, Pascoe Pleasence and Nigel Balmer, 'The Audacity of Justice: Recession, Redundancy, Rights and Legal Aid' (2010) 9(4) *Social Policy and Society* 475; Joanna Miles et al, 'When Exceptional is the Rule: Mental Health, Family Problems and the Reform of Legal Aid in England and Wales' (2012) 24(3) *Child and Family Law Quarterly* 320.

[65] Amnesty International, *Cuts That Hurt: The impact of legal cuts in England on Access to Justice* (Amnesty, 2017; Natalie Byrom, *The Impact of Cuts to Civil Legal Aid on Practitioners and Their Clients* (Warwick Centre for Human Rights, 2013).

[66] Hazel Genn, *Paths to Justice* (Oxford University Press, 1998).

[67] James Organ and Jennifer Sigafoos, *The Impact of LASPO on Routes to Access to Justice* (EHRC, 2018).

[68] See, eg, Ministry of Justice, *Post-Implementation Review of LASPO Part 1* and *Legal Support: The Way Ahead, An Action Plan to Deliver Better Support to People Experiencing Legal Problems* (HMSO, February 2019); Equality and Human Rights Commission, *Access to Legal Aid for Discrimination Cases* (EHRC, June 2019).

[69] Chris Minnoch and Rohini Teather, *The Time has Come to Bring the Legal Aid Sector's Sustainability Issues into the Public Domain* (Legal Action Group, July 2020); *Justice Committee Announces Inquiry into the Future of Legal Aid* (Legal Action Group, September 2020).

[70] Monidipa Fouzder, *Judicial Review Panel Set for Evidence Deluge* (*Law Society Gazette*, 26 October 2020).

have been acting unlawfully if it made the decision not to house them without having the power to do it (illegality), if by denying housing they made a decision no reasonable decision maker would have made (unreasonable), if they somehow failed to observe the rules of natural justice (procedural impropriety) or if they acted incompatibly with the Human Rights Act 1998. The final ground for judicial review in relation to human rights is central to the more recent practice of progressive lawyers in the UK. The Human Rights Act 1998 is a significant contemporary factor, 'bringing rights home' to such an extent as to make those rights entrenched in the European Convention on Human Rights (ECHR) enforceable in UK courts. Under the HRA 1998, lawyers can pursue human rights at any level of court proceedings. For example, a successful review of the decision above on human rights grounds could positively impact a much wider group of people in similar circumstances by holding other local authorities to account.

The links between judicial review and legal aid are therefore significant in terms of facilitating public law remedies for vulnerable and excluded groups.[71] It is in this context that the iterative process of strategic litigation must also be examined. While progressive lawyers increasingly battle against the government, the government in turn attempts to curb their litigation. Parallels between today's context and that of US constitutional litigation in the 1970s and 1980s are stark: just as liberal public interest law programmes took hold in the US, they became victims of their own success. In fact, Cummings notes how success 'turned into a liability as the political current shifted in the direction of increasing conservatism' and restrictions were placed on the use of Government funding.[72] For example, in 1996 a US congressional restriction banned funded organisations from 're-districting challenges, lobbying, class action suits, representing most aliens, political advocacy, collecting attorney's fees, abortion litigation, prisoner representation, welfare reform activities and defending public housing tenants evicted for drugs'.[73] Further, the restrictions banned lawyers in organisations that were otherwise funded by the Legal Services Corporation from engaging in *any* of these activities, even if those lawyers were using non-LSC funds.

We can draw comparison with the context in England and Wales. The areas that fell out of scope for legal aid by virtue of Part 1 of LASPO are almost identical to those described above (eg, prison law, welfare benefits, housing matters). Similarly in respect of 'representing aliens', the government

[71] One study demonstrated that legally aided claimants were more likely to obtain tangible benefits than those pursuing claims in a private capacity. It highlighted the 'good value' of potential high cost to the legal aid fund in view of the range of benefits received. The study did not support findings, made on behalf of the government in support of changes to judicial review, that the system was being abused: Maurice Sunkin et al, *The Value and Effects of Judicial Review: The Nature of Claims, their Consequences and Outcomes* (The Public Law Project, 2015).

[72] Scott Cummings, 'The Politics of Pro Bono' (2004) 52(1) *UCLA Law Review* 1, 21. See also, Garth (n 29) 175–76.

[73] ibid 22.

introduced a residence test to limit civil legal aid to those who had been resident in the UK for 12 months (it was declared unlawful by the Supreme Court in 2016).[74] Provisions of the Criminal Justice and Courts Act 2015 aimed to curb challenges to the government by limiting powers to intervene and imposing more prohibitive time limits in judicial review. It raised costs risks for organisations pursuing third party interventions (often third sector) and made it easier for the court to refuse remedies in favour of successful claimants.[75] Samuels concludes that overall these changes have narrowed the legal opportunity structure, which may lead to 'a long term weakening of CSOs [civil society organisations] capacity to advocate for their clients and hold the government to account'.[76] Similar to the conservative current in the US in the mid-1990s, there can be little doubt as to the political purpose of the reforms in the UK with the then Lord Chancellor sharing his perception that judicial review is a 'promotional tool for countless left-wing campaigners' who are 'growing in number, taking over charities, dominating BBC programmes and swarming around Westminster'.[77] A further relevant political clash rested with the earlier conservative (and later coalition) government's Big Society agenda. It promoted a wide vision of citizenship, volunteerism and 'self-reliance' but this did not accommodate well those civil society organisations that 'went beyond service provision and had their own agendas, pursued through political and legal forums'.[78] According to Samuels, the restrictions placed on judicial review were part of a wide suite of reforms intended to 'put obstacles in the path' of civil society organisations.[79] These restrictions, including those under the Lobbying Act, she argues have had a chilling effect on organisations that are now more hesitant to use legal tactics.

Opposing changes to legal aid and judicial review,[80] strengthening the domestic human rights framework and lobbying against cuts to social welfare

[74] *R (Public Law Project) v Lord Chancellor* [2016] UKSC 39.

[75] Harriet Samuels, 'Public Interest Litigation and the Civil Society Factor' (2018) *Legal Studies* 1, 5.

[76] ibid 6.

[77] Chris Grayling, 'The Judicial Review System is not a Promotional Tool for Countless Left-Wing Campaigners' (*The Daily Mail*, 11 September 2013).

[78] Samuels (n 75) 6.

[79] ibid. It is notable that similar restrictions have recently been observed in Australia with one study showing the interplay between community lawyers who pursue systemic change and the curbing of their activities through government decision making: 'Submissions to parliamentary and government inquiries [by lawyers] are acceptable, and often sought by government, regardless of the fact that they distract from the 'flesh and blood individual' in need of help. Lobbying and campaigning – speaking out – is not acceptable. In this regard, the restrictions appear to be ideologically based … [they] prevent public critique of government policy and practice, and silence dissent': Liana Buchanan, 'Community Lawyers, Law Reform and Systemic Change: Is the End in Sight?' in Flynn and Hodgson (n 61) 154.

[80] The case of *R (Ben Hoare Bell Solicitors & Others) v Lord Chancellor* [2015] EWHC 523 (Admin) [2015] 1 WLR 4175 provides a clear example of the interplay between proposed restrictions on both legal aid and judicial review. In this case a proposed rule that legal aid providers would not be paid for work in applying for judicial review unless it was later granted was quashed by the Divisional Court.

provision comprised a large part of the access to justice campaigning by lawyers during the fieldwork phase of this study from 2015 to 2017. In 2016, a new collective wave of lawyers self-identifying as 'activist lawyers' in the public domain emerged. This comprised a social media campaign largely in response to critical comments made by Theresa May, in reference to the investigation of public interest lawyer Phil Shiner who has subsequently been struck off for dishonest conduct, at the Conservative party conference in 2016: 'We will never again – in any future conflict – let those activist, left-wing human rights lawyers harangue and harass the bravest of the brave – the men and women of Britain's armed forces'.[81] To cite a few further examples of lawyer's campaigning on access to justice issues: in July 2015 legal aid solicitors conducted a 52-day strike to protest further cuts to legal aid and a book about the pressures faced in the criminal justice system has received widespread attention.[82] Whistleblowers have spoken out about the unfair allocation of legal aid contracts[83] and judges have made repeated calls to alleviate the difficulties created by increasing numbers of litigants in person.[84] A human rights crowdsourcing campaign 'Act for the Act' established by barristers working together with a legal journalist told 'ordinary, real stories' about the impact of the Human Rights Act.[85] The objective of the campaign was to raise awareness of the ways in which the Human Rights Act was important to ordinary people, countering the mainstream notion that the Act only assists, for example, terrorists or 'illegal' immigrants. Interestingly, the lawyers used their own clients' cases as narrative examples in an attempt to influence public debate and, in turn, the decision making process as to scrapping the Human Rights Act. Figure 2 below describes a campaign in relation to a strategic case conducted by lawyers at the charity Just for Kids Law (and the barristers they instructed) and supported by a number of other children's charities that successfully ensured better support for young people in custody.[86] The left hand image in Figure 3 below describes an extensive campaign by the same charity that changed the law to prohibit holding vulnerable 17-year-olds in custody overnight and ensure transfer to local authority accommodation. The right-hand image at Figure 3 below concerns a case taken by a disabled woman who relied on Article 8 ECHR to ensure her local authority met her

[81] For discussion of this politico-legal culture see, Conor Gearty, 'British Torture, Then and Now: The Role of Judges' *Modern Law Review* (10 September 2020, online record before inclusion in an issue), available at www.onlinelibrary.wiley.com/doi/full/10.1111/1468-2230.12578.

[82] The Secret Barrister, *Stories of Law and How It's Broken* (Picador, 2018).

[83] Sarah Downey, 'Legal Aid Agency Faces 100-firm Challenge over Criminal Contract Cuts Amid Whistleblower's Call for an External Investigation' (*Legal Business*, 8 November 2015).

[84] The Judiciary of England and Wales, Report on Litigants in Person (Judicial Working Group, 2013), available at www.judiciary.uk/wp-content/uploads/JCO/Documents/Reports/lip_2013.pdf.

[85] See further 'Act for the Act' crowdsourcing campaign www.crowdfunder.co.uk/actfortheact.

[86] The *context* of judicial decision making continues to be relevant in that this case involved (unsuccessful) arguments on behalf of the government that they could not provide support to vulnerable young people because of a lack of resource at a time of austerity driven cuts. See R *(on the application of HC) v Secretary of State for the Home Department & Another* EWHC 982 (Admin).

care needs.[87] The lawyers' legal advice and representation in several of these cases was integral to a much broader cultural political exercise aimed at preserving domestically enforceable rights, and available remedies, within the current human rights framework.

Figure 2: Act for the Act Campaign Image, Article 2
Source: www.actfortheact.uk 2015, image by Pete Moss.

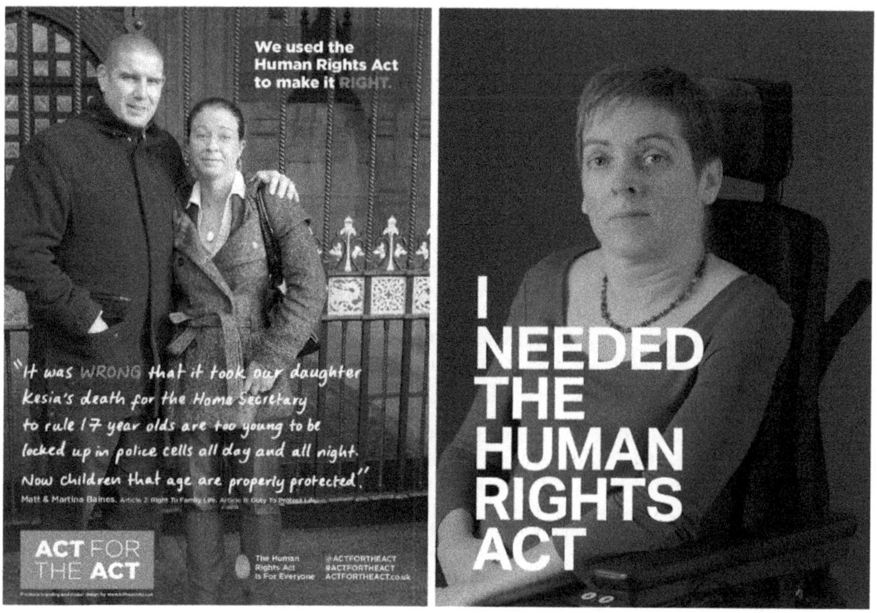

Figure 3 Act for the Act 'Right and Wrong' Campaign Images (Act for the Act, 2015)

[87] This case was used as a case study in another related campaign (Equally Ours) set up by eight national charities to show the importance of human rights and its relevance to everyday life: www.equallyours.org.uk.

The human rights and social welfare reforms relevant to austerity measures have led some lawyers to challenge policy developments both in the courts and in the public sphere. Human rights have repeatedly been the framework upon which to challenge the status quo and, increasingly, this is true of both radicals and reformers.[88] The use of strategic litigation and third party interventions in the UK, in particular in relation to access to justice issues and challenging unlawfulness of the legal aid regime, characterised the fieldwork phase of this study.[89] The cultural political realm in which lawyers pursue casework, especially on human rights grounds,[90] is arguably one of ever increasing sensitivity and polarised perspectives on welfare entitlement. In political and constitutional terms there is no doubt that the battles in which lawyers engage may well *create* further sites of conflict. The separation of powers of course demands a legislative, judicial and executive divide that some argue is subverted by strategic litigation.[91] An academic led project funded by Policy Exchange, the Judicial Power Project, expressly aimed to examine the proper limits of judicial power and balance the constitution. In doing so, it published a list of 50 'problematic' cases which they argue disrupt the balance of constitutional power.[92] Yet, many progressive lawyers who carry their causes to the courts argue that they do so in order to uphold the rule of law and to maintain the institutional autonomy of the courts.[93] The extent to which lawyers accept their professional activities being framed and labelled in 'activist' terms will be further explored in this book.

[88] Kate Nash, *The Political Sociology of Human Rights* (Cambridge University Press, 2015) 172.

[89] Alison Pickup, *Top Legal Aid and Access to Justice Cases of Recent Years* (The Public Law Project, 2018), available at https://publiclawproject.org.uk/wp-content/uploads/2018/08/Top-legal-aid-and-access-to-justice-cases-of-recent-years.pdf. See, eg, the successful challenge to the exceptional funding regime in *IS v Director of Legal Aid Casework & Anor* [2015] EWHC 1965 (Admin); challenges to cuts to legal aid for prisoners, R *(Howard League for Penal Reform and another) v Lord Chancellor (Equality and Human Rights Commission Intervening)* [2017] EWCA Civ 244 [2017] 4 WLR 292. In the UKSC see *R (on the application of SG and others (previously JS and others)) v Secretary of State for Work and Pensions* [2015] UKSC 16 concerning the legality of the benefits cap for single mothers; the successful challenge to Employment Tribunal fees, *R (UNISON) v Lord Chancellor (Equality and Human Rights Commission and another intervening) (Nos 1 and 2)* [2017] UKSC 51 [2017] 3 WLR 409; and the unanimous decision that the residence test for legal aid was unlawful *R (Public Law Project) v Lord Chancellor* [2015] EWCA Civ 1193 [2016] UKSC 39 [2016] AC 1531.

[90] The right to a fair and public hearing, within a reasonable time by an independent and impartial tribunal under Article 6 ECHR is particularly important in the context of cuts to legal aid.

[91] Mr Justice Cranston noted in a 2014 case concerning prison reform regulations limiting legal aid that, while he understood the concern that the changes could have a serious adverse effects for prisoners, 'for the time being, the forum for advancing these concerns remains the political': *R (Howard League for Penal Reform and Prisoners Advice Service) v the Lord Chancellor* [2014] EWHC 709 (Admin). His findings echo that of Lord Sumption in a different context but declaring courts are 'not [here] concerned with social or economic issues or other issues of macro-policy which are classically the domain of Parliament', *R (on the application of Prudential PLC) v Special Commissioner of Income Tax* [2013] UKSC 1 [131].

[92] Richard Ekins and Graham Gee, Judicial Power: 50 Problematic Cases (Policy Exchange, 2016). available at http://judicialpowerproject.org.uk/judicial-power-50-problematic-cases/.

[93] Terence Halliday, 'Politics and Civic Professionalism: Legal Elites and Cause Lawyers' (1999) 24(4) *Law and Social Inquiry* 1013, 1056.

As I explore in chapter five, it is also unclear how lawyers view themselves in this contemporary context juxtaposed with the progressive, strategic lawyer who emerged in the 1970s. I argue it is important to consider whether lawyers' own perceptions of impact and strategic change, as described through their personal narratives, can inform our understanding of the progressive lawyer over time.

CAUSE LAWYERING AND LEGAL MOBILISATION

Unlike conventional lawyers, a cause lawyer views the law as a tool for achieving desired political, cultural, economic or social ends and aims to facilitate social change through their casework and related activities.[94] Closely tied to the civil rights movement and to the well-accepted notion of lawyers acting in the 'public interest' in the US, cause lawyering has a 'place of honour' in the American legal system: law schools are said to be quick to 'celebrate judicial decisions that resulted from cause lawyering' and academics increasingly contribute to its 'sometimes mythical' culture.[95] Yet in the UK we do not yet have a sociological or theoretical space within which to discuss this important and comparable area of legal practice. It has been said that the lack of cultural and professional recognition of cause lawyering is in part due to the UK's system of legal aid, where lawyers are dependent on the state[96] as well as the 'cold climate' of 'quiet conservatism' and bureaucratic legal aid management.[97]

Cause lawyering theory derives from the collected work of socio-legal scholars Austin Sarat and Stuart Scheingold and their collaborators in a series of edited volumes. It describes those lawyers who use 'legal skills to pursue ends and ideals that transcend client service'.[98] The term has developed over almost three decades to encompass disparate activities and been adopted in several other jurisdictions, such that it has no clear definition. Lawyers who broadly pursue social change are labelled in many different ways and terms can be used interchangeably to describe different interpretations of cause lawyering approaches: the rebellious lawyer,[99] the critical lawyer,[100] the

[94] Sarat and Scheingold (n 3).

[95] Lynn Wardle, 'The Use and Abuse of Cause Lawyering: The Bad Example of Roe v Wade' (2014) 35 *University La Verne Law Review* 217. I acknowledge the different constitutional context in the US having a bearing upon the development of the theory, not least in relation to the court's role in interpreting a codified constitution.

[96] Francis (n 35) 109.

[97] Boon (n 45) 143.

[98] Sarat and Scheingold (n 1) 3.

[99] Gerald Lopez, *Rebellious Lawyering: One Chicano's Vision of Progressive Law Practice* (Westview Press, 1992).

[100] Louise Trubek and M Elizabeth Kransberger, 'Critical Lawyers: Social Justice and the Structures of Private Practice' in *Cause Lawyers: Political Commitments and Professional Responsibilities* (Oxford University Press, 1998).

community lawyer,[101] the political lawyer,[102] the radical lawyer,[103] and the progressive lawyer.[104] Arguably none of these labels have taken the equivalent *scholarly* hold of the cause lawyer. Cummings provides an explanation for the powerful emergence of cause lawyering theory in US scholarship, which he relates to the development of socio-legal studies and empirical legal research. He argues that those scholars who felt limited by the 'normative orientation of new progressive theories' turned to cause lawyering in the 1990s to change the field of research by 'distinguishing legal advocacy on the basis of lawyer *motivation* rather than a particular conception of the good society or a specified political agenda'.[105]

Likewise, a focus on *lawyer motivation* is central to this book. It relates to an acceptance that law and legal institutions are not static but ever changing and that lawyers working within them have values, goals and perspectives (however mixed) that influence the choices they make.[106] While progressive lawyers might use the law, they are motivated to look *outside* the law to achieve desired ends. A rejection of positivism, as theoretically expressed through legal realism, and the growing dissatisfaction with formalism further characterises the development of cause lawyering theory. The gap between 'law in books' and 'law in action' historically created new theoretical and empirical shifts among socio-legal scholars[107] and led to a 'radical decentering of law'[108] taking greater account of personal, social and cultural factors that have a bearing upon our understanding of law's role in society and also of lawyers pursuing social change. Etienne's empirical study in the US criminal cause lawyering context is useful in terms of determining some common motivational factors. The categories that emerged from the study were 'ideological', 'personality-based', 'experiential', 'ambition-orientated' and 'group-identities'. While the study found that the motivations of criminal cause lawyers within these categories were richly varied, several common traits were identified. These were: (i) a shared ideology or worldview combined with scepticism of government action; (ii) belief in the process of representation; (iii) sharing a group identity.[109] This book similarly considers the

[101] Karen Tokarz et al, 'Conversations on "Community Lawyering": Conversations on the Newest (Oldest) Wave in Clinical Legal Education' (2008) 28 *Washington University Journal of Law and Policy* 359.

[102] Martha Minow, 'Political Lawyering: An Introduction' (1996) 31 *Harvard Civil Rights-Civil Liberties Law Review* 287; Terence Halliday et al (eds), *Fighting for Political Freedom: Comparative Studies of the Legal Complex and Political Liberalism* (Hart, 2007).

[103] Carrie Menkel-Meadow, 'The Causes of Cause Lawyering: Toward an Understanding of the Motivation and Commitment of Social Justice Lawyers' in Sarat and Scheingold (n 1).

[104] Lucie White, 'Creating Models for Progressive Lawyering in the 21st Century' (2001) 9 *Journal of Law and Policy* 297.

[105] Scott Cummings, 'The Pursuit of Legal Rights and Beyond' (2012) *UCLA Law Review* 506, 512.

[106] Menkel-Meadow (n 103) 31–68.

[107] William Twining, 'Remembering 1972: The Oxford Centre in the Context of Developments in Higher Education and the Discipline of Law' (1995) 22(1) *Journal of Law and Society* 35.

[108] Scheingold (n 2) xxii.

[109] Margareth Etienne, 'The Ethics of Cause Lawyering: An Empirical Examination of Criminal Defense Lawyers as Cause Lawyers' (2005) 95 *Journal of Criminal Law and Criminology* 1195, 1209.

shared experiences that relate to lawyers' ability to sustain their work over time. My argument is that in light of changes since the 1970s what motivates lawyers to *choose* the progressive professional path and what motivates them to *stay* are distinct and important.

The practice of public interest law in the US relates to the socio-legal scholarly shift towards research on cause lawyers. This term describes 'legal practice that advances social justice and other causes for the public good'[110] and, while it can be traced to the abolitionist movement, also relates to the work of a movement of lawyers who sought to overcome social injustice in the 1960s.[111] In the 1980s and 1990s, the rise of neighbourhood law practices, a recognition of the ambitions of lawyers working in the fight against poverty, and significant funding from the Ford Foundation to establish 'elite' programmes of public interest activity, all accelerated the development of cause lawyering as scholars sought to theoretically describe new and emerging types of legal practice. However, the terminology presents problems in terms of professional identification. Chen and Cummings have argued that the label 'public interest law' has shown great resilience and been adopted globally[112] but its prevalence in the UK is debatable. Sarat and Scheingold also point to problems with the theory of public interest law and argue that cause lawyering is more 'inclusive' by going beyond a particular conception of what is simply in the public interest:

> [C]ause lawyering conveys a determination to take sides in a political or moral struggle without making distinctions between worthy and unworthy causes ... to talk about public interest lawyering is to take on irresolvable disputes about what is, or is not, in the public interest. Whether the pursuit of any particular cause advances the public interest is very much in the eye of the beholder.[113]

This tension is interesting because it goes to the heart of questions addressed in this book. Progressive lawyers *do* take sides in a struggle by distinguishing a 'worthy' cause. By exploring the influences that are brought to bear on their decision-making and how they frame and negotiate these decisions we gain a deeper understanding of the construction of causes that are deemed 'worthy'. It is important to interrogate in particular how their values relate to their choice to pursue particular causes, how they perceive their decision-making to be influenced by the progressive networks to which they belong, and how individual and collective motivations interrelate and might mutually reinforce one another. As Francis asserts in his study of Canadian progressive lawyers, they are at the edges of the legal profession but are in fact empowered by their status: '[they] have developed an alternative conception of lawyering which draws heavily on political activism and enables them to demonstrate creativity, reflexivity

[110] *Black's Law Dictionary* (Thomson Reuters, 2011) 612.

[111] Ann Southworth, 'What is Public Interest Law? Empirical Perspectives on an Old Question' (2013) 62 *De Paul Law Review* 493.

[112] Alan Chen and Scott Cummings, *Public Interest Lawyering: A Contemporary Perspective* (Walters Kluwer, 2013).

[113] Sarat and Scheingold (n 3) 5.

and entrepreneurship'.[114] Similarly, this book describes and explores collective empowerment in the current UK context where cuts to legal aid and pressures on the justice system have created a perceived urgent need for collaboration in order to challenge the status quo.

A number of different cause lawyering typologies have developed over the last two decades. For example, Luban describes two broad types of radical and reformist cause lawyers in his discussion of government lawyers in the US.[115] McEvoy, in his study of lawyers working in conflicted and authoritarian societies, identifies three cause lawyering types: 'struggle lawyers', 'human rights activists' and a 'pragmatic moral community'.[116] I consider Hilbink's typology, based on his doctoral work, to be particularly useful in the context of this study: (i) proceduralist lawyering (ii) elite/vanguard lawyering and (iii) grassroots lawyering.[117] The proceduralist lawyer is the closest to the traditional notion of the lawyer: someone who upholds the rule of law (that being their 'cause') by fairly representing clients and 'marked by a belief in the separation of law and politics, and a belief that the legal system is essentially fair and just'.[118] Elite/vanguard lawyering in contrast views the law as a superior form of politics and rests in the belief that the law itself can be used to render substantive justice such that it will change society. Elite lawyers seek to move change 'upwards' towards elites in law and politics generally.[119] Rather than adopting the neutrality of the proceduralist lawyer they are motivated by political goals and often work in conjunction with advocacy groups on litigation. The final cause lawyer type describes those lawyers working at grassroots level to achieve substantive social justice but, unlike the elite lawyers, they use the law in combination with other grassroots activism tools. Grassroots lawyers believe in empowering individuals and communities to achieve change and rely on the collective power of social movements because legal action is seen as only one of several ways to achieve social change.[120] Hilbink noted (in 2004) that 'the grassroots model, in increasingly conservative political climates around the world, represents the most viable and thus, most prevalent approach.'[121] Underlying each of these cause lawyering typologies lies the important question of how lawyers view the law and a

[114] Francis (n 35) 87. A recent legal mobilisation study across environmental NGOs in four jurisdictions also highlighted the importance of 'strategy entrepreneurs' to promote the use of particular legal tools and tactics within organisations: Lisa Vanhala, 'Is Legal Mobilization for the Birds? Legal Opportunity Structures and Environmental Non-Governmental Organisations in the United Kingdom, France, Finland and Italy' (2017) 51(3) *Comparative Political Studies* 380.

[115] David Luban, 'The Moral Complexity of Cause Lawyers Within the State' (2012) 81 *Fordham Law Review* 705.

[116] Kieran McEvoy, 'Cause Lawyering, Political Violence, and Professionalism in Conflict' (2019) *Journal of Law and Society* 529.

[117] Hilbink (n 4) 661.

[118] ibid 668.

[119] ibid.

[120] ibid 681.

[121] ibid 682.

further distinguishing feature is the extent to which lawyers' work is politically embedded,[122] which in turn impacts upon the tools that they use to achieve change.

Michael McCann addresses the way in which legal discourse can be 'constitutive of practical interactions among citizens'[123] by studying how litigation provides empowering and identity-constituting experiences for social movements. Unsurprisingly, the tools adopted within theories of legal mobilisation considerably overlap with those of cause lawyering and are useful in terms of identifying types of progressive practice: 'raising consciousness among particular communities or the public, delivering public legal education or specialized legal education, lobbying for law reform or changes in the levels of access to justice, providing summary legal advice and referral services, and undertaking strategic or test case litigation'.[124] Of particular interest, and consistent with Sarat and Scheingold's approach, is the assertion that lawyers create a legal and political consciousness[125] that leads citizens to participate in political processes. However, the theoretical focus of much of the work on legal mobilisation is primarily on how the law is used to mobilise *citizens* in a broadly constituted sense. My approach is distinct from these studies by moving the critical lens to *lawyers* and the decisions they make in order to strengthen ties to one another. While there have been some studies addressing lawyer mobilisation in the past[126] none provide a comprehensive analysis across subsets of practice in a UK context.

It is unclear whether the cause lawyering typologies align with how lawyers view themselves, their own work and their broader collective identity. I acknowledge that an analysis of these self-perceptions is complex given that how a lawyer perceives their own work may change over time or in particular contexts.[127] However, I argue it is nonetheless important to capture how lawyers in the UK work within and across these cause lawyering types, even where there is movement between them, because lawyers' own voices and experiences are central to overcoming the challenges to sustaining the profession in future and to better

[122] Sida Liu and Terence Halliday, 'Political Liberalism and Political Embeddedness: Understanding Politics in the Work of Chinese Criminal Defense Lawyers' (2011) 54 *Law & Society Review* 831, 835.

[123] Michael McCann, *Rights at Work: Pay Equity Reform and the Politics of Legal Mobilization* (Chicago University Press, 1994) 8.

[124] Lisa Vanhala, *Making Rights a Reality: Disability Rights Activists and Legal Mobilization* (Cambridge University Press, 2011) 6.

[125] Michael McCann and Helena Silverstein, 'Rethinking Law's "Allurements": A Relational Analysis of Social Movement Lawyers in the US' in Sarat and Scheingold (n 1) 262.

[126] See, eg, Kieran McEvoy and Rachel Rebouche, 'Mobilizing the Professions: Lawyers, Politics and the Collective Legal Conscience' in John Morison et al (eds), *Judges, Transition and Human Rights* (Oxford University Press, 2007); Kilwein, 'Still Trying: Lawyering for the Poor and Disadvantaged in Pittsburgh, Pennsylvania' in Sarat and Scheingold (n 1); Devyani Prabhat, *Unleashing the Force of Law: Legal Mobilization, National Security and Basic Freedoms* (Palgrave Macmillan, 2016).

[127] Francis (n 35) 94.

aligning legal education with the work that lawyers do. As I outline in chapter three, my focus on identity in fact seeks to take account of the fact that there are no fixed identities but aims to better capture how they are subject to change. It is further important to probe the extent to which UK lawyers rely on social movements to pursue change, or whether they perceive themselves to be part of a network pursuing social change such that they might in itself constitute a social movement. Notwithstanding the shifting context and changing perceptions this book argues that the relational, interconnected aspects of their work:

> The relationship of progressive law practices to social activist groups, their choice of legal strategies, and their internal relationships are what define them and differentiate them from the rest of the profession. These characteristics also shape their interaction with other significant institutions: the state and its legal aid program, the legal profession and the academy, and other progressive lawyers.[128]

To summarise, this books explores the relationships and the networks of interaction that exist to sustain progressive lawyering. The central concern, consistent with the focus of cause lawyering, is on lawyer motivation and how lawyers in the study construct their work, as well as the extent to which they create legal and political consciousness in so doing.

THE CONTROVERSIES OF PROGRESSIVE LAWYERING

Cause lawyering theory interrogates the ways in which lawyers pursue ends that transcend client service.[129] This question points to the contradictions at the heart of progressive practice whereby lawyers might struggle to uphold the clients' best interests as a neutral advocate while at the same time being committed to their *own* goals. A number of related issues stem from this struggle including, for example, the ability and willingness to accept or decline instructions on cases; direct conflicts between a client's case and 'the cause'; tensions between meeting individual client needs and pursuing wider systemic change; and disputes about who speaks 'for' individuals and groups, including the extent to whether (and on what basis) lawyers have the legitimacy to speak on behalf of others at all.

It is useful to think about the extent to which cause lawyering theory can help us understand the controversies of progressive legal practice in the UK. To begin to understand the ethical controversy of progressive lawyering, the underpinning regulatory regime on independence for lawyers in UK practice is important. The principles governing solicitors' conduct clearly state that they 'must not allow their independence to be compromised.' They must behave in a way that maintains the trust of the public and act in the best interests of each client

[128] Abel (n 35) 11.
[129] Cummings (n 105) 521.

while upholding the rule of law and the proper administration of justice.[130] The Barristers' Code of Conduct contains similar provisions within its core duties and states that barristers must 'promote *fearlessly* and *by all proper and lawful means* the client's best interests'[131] alongside their overriding duty to the court. Barristers must in fact put their client's interests ahead of their own and of any other person.[132] They are also required not to withhold their services 'on the ground that the nature of the case is objectionable' or the 'conduct, opinions or beliefs' of the prospective client are unacceptable'.[133] This is known colloquially as the 'cab-rank rule' whereby barristers must take the next case that comes along regardless of their own interests. Lawyers are therefore required to put any personal opinions or moral objections to the status of their client to one side.[134] Consistent with the proceduralist lawyer described above[135] and the notion of zealous advocacy,[136] lawyers generally should be fearless, but neutral, in the pursuit of their clients' interests. Solicitors in the UK are not formally *bound* by the same requirement as to neutrality as barristers.[137]

Even in the traditional sphere of legal practice, a number of influences and interactions at the heart of ethical decision-making are described in the relevant literature. One report sought to present a model of ethics 'indicators' and highlighted three themes of relevance to this study:[138]

1. character (individuals and professional dispositions to regard something as ethical or unethical);
2. context (incentives, infrastructure and culture); and
3. capacities (how we recognise and reason decisions).

The report emphasises that for lawyers these three 'precursors to behaviour' interact with behaviour itself: 'so our tendency to see something as ethical or unethical is determined by our own character; the context within which we work and our capacities'.[139] Therefore, behaviour itself can influence context,

[130] Solicitors Regulation Authority Standards and Regulation, Principles (SRA, 2011).

[131] Bar Standards Board, Code of Conduct, Rule C15 (BSB, 2015).

[132] ibid.

[133] BSB (n 131) Rule C28.

[134] Schneyer, 'Moral Philosophy's Standard Conception of Legal Ethics' (1984) *Wisconsin Law Review* 1529, 1534.

[135] Hilbink (n 4).

[136] In the US, the equivalent of a duty to fearlessly act in the best interests of the client is promoted in the zealous advocacy duty. This is enshrined in the Preamble and Scope of the ABA Model Rules of Professional Conduct (1983) at para 2: 'as advocate, a lawyer zealously asserts the client's position under the rules of the adversary system'. The concept is elaborated at para 8: 'a lawyer's responsibilities as a representative of clients, an officer of the legal system and a public citizen are usually harmonious. Thus, when an opposing party is well represented, a lawyer can be a zealous advocate on behalf of a client and at the same time assume that justice is being done'.

[137] Boon (n 45) 152.

[138] Richard Moorhead et al, *Designing Ethics Indicators for Legal Service Provision* (The Legal Services Board, 2012) 4.

[139] ibid 5.

and vice versa. This is of particular interest in light of the historical and contemporary issues described above but also in considering how lawyers must try to apply static principles of conduct within an ever-shifting context, while also influenced by their own personal, unique character and capacities. The questions in this study similarly seek to address how the cultural *context* of decision-making might influence the *character* of the decision (ie, whether lawyers perceive themselves to have made an ethical choice) and especially so where that context is one in which values based collective decision-making may be brought to bear.[140]

I also explore the extent to which lawyers perceive and acknowledge their decision-making to be influenced by political factors. Much of the literature implicitly assumes that cause lawyers prioritise the cause above the client, although the clients themselves may in fact be or represent the cause.[141] For many cause lawyers, a whole community serves as the client. Cause lawyers tend to be set apart from the rest of the profession and have been said to work at the edge, rather than the core[142] but for many, their unique position means they can take risks and innovate more than other lawyers. The very concept of the cause lawyer challenges the traditional ethical assumptions of what it means to be a detached lawyer. Their independence and ability to firmly uphold the best interests of their client is called into question such that their partisanship is said to subvert the accepted norms of professional ethics. As Rosen attests, judgements on this transgression may not be consistently applied. He suggests that lawyers in traditional private practice are guilty of similar ethical infractions, yet it is seen as being more acceptable than apparent breaches made by lawyers on the 'fringes' of legal practice.[143] Similarly in the UK context, research conducted on the cab rank rule for barristers suggests that while 'as a principle it is to be applauded, as a rule it fails lamentably because there is no apparent application of enforcement procedures'.[144] On one view, it is of course at times accepted that lawyers might fail to be impartial: 'a lawyer need not be apologetic for not being partisan, for identifying. That is his function'.[145] Nonetheless there are obvious moral tensions where lawyers put causes above their clients[146] and also,

[140] See also, Mather et al (n 9). For discussion in the in-house corporate context see, Richard Moorhead et al, *In-House Lawyers' Ethics: Institutional Logics, Legal Risk and the Tournament of Influence* (Hart, 2018).

[141] Stuart Scheingold and Anne Bloom, Transgressive Cause Lawyering: Practice Sites and the Politicization of the Professional (1998) 5 *International Journal of the Legal Profession* 209.

[142] Francis (n 35).

[143] Robert Rosen, 'Book Review: On the Social Significance of Critical Lawyering' (2000) 3(2) *Legal Ethics* 267.

[144] John Flood and Morten Hviid, *The Cab Rank Rule: Its Meaning and Purpose in the New Legal Services Market* (Legal Services Board, 2013) 22.

[145] Edgar Cahn and Jean Cahn, 'The War on Poverty: A Civilian Perspective' (1964) 73 *Yale Law Journal* 1317, 1335.

[146] David Luban, *Lawyers and Justice* (Princeton University Press, 1988) 293.

especially for barristers, where they might refuse instructions expressly because of a commitment to a cause or political belief.

As a means of bringing together the ethical and personal aspirations of cause lawyers, Sarat argues that cause lawyers use their professional skills to move towards 'a particular vision of good' and their legal knowledge 'to give life to law's ethical aspirations'.[147] Lawyers work to uphold justice, and its fair administration, consistent with other ethical requirements but they do so with a heightened sense of what is right. The lawyer must therefore have an intrinsic sense of what is 'good'.[148] Can it really be said that cause lawyers have a more developed sense of morality? There are obvious tensions here: while on the one hand cause lawyers are said to be set apart and excluded from the rest of the legal profession by virtue of the work they do, they are arguably presented as a moral elite in comparison to other lawyers who do not pursue societal change in the same way. Rosen comments that Sarat's conception of the 'good' lawyer is problematic not only because it 'drives a wedge between cause lawyers and the rest of the legal profession', but because it 'too quickly moves between political causes and moral requirements'. Rosen tackles the ethical mire of whether lawyers choose the 'right' side and rejects any notion of cause lawyering where the 'defining moment' is to somehow reject clients who are on the 'wrong' side.[149]

The discussion above perhaps illustrates that *all* lawyers are trained to be committed both ethically and morally and a separation of politics and morality is a struggle for any lawyer. Sarat and Scheingold's points of distinction do appear flawed: while in some respects they highlight the overlaps with conventional lawyering[150] by predominantly focusing on the ways in which cause lawyers and traditional lawyers are different, they may have neglected the ways in which they are in fact the same. Bloom, for example, points to some similar practice styles between cause lawyers and conventional lawyers including 'high levels of prestige' and 'repeat player status' where lawyers are reinstructed in the same matters.[151] In the UK context, Boon identifies that the notion of cause lawyering forces us to ask whether a *common* conception of justice even exists for lawyers, one that serves as a 'touchstone for their distinctive professional values'.[152] Like Sarat, Boon asserts that if it does exist, it might be said that

[147] Austin Sarat, 'Between the (Presence of) Violence and the (Possibility of) Justice' in Sarat and Scheingold (n 1) 318.

[148] Legal ethics is not a mandatory part of qualifying law degrees in the UK and some have argued that to better instill the ethical values upon which the Codes of Conduct rest it should be included in the foundational stage. See, eg, Andrew Boon, *A Model Curriculum for Legal Ethics* (The Law Society, 2010).

[149] Rosen (n 143) 175.

[150] Austin Sarat and Stuart Scheingold, 'State Transformation, Globalization and the Possibilities of Cause Lawyering' in Sarat and Scheingold (n 45) 13.

[151] Anne Bloom, 'Practice Style and Successful Legal Mobilisation' (2008) 71 *Law and Contemporary Problems* 1, 3.

[152] Andrew Boon, 'Cause Lawyers and the Alternate Ethical Paradigm' (2004) 7 *Legal Ethics* 251.

cause lawyers transgress or move beyond this traditional boundary and do so in the interests of justice itself: albeit with reference to their own conception of what 'justice' is.[153]

There can be no doubt that progressive lawyers bring something unique to the law in light of their character and capacities. Their practice is personally meaningful, in whatever subjective sense,[154] and it is important to grasp and articulate the ethical constraints at play. Do progressive lawyers in the UK see themselves as 'set apart' from the rest of the profession? Do *they* believe themselves they hold higher ethical and moral standards? How do progressive lawyers balance their duties to clients with overarching convictions as to the role of law in society when they are in conflict? How much control do progressive lawyers exercise over how their client's cases develop? This study is not exclusively one of legal ethics, nor does it attempt to empirically measure professional decision-making in ethical terms. It does however seek to capture the lawyer's experience of, and perspective on, the dilemma of representing individual client interests while pursuing social change and will interrogate whether a common conception of justice exists for progressive lawyers, or whether it is bounded by the different subsets of practice. In this context personal background and beliefs are relevant in determining what reference points progressive lawyers use for what 'justice' even is and how they locate and frame them.

Closely situated within the ethical controversy of cause lawyering rest two further professional controversies relevant to this study. First, the question of whether cause lawyers are viewed as being within or outside the profession itself and the related definitional constraints as to whether their activity actually forms part of their professional practice. Secondly, whether progressive practice in fact entrenches professionalism and further disempowers clients (this controversy is clearly related to the ethical tensions described above). With respect to the first issue, the extent to which cause lawyers operate on the fringes of professional practice depends on the type of work they do and the role that activism and campaigning plays in their work. It is important to outline clearly *who* counts as a progressive lawyer for the purposes of the study. Boon asserts that 'treating lobbyists or activists as cause lawyers merely because they are lawyers undermines the relevance and significance of their activity to legal ethics'.[155] In terms of research methodology, I have in fact chosen to include lawyers in charities, NGOs and law school clinics in the study notwithstanding the fact that a minority may no longer represent individual clients or technically 'practice' law.[156] Boon appears to suggest that because these lawyers are not

[153] Scheingold and Bloom (n 141) 220.
[154] Duncan Kennedy, 'The Responsibilities of Lawyers for the Justice of Their Causes' (1987) 18 *Texas Tech University Law Review* 1157.
[155] Boon (n 152) 252.
[156] It is not uncommon for in-house lawyers in NGOs and law school clinics to temporarily or permanently suspend their practising certificates if they are not conducting client facing legal work

bound by the strict regulatory codes of conduct described above they should not be captured within the definition of 'cause lawyer'. I adopt a wide approach in light of experientially informed assumptions made *by lawyers* in the field of activity and in light of the importance of individual and collective perceptions to the study. Participants selected for the study self-identify as 'lawyers' and are professionally qualified (or intend to be) as either solicitors or barristers. Their *legal* knowledge and expertise underpins their professional lives. As I set out in chapter three, how practice sites and areas of work are delineated is shaped by their legal identity such that the study focuses on whether progressive lawyers *themselves* think they are within or outside the profession as a whole and to what extent they are conscious of their positioning. A further focus is on how they determine their own position within the network of practice with reference to one another as progressive lawyers.

The second professional controversy relates to law, and lawyer, empowerment. This criticism is often directed at impact litigation strategies but some critics also highlight the disempowerment inherent in lawyers giving general legal advice. Diana Leat commented in 1975, not long after the establishment of the first UK law centres, that 'the neighbourhood law centre is not merely insufficient for the task of [reducing social inequality] but it is counterproductive insofar as it actually serves to stabilise if not to increase the legal profession's dependents'.[157] Leat asserted that 'where there is a conflict between the lawyer's (radical) analysis and the client's self-interest it would appear that the latter is bought for the price of the former'.[158] She called for a re-examination of the notion of the neighbourhood law centre as a means of achieving social equality. She argued that communication 'implies selection and organisation' of information already carried out by the lawyer,[159] thus not empowering the client at all, but rather concealing further inequality 'beneath a façade of empirical objectivity'.[160] Grace and Le Fevre, writing a decade later, similarly argued that law centre lawyers should be instruments for community activism rather than merely activists themselves.[161] This is a common criticism within the legal mobilisation and cause lawyering literature: that legal professionalism simply heightens *the lawyer's* position of power and

on a regular basis. This is because their work might fall outside of *regulated* legal activity (common for pro bono projects, social welfare advice, policy work and some work at an international level). Nonetheless the study adopts a focus on the 'credential' of lawyer as conferred by the profession. See further, Sommerlad and Hammerslev (n 60) 4.

[157] Diana Leat, 'Rise and Rôle of the Poor Man's Lawyer' (1975) 2 *British Journal of Law and Society* 166, 177.

[158] ibid 179.

[159] See further, Martha Minow and Elizabeth Spelman, 'In Context' (1990) 63 *Southern California Law Review*, 1597: 'The very process of categorization, of selecting some facts and not others, involves choices, values, judgments, preconceptions and moral positions'.

[160] Leat (n 157) 179.

[161] Clive Grace and Patrick LeFevre, 'Draining the Swamp' (1985) 7 *Law & Policy* 97. See also, Garth (n 29) 171–73.

diminishes that of the client.[162] Handler endorses this view: 'legal symbols may serve to raise grievances, diminish acquiescence, and build hopes, but they are not sufficiently strong enough to overcome barriers to mobilisation'.[163] Rhode also argues that 'any approach that keeps lawyers in a position of dominance may perpetuate the position of powerlessness that they seek to address'.[164]

With aims, objectives and overall political and social goals being set by lawyers themselves it is importance to ask whether lawyers might have divergent goals and vested interests. Some law centres, charities and law school clinics providing legal services seem, on the face of it, reserved in outlining their procedure for case selection and where policy goals and individual client cases coincide the selection criterion become blurred. The basic question of *why* lawyers pursue the cases they do, *when* they do is pertinent. How do lawyers both perceive and identify legal need? In the context of day-to-day casework how are cases selected? This study will explore the lawyer's own perception of professional norms where strategic cases may well take priority over those of individual clients. It is unclear whether lawyers themselves self-identify as having cause orientated priorities and to what extent their case selection and strategy adopted operates on a conscious and self-directed level related to their own motivations.

In relation to client disempowerment there is some further related controversy by way of the critique of high impact or strategic litigation. While this study is not concerned with the success of cause lawyers engaging in litigation per se, to better understand the relationship between success, or failure, on cause lawyers' perceptions of themselves and their own understanding of the casework choices they make, it is useful to take note of the critique. Scheingold's seminal analysis of what he termed 'the myth of rights' argued that lawyers who pursue activism have an overly simplistic view of the interaction between litigation and other methods of social change.[165] Appreciating he is writing in the US context with a codified constitution and where the review powers of the courts are different to the UK,[166] he nonetheless argues that rights as articulated by the courts often fail to be realised where they are intertwined with contested matters of public policy. Heavily influenced by Judith Shklar's work on legalism,[167] Scheingold asserted that lawyers all

[162] Angelo Acheta, 'Community Lawyering Review Essay' (1993) 81 *California Law Review* 1363, 1375.

[163] Joel Handler, *Social Movements and the Legal System: A Theory of Law Reform and Social Change* (New York Academic Press, 1978) 219.

[164] Deborah Rhode, 'Access to Justice: Connecting Principles to Practice' (2004) 17 *Georgetown Journal of Legal Ethics* 369, 385.

[165] Scheingold (n 2).

[166] See, eg, Lord Carloway, *Constitutional Principle and the Rule of Law* (Lord Rodger Memorial Lecture, 29 October 2020) 5. Available at www.judiciary.scot/docs/librariesprovider3/judiciary documents/lord-rodger-memorial-lecture---29-october-2020-deb.pdf.

[167] Judith Shklar, *Legalism: Law, Moralism and Political Trials* (Harvard University Press, 1964).

too often approach casework with a naïve view that fails to take the 'politics of rights' into account. He further argued that the 'the myth of rights' was incorrectly premised on 'a direct linking of litigation, rights, and remedies with social change'.[168] In fact, Garth surmised that the failure to adopt test case litigation in the early years of the UK law centre movement's history was, in part, due to an awareness of the 'disenchantment' expressed in critical literature in the US.[169] Notwithstanding that care should be taken where lawyers might well either exaggerate or minimise their own roles, lawyers' *own* narratives as to strategic choice and the any perceived inadequacy of litigation and related strategies is important for adding texture and insight into the decisions that lawyers make about the tools they use, as I explore further in chapter five.

Southworth's study of right-wing cause lawyers is instructive here as she sought to address two important questions in light of the myth of rights critique: (1) What strategies did [these] lawyers pursue? and (2) What did they *believe* they were accomplishing? Her study suggests that lawyers evaluated their own work according to the benefits that clients received, rather than overarching favourable precedent being achieved. Moreover, lawyers' tactical choices seemed to 'reflect the institutional attributes of the practice settings in which they worked as well their views about the efficacy of alternative strategies'.[170] Southworth asserts that generally lawyers were aware of the limitations of litigation and 'understood the difference between judicially prescribed rights and real power'.[171] Very few lawyers sought to achieve their clients' goals using litigation alone.[172] Rather, they might have helped a client obtain resources, educated the public about the work of an organisation, mobilised grassroots campaigns or created leverage in negotiations.[173] Likewise, lawyers described a range of other activities they were engaged in, which often served to complement their litigation, such as lobbying, community organising and education, influencing government policy implementation or simply gaining publicity.[174]

Social Movements and Collective Identity

The contemporary *organisational* practice of progressive lawyering bears some resemblance to the intensive 1970s model described above. The particularities

[168] Scheingold (n 2) 5.
[169] Garth (n 29) 64.
[170] Ann Southworth, 'Lawyers and the Myth of Rights in Civil Rights and Poverty Practice' (1999) 8 *Boston University Public Interest Law Journal* 473.
[171] ibid 477.
[172] ibid 478.
[173] ibid 491.
[174] ibid 482–84.

of progressive practice sites reveal why and how lawyers might be attracted to working on certain types of cases or causes. Whether this is due to geographic location, personal background, pre-existing relationships with other lawyers, media attention, the type of general client casework or potential for high level strategic litigation; why lawyers make the decisions to use the legal tools they do, the way they do and when they do is critical to deepening our understanding of this culturally impactful area of legal practice. In this context, the collective identity of lawyers as a movement pursuing social change demands further critical exploration.

A comparative UK legal mobilisation study demonstrates well the relationship between law and social movements. Vanhala followed disability activists and lawyers as they negotiated political issues in a legal context to investigate why they chose to pursue legal remedies.[175] Using a sociological theory of institutions, Vanhala points to the ways in which litigation strategies can shape collective identity and illustrates that consensus, or lack thereof, influences whether or not an organisation 'turns to law' in the first place in pursuit of its goals. She finds that although the issues in cases impact individuals, it is how they affect the *collective* identity that demonstrates the role of legal mobilisation in achieving social change. By taking social movement identity politics into account Vanhala's concern is to trace the identity and institutionalised norms that influence strategic choices. While I am more concerned with the construction of meaning through experience rather than outcomes, I am similarly guided by the consideration of frames and how collective values influence decision-making. My related focus is on how *lawyers* contest, negotiate, articulate and rearticulate meaning in the context of their work and across different organisational settings within their networks of legal practice.

The study of social movements presents a meaningful exploration of shared collective identities and their related cultural reproduction. The ways in which law reformers use the law to achieve social change within the context of social movements has long been recognised.[176] Traditionally, social movement scholars analysed movements as a form of political activity by grassroots rather than powerful or elite groups.[177] Some scholars refer to socially disruptive tactics in their definition either as a violation of legal rules or as a disruption of social practice; yet 'most social movements balance disruption and confrontation with cooperation, legality and consensus building'.[178] There have been divergent developing trends in social movement theory,[179] however, in 'The Concept of a

[175] Vanhala (n 124).

[176] Handler (n 163).

[177] J Craig Jenkins, 'Sociopolitical Movements' in Samuel Long (ed), *The Handbook of Political Behaviour* (Plenum Press, 1981) 81; Cyrus Zirakzadeh, *Social Movements in Politics: A Comparative Study* (Longman, 1997).

[178] ibid 5.

[179] Diani consolidates four main theories: The Collective Behaviour Perspective, The Resource Mobilization Theory, Political Process Perspective and New Social Movements.

Social Movement' Mario Diani sets out a persuasive unifying theory that identifies common threads across the four leading theoretical approaches:

1. networks of informal interaction;
2. shared beliefs and solidarity;
3. collective action on conflictual issues;
4. action which displays largely outside the institutional sphere and routine procedures of daily life.[180]

The final feature, lack of institutionalisation, is ultimately disputed by Diani (in light of the differing degrees to which institutionalism can ultimately influence the development of social movements). He therefore arrives at the following definition:

> Social movements consist in networks of informal interaction between a plurality of individuals, groups and organizations, engaged in a political and/or cultural conflict, on the basis of a shared collective identity.[181]

Importantly, Diani focuses on a looser 'network of informal interactions between individuals, groups and/or organisations' with the boundaries of the movement itself being defined not so much by action or organisation but by 'the specific collective identity shared by actors involved in the interaction'.[182] Friedman and McAdam describe collective identity as a 'shorthand designation for announcing a status' that can be comprised of a set of attitudes, commitments or values.[183] They too outline the relationship between collective identity and a networked conception of social movements.[184] For Diani, collective identity is both internal and external, thus actors 'must define themselves as part of a broader movement, and, at the same time, be perceived as such, by those within the same movement, and by opponents and/or external observers'. While a diverse range of views might be held within the group, the collective identity is pertinent. It is upon the basis of this shared identity, and beliefs, that actors are engaged in political or cultural conflict.

The most prescient point in respect of Diani's definition is that he moves away from a set notion of organisational structure and formal institutions. This is important in the context of progressive lawyering: I interrogate where activities rest outside and across organisations and build on Diani's work to show that social movements exist (and may persist) across a wide spectrum. We should not overly focus on structure to the detriment of more nuanced identifying features, nor should we be restricted even by traditional boundaries of professionalism.

[180] Mario Diani, 'The Concept of a Social Movement' (1992) 40(1) *Sociological Review* 7.
[181] ibid 13.
[182] ibid 8–9.
[183] Debra Friedman and Douglas McAdam, 'Collective Identity and Activism: Networks, Choices and the Life of a Social Movement' in Aldon Morris et al (eds), *Frontiers in Social Movement Theory* (Yale University Press, 1992) 156, 157.
[184] ibid 170.

Diani relies on network theory, that is to say the social interactions that exist between people both as individuals but also within and across organisations or groups.[185] Networks consist of sets of nodes that are linked by relationships and are often differentiated and delineated in some way:

> In social movement networks, nodes usually consist either of the individuals who mobilize or sympathize with a certain cause or subscribe to certain alternative lifestyles, or of the organizations that promote collective action on such issues or encourage alternative cultural practices.[186]

The network nodes are connected by ties that might be direct (for example, two lawyers who know each other) or indirect (eg, where an activity or resource is shared). These network ties are important to collective identity, as well as to the ideology, symbols and tools that movements rely upon.[187] Importantly, Diani's 'networks of interaction' approach therefore demonstrates that an organisation itself cannot be a social movement simply by virtue of its organisational structure. Even the term 'public interest group' fails to adequately capture the processes of interaction across and within different network nodes. It is this interactive process that determines the shared system of belief and sense of belonging so central to the concept of a social movement.

The cause lawyering literature also points to the importance of networks in creating opportunities for lawyers to benefit from alliances.[188] There are also several possible reasons for the rigorous and persistent pursuit of change within intensive settings within and across networks. Sarat and Scheingold identify a 'relative congenial context' in small, focused environments, which gives a 'sense of being part of an egalitarian, democratic, political movement that was making political progress'.[189] The mix of 'autonomy and choice' and 'purposeful solidarity and accomplishment' is further rewarding for lawyers. Cause lawyering networks had particular success in the 1960s and 1970s in the US given that historically the civil rights movement had a role to play in establishing smaller sites of activity. These were grassroots lawyers whose work was linked to social movements in an attempt to bring about change using a variety of tools. Smaller organisations in the US were micro-sites of influential activity representing cultural and political issues that also translated to more elite settings. The UK law centre movement replicated this model and the solidarity of networks was

[185] Charles Kadushin, *Understanding Social Networks: Theories, Concepts and Findings* (Oxford University Press, 2012). Networks also have a particular role to play in the narrative constitution of identity: Margaret Somers, 'The Narrative Constitution of Identity: A Relational and Network Approach' (1994) 23(5) *Theory and Society* 605; Andrew Brown, 'A Narrative Approach to Collective Identities' (2006) 43(4) *Journal of Management Studies* 731.

[186] Mario Diani, 'Social Movements and Networks' in the *Blackwell Encyclopaedia of Sociology* (Wiley and Sons, 2015).

[187] Sarah Soule, 'Diffusion Processes Within and Across Movements' in David Snow et al, *The Blackwell Companion to Social Movements* (Blackwell, 2004) 294, 297.

[188] Stephen Meili, 'Latin American Cause Lawyering Networks' in Sarat and Scheingold (n 45) 307.

[189] Sarat and Scheingold (n 3) 91.

fundamental in its early success.[190] For many law centres, the features of the local activist community had obvious influence. Abel describes the example of Brent Community Law Centre in the 1980s in the UK, which engaged in progressive activities due to 'strong trade union and tenant groups, a Labour-dominated local council, and a large organized black community'.[191] The apparent shared interactions within and across these settings is salient. Whether through friendships, employment links or professional networks such as the Haldane Society of Socialist Lawyers, The Human Rights Lawyers Association or the Young Legal Aid Lawyers Association they serve to strengthen solidarity. Within these networks, this book identifies how the values and motivations of lawyers are illustrative of the choices they have made in their professional lives and are interwoven with personal and political perspectives.

The questions that Diani therefore poses are instrumental in the context of this research: 'how do actors, who are broadly interested in similar issues, yet from different perspectives, come to think of themselves as part of a broader movement, while preserving their peculiarity?' Furthermore, 'how to they manage to preserve their collective identity?'[192] These questions move away from examining strict function to interaction and guide the research questions at the heart of the study. What beliefs do progressive lawyers share across different organisational settings (NGOs, charities, law firms and law centres)? What processes and experiences lead to their sense of collective identity? Diani's definition also facilitates consideration of how ideas and values are sustained over time. Diani encourages attending to 'network processes connecting events, activities, and ideas' and not simply to those processes that might link individuals to institutions and organisations. Further he asserts that the *multiplicity* of networks should not be overlooked, different actors and events may be linked by disparate activities.[193]

CONCLUSIONS

I have outlined the ways in which the controversies identified in socio-legal studies of cause lawyers can provide a framework for exploring how UK lawyers seek to pursue broader social change. How cause lawyers organise themselves collectively as professionals is significant. The ethical controversies directly relate to the question of why lawyers are motivated to pursue the cases they do and what ethical frameworks they adopt in order to do their work. While lawyers can be

[190] Garth (n 29) 67.
[191] Abel (n 35) 6.
[192] Diani (n 180) 18.
[193] Mario Diani, 'Networks and Social Movements: A Research Programme' in Mario Diani and Douglas McAdam (eds), *Social Movement Analysis: The Network Perspective* (Oxford University Press, 2003) 318.

grouped together and assigned any one of a number of indeterminate labels, a salient issue is whether the lawyers in this study understand *themselves* to be part of a collective movement, and whether they are perceived as such by others. Diani demands this *dual* definitive clarity and provides a useful starting point towards investigating the cultural and political identification lawyers have with projects, causes, campaigns and casework strategies and, in turn, whether they are identified by them. As McEvoy and Rebouche assert in the cause lawyering context: 'not only does law matter, but so do lawyers and so does what they say'.[194] The stories in this book intend to capture lawyers' voices; the fluidity of their perspectives and changes over time in order to probe how progressive legal identity is formulated and the necessary conditions for sustaining it.

Processes of legislative action and administrative decision-making are inevitably interwoven with social, political and economic constraints and a recent context of legislative change has brought about a renewed wave of professional discontent in the UK. While, of course, lawyers have often historically been engaged in political wars, the battleground presents new complexities that this study aims to explore. Lawyers are fighting for access to justice on behalf of vulnerable clients, while fighting for *themselves* to have continued access on their clients' behalf. Further, while battling over rights entitlements, progressive lawyers are at the same time advocating for the future of the very framework that upholds those rights. It appears that this is not an individual fight, but one of a collective. It lies not in the courtroom alone but across multiple sites of socio-political production. I am concerned with the interplay between the lawyer, the client and the state, as these battles have been fought (whether won or lost) over the last five decades to the present day. This book interrogates the ways in which personal and professional life is constitutive of political culture by examining the networks of interaction that influence change. Across different practice sites the choices that lawyers make in the context of both their day-to-day and high impact work are far reaching in terms of shaping the nature of their own legal practice, their relationships with other civil society organisations and with social activists working within them. This study is therefore situated in the contemporary context of progressive legal practice and is alive to the controversies upon which it rests. It looks to the foundations of legal aid in the past but traces its future in order to better identify the individual and the collective pursuit of social change as perceived and experienced by UK progressive lawyers within and across their networks.

[194] McEvoy and Rebouche (n 126) 310.

3

Identifying Progressive Lawyers

THIS BOOK DEMONSTRATES that, perhaps unsurprisingly, lawyers like telling stories about themselves and there is an enhanced element of performance in this research.[1] The importance of storytelling in legal practice cannot be overstated: there is a personal story at the root of every legal problem, often persuasively told and retold by way of competing narratives in an effort to 'find truth' and to 'do justice'.[2] Lawyers are expert storytellers and their narratives reveal a rich multi-layered process of telling their clients' stories such that those stories, and the values expressed through them, can potentially become entwined in their own. In this study, narratives are more than a text to be analysed; they form part of a social performance that is interactively constructed.[3]

This chapter outlines the research methodology for the study and its relevance to developing an in-depth understanding of lawyers' experiences and perceptions of themselves and others. Qualitative research design is apt in providing an adaptive framework that can be reconstructed in response to changing conditions such that it is in itself *interactive*.[4] The qualitative approach adopted rests firmly in the sociology of law and is influenced by socio-legal studies, it attempts to understand the social order through law and to enhance our understanding of legal practice within a wider social structure.[5] More specifically, narrative qualitative research captures the nuances of experience and perception so crucial to the study of progressive lawyering identity. It takes account of motivation and

[1] Erving Goffmann, *The Presentation of Self in Everyday Life* (Random House, 1956). For a study of how legal professional identity might be developed through performance see Desmond Manderson and Sarah Turner, 'Coffee House: Habitus and Performance Among Law Students' (2006) 31(3) *Law and Social Inquiry* 649.

[2] See, eg, W Lance Bennett and Martha Feldman, *Reconstructing Reality in the Courtroom: Justice and Judgment in American Culture* (Rutgers University Press, 1981); Peter Brooks and Paul Gewirtz, *Law's Stories: Narrative and Rhetoric in Law* (Yale University Press, 1998). Legal education literature has long explored applied legal storytelling as educational method, see Anthony Amsterdam, 'Telling Stories and Stories About Them' (1994) 1 *Clinical Law Review* 9; Nigel Duncan, Editorial, (2007) 41 *Law Teacher* 3.

[3] Francesca Polletta et al, 'The Sociology of Storytelling' (2011) 37 *Annual Sociological Review* 109–30.

[4] Joseph Maxwell, *Qualitative Research Design: An Interactive Approach* (Sage, 2013) 3.

[5] Colin Campbell and Paul Wiles, 'Study of Law in Society in Britain' (1976) *Law and Society Review* 547, 553.

change by providing an analytical basis for capturing it and the ways in which beliefs are sustained over time.[6] This is central to understanding how progressive legal identity has evolved over the last five decades in response to, for example, cuts to legal aid and emergent human rights norms. The fieldwork illustrates overlaps between conversation and storytelling and between interviews and encounters, all of which can be accommodated and enhanced through narrative methodology.

This chapter seeks to explain how we might conceive of narrative sociological method in the context of this study. The chapter first explores the reflexivity and subjectivity at the heart of the research. I then discuss the rationale behind the decision to use narrative research and autoethnography in order to accommodate the unique reflexivity inherent in the study. In doing so, the process of identifying, and continually revisiting consciousness in the research process is explained. Secondly, the chapter outlines the research design by giving an account of ethnographic exposure to progressive practice sites, otherwise known as 'network nodes' and the types of legal advice, representation, campaigning and policy work that progressive lawyers do within and across them.[7] Finally, I outline the research findings in relation to contested labelling of lawyering identity. The importance of network identification, and its relationship to the theoretical assumptions upon which the study is grounded, is also woven throughout.

NARRATIVE METHODOLOGY

If one accepts that narrative and life are intertwined such that we can locate narratives in our everyday interactions, my own interactions with progressive lawyers facilitate the storytelling in this study. In fact, some stories I already knew well given that the paths and turning points were closely intertwined with my own. Other stories were voices of experience from the past that could inform the present and speak to the future. Reflexivity (or 'reflective' research)[8] therefore forms an inherent part of this research and has implications for the research methodology. The context of the fieldwork has a significant role to play with methods being situated in lived experience.

Reflexivity in qualitative research promotes self-reflection such that the context of fieldwork is foregrounded in the research process. Situated judgements

[6] Molly Andrews, *Lifetimes of Commitment: Ageing, Politics and Psychology* (Cambridge University Press, 1991).

[7] Charles Kadushin, *Understanding Social Networks: Theories, Concepts and Findings* (Oxford University Press, 2012); Paul McLean, *Culture in Networks* (Polity Press, 2017).

[8] The terms *reflexive* and *reflective* are used interchangeably. They have at times been distinguished such that reflexive research can be seen as a specified *type* of reflective research, which involves reflection on various levels or across themes. See Mats Alvesson and Kaj Skoldberg, *Reflexive Methodology: New Vistas for Qualitative Research* (Sage, 2009).

are confronted and demand a realisation of one's own background, values, assumptions and interests in the research agenda. Put simply, reflexivity requires the researcher to give attention to how to 'think about thinking' and recognises that all research 'is driven by an interpreter'.[9] Paradoxically reflexivity has the potential to expand the possibilities of research through identification and accommodation of what might otherwise be perceived to be its limitations:

> As we see it, the process of reflexivity is an attempt to identify, do something about, and acknowledge the limitations of the research: its location, its subjects, its process, its theoretical context, its data, its analysis, and how accounts recognize that the construction of knowledge takes place in the world and not apart from it. ... For us, being reflexive in doing research is part of being honest and ethically mature.[10]

This study acknowledges and recognises the layers of meaning, as well as the creation of self, by virtue of reflective involvement in the research process.[11] The reflexivity of the study is multi-layered: while I develop my own reflective response within the context of the research, participants are encouraged to be 'reflective practitioners' who probe their own experiences such that they confront their own judgements and actions.[12] As participants in the research, there is potential to be 'action-present' in one's professional life:

> When someone reflects-in-action, he becomes a researcher in the practice context. He is not dependent on the categories or established theory and technique, but constructs a new theory of the unique case.[13]

A reflexive approach draws upon the 'natural settings' of the research. In this respect, ethnography provides an in-depth understanding of *experience* in the context in which that experience occurs: it is the 'first-hand experience and exploration of a particular social or cultural setting on the basis of (though not exclusively by) participant observation'.[14] It is particularly appropriate when seeking to understand how people make sense of social experience and the structures within which they encounter and share that experience.[15] Likewise, ethnography offers a way to capture and explore how political changes might affect the work of legal institutions and the identity of lawyers within them.[16]

[9] ibid 11.

[10] Geoffrey Shacklock and John Smyth, *Being Reflexive in Critical Educational and Social Research* (Falmer, 1998) 6–7.

[11] Maxine Birch, 'Re/constructing Research Narratives: Self and Sociological Identity in Alternative Settings' in Rosaline Edwards and Jane Ribbens (eds), *Feminist Dilemmas in Qualitative Research: Public Knowledge and Private Lives* (Sage, 1998).

[12] Stephen Brookfield, *Understanding and Facilitating Adult Learning* (Open University, 1986) 247.

[13] Donald Schon, *The Reflective Practitioner: How Professionals Think in Action* (Temple Smith, 1983) 68.

[14] Paul Atkinson et al (eds), *Handbook of Ethnography* (Sage, 2001) 4.

[15] Kees Van der Waal, 'Getting Going: Organizing Ethnographic Fieldwork' in Sierk Ybema et al (eds), *Organizational Ethnography: Studying the Complexity of Everyday Life* (Sage, 2009).

[16] See, eg, Hagan et al 'Swaying the Hand of Justice: The Internal and External Dynamics of Regime Change at the International Criminal Tribunal of the Former Yugoslavia' (2006) 31(3) *Law and Social Inquiry* 585.

While the data collection by way of face-to-face interview in this study comprises an 18-month long period, in fact the fieldwork period is much longer by virtue of my encounters over many years with practitioners in different contexts. On the continuum of ethnographic research participation, my role lies beyond being an 'observer' such that I am a participant in the research by virtue of my own experience.[17]

Ethnography therefore offers rich possibilities by virtue of its exploratory nature and its facilitation of research participation. As a step further, if we accept that ethnography can be understood as knowledge informed by experience and relies to some extent on the researcher having experiences similar to those of the research participants, we must also confront the issue of *subjective* representation of social reality which may lead to research bias. I acknowledge that some socio-legal scholars reject narrative research methodology on this basis; or simply dislike it, and that it has often been 'scorned by scholars aspiring to scientific authority'.[18] However, I have been long drawn to the depth of analysis that such research methods offer by way of complement to other empirical research methods. Drawing upon similar studies in the field of social psychology this research adopts a participatory approach that acknowledges subjectivity and purports that the research might be enhanced by it:

> It is through establishing rapport, or 'bias' as some may call it that interviewers come to understand interviewees … interviews can be understood as related to though not identical with, other, more familiar forms of human communication; from this perspective, rapport is not regarded as something to be avoided but rather as a resource that has the potential to enhance the quality of the interview.[19]

Autoethnography is also relevant to the study and, through self-reflection, connects personal experience and autobiography to the research. It has been a burgeoning research method in the field of clinical legal education in the UK[20] and can be drawn upon as an immersive method that 'treats research as a political, socially-just and socially conscious act' and promotes the accommodation of experience, emotion and subjectivity.[21] It also acknowledges that the researcher may come to the research with values, beliefs and experiences that cannot simply be dismissed but have the potential to form an integral part of the research as a process of self-conscious learning.[22] Autoethnography looks both

[17] Raymond Gold, 'Roles in sociological field observation' (1958) 36 *Social Forces* 217.

[18] Patricia Ewick and Susan Silbey, 'Subversive Stories and Hegemonic Tales: Towards a Sociology of Narrative (1995) 29(2) *Law & Society Review* 197, 197. See also Jonas Bens and Larissa Vetters, 'Ethnographic legal studies: reconnecting anthropological and sociological traditions' (2018) 50(3) *The Journal of Legal Pluralism and Unofficial Law* 239.

[19] Andrews (n 6) 51–52.

[20] Elaine Campbell, 'Should I share my journal entry with you? A critical exploration of relational ethics in autoethnography' (2017) 6(4) *Departures in Critical Qualitative Research* 4.

[21] Tony Adams and Stacey Holman Jones 'Autoethnography is queer' in Norman Denzin et al (eds), *Handbook of Critical and Indigenous Methodologies* (Sage, 2008).

[22] Carolyn Ellis and Arthur Bochner, 'Autoethnography, personal narrative, reflexivity' in Norman Denzin et al (eds), *Handbook of Qualitative Research* (Sage, 2000) 737.

outward and inward such that the line between personal and cultural aspects of research may become blurred.[23] This is particularly appropriate in a storytelling context. Indeed, it has long been recognised that personal narrative research lends itself well to autoethnography.[24] The presentation of relevant autobiographical details provides tools by which to analyse lived experience in order to recognise cultural identity within the broader context of the research. Using these methods it should be stressed that they do not purport to expose definitive truth, rather a construction of truth rooted in personal experience.

Notably, the narrative turn in sociology in the 1980s recognised in particular the ways in which narrative could give us insight into the how people 'fashioned identity from available cultural identities' and especially so in relation to collective identity.[25] Narratives can help us understand how individuals inhabit their own sense of self while navigating their broader social world and the spaces between them. Interactions, perceptions, expectations and disappointments are just some of the features that can be captured in the space between actual experience and the retelling of that experience. Narratives are also useful in simply exploring why life might go in a particular direction, not just causally but morally.[26] In this study, narratives have potential therefore to describe lessons derived from progressive lawyers' experiences as turning points in their lives, as well as how those turning points might be linked to their own sense of right and wrong.

In this regard the research is guided by the broader narrative thesis of *continuity*. Embedded in constructivism, and in much of Jerome Bruner's work, the continuity thesis argues that 'narrative draws on life for inspiration to create an imagined world that has substance, colour, texture and meaning'.[27] It purports that life gives meaning to narrative, and narrative gives meaning to life, facilitating a fertile process of creativity. As Ellis and Bochner identify, the question to consider is not 'does my story reflect my past accurately?' but rather, 'what are the consequences my story produces?' and 'what new possibilities does it offer for living my life?'[28] The *discontinuity* thesis on the other hand argues that while narrative seeks to describe life, it is set apart from life itself. Narrative can enforce meaning that may not have actually been there in the first place; it surfaces only in the retelling such that narrative and life cannot be described as a continuous process.

[23] Deborah Reed-Danahay, *Auto-ethnography: Rewriting the Self and the Social* (Routledge, 1997).

[24] Norman Denzin, *Interpretative Biography* (Sage, 1989).

[25] Francesca Polletta et al, 'The Sociology of Storytelling' (2011) 37 *Annual Sociological Review* 109, 112.

[26] Molly Patterson and Kristen Monroe, 'Narrative in Political Science' (1998) 1 *Annual Review of Political Science* 315, 316.

[27] Brian Schiff et al, 'Life and Narrative: A Brief Primer' in Brian Schiff et al (eds), *Life and Narrative: The Risks and Responsibilities of Storying Experience* (Oxford University Press, 2017) xxxii.

[28] Ellis and Bochner (n 22) 744.

The connection between personal and professional lives is therefore key to the exploration of identity and centres around collective values, shared experiences and interactions. The continuity thesis offers a connection between story and life experience that also relates to the 'life history' approach adopted in this book, which is apt for both categorising and connecting the personal narratives shared.[29] Historicism – how social and cultural phenomena might be related to history – is particularly relevant to participants pursuing change in view of the fact that at the time of my fieldwork the research environment is itself subject to unprecedented change and upheaval. Lawyers' own observations are set within a particular context that takes account of the unique time and place of the study. For many participants, today's particular challenges are compared and contrasted to the past and viewed through that prism. The research moves with the participants' own progression. As their stories are shaping and evolving so too are their careers and the lives of their clients and the causes they pursue. In analysing their narratives, I sense a continuous striving and a never standing still: a desire to do better, to achieve more, to positively change the lives of clients or pursue impactful societal change. The moving and turning of lawyers' stories within this broader desire for change is revealing. Even when drawn back, the stories continue to evolve forward while participants strive for change. The research therefore demands a storied methodology that is alive to the process of change and also to participants' struggle to resist its negative impact.

REFLEXIVITY AND ELITE INTERVIEWING

In every research context, whether in an interview or in the archive, we are affected: moved, changed, transformed. Attentiveness to these dynamics in practices of 'reflexivity' involves a critical stance to research methods and to knowledge making practices, seeking to make more explicit how we produce what we come to know.[30]

A sense of equality between researcher and the research respondents is particularly important in narrative research.[31] This is in part due to the open and personal nature of the research and the need for participants to feel at ease in order to facilitate storytelling in a personally meaningful way. In narrative research, a joint understanding of the narratives created in the research process facilitates the functioning of that very process, which also resonates with the accepted contention that narrative research methodology must be seen as collaborative.[32]

[29] Brian Alleyne, *Narrative Networks: Storied Approaches in a Digital Age* (Sage, 2015) 141.

[30] Joan Anim-Addo and Yasmin Gunaratnam, 'Secrets and lies: Narrative methods at the limits of research' (2012) 5(3) *Journal of Writing in Creative Practice* 387, 391.

[31] David Fetterman, *Ethnography: Step by Step* (Sage, 1998) 129.

[32] D Jean Clandinin and F Michael Connelly, *Narrative Inquiry: Experience and story in qualitative research* (Josey-Bass, 2000); D Jean Clandinin and Jerry Rosiek, 'Mapping a landscape of

As described above, my own role is one of a researcher-participant such that the study can be described as reflexive ethnography. My background of working for charities and NGOs, and in law school clinics, places me within one of the subsets of practice with experience of others in the study. My colleagues generally work in legal aid, civil liberties or human rights. Participants in the study are willing to share their own experiences on a level that necessitates a shared understanding of those experiences and the values that shape them. The insights derived from that shared understanding come from active *participation* in the research process, which in turn facilitates further narrative construction. Lawyers in the study often described feeling validated and motivated by the act of sharing their stories, and I acknowledge that this process equally applies to me and that methodological implications flow from it. For example, it is important to resist any attempt to order narratives on behalf of others as well as 'the cleaning-up and pulling-together impulses of the researcher in seeing out unifying story-line/s'.[33] The narrative process accepts that 'all tellings are unique, incomplete and inaccurate' and in fact, the more a story might deviate from historical 'accuracy', the more it simply 'depicts norms, values and beliefs because these accounts more fully embody the storyteller's interpretation of events'.[34] Ethnography lends itself well to accommodating these elements of disruption due to what has been described as its 'anarchic atmosphere' compared to other types of qualitative research.[35]

As such, the narrative interviews were conversational and collaborative. This approach is reflected in my decision to use the word 'participant' throughout this study to describe what might otherwise be termed 'respondents', 'interviewees' or 'research subjects'. The terminology better reflects the participatory nature of the project as well as my own role within it: I aim to put others at ease by creating a mutually reinforcing dialogue that is shared rather than owned. However, I note that claims as to prior knowledge can influence power relations – both perceived and actual – during fieldwork, especially in the context of elite interviewing. Interviews in this study are exclusively with 'elite' participants who are considered elite in research terms because they have been selected for a particular reason by virtue of their professional position and because of their high social importance.[36] Many of the participants enjoy high levels of prestige in their professional lives. Lawyers form part of a professional elite and hold a set of beliefs, whether consciously or not, to the exclusion of other individuals

narrative inquiry: Borderland spaces and tensions' in D Jean Clandinin (ed), *Handbook of narrative inquiry: Mapping a methodology* (Sage, 2006) 35.

[33] Anim-Addo and Gunaratnam (n 30) 392.

[34] Anthony v Alfieri, 'Welfare Stories' in Martha Minow and Gary Bellow (eds), *Law Stories* (University of Michigan Press, 1996) 30–32.

[35] John Flood, 'Socio-legal ethnography' in Reza Banaker and Max Travers (eds), *Theory and Method in Socio-Legal Research* (Hart, 2005) 34.

[36] David Richards 'Elite interviewing: Approaches and Pitfalls' (1996) 16(3) *Politics* 199.

or groups of people.[37] Throughout the research process I was acutely mindful that unlike a 'detached observer' expectations and assumptions flow from my identification with the group and imbalances of power are arguably experienced more acutely in an elite context. This is of course also true of power imbalances of age and gender and, added to the weight of intellectual or experiential elitism in the legal profession, these imbalances can at times seem overwhelming given that judgements are frequently made based on achievements, experiences and connectivity to a network of practitioners who have the capacity to hold each other in very high esteem.

In many respects, the experience of this research has highlighted the elitism of the legal profession by giving me a view from both *within* and *outside* it. During the fieldwork, I often sensed my role as a researcher shifting. While in some contexts I was an insider looking in, in others my role was reconfigured and I might experience exclusion from a particular subset of practice. To clarify, that is not to say I experienced my research role as a detached observer: I still considered myself a participant in the research. It is simply that the vantage point shifted such that power relations changed. In light of these observations, I was often struck by the response of some practitioners who revealed their own insecurities when I have approached them for interview. In what can be a competitive field of practice, many expressed uncertainty as to whether their own work is esteemed or valuable enough to fit within the remit of the study. Given that this study is ultimately concerned with collective identity it is important to consider how those who objectively 'belong' might feel a sense of fragility about that very belonging. In my experience, progressive practitioners often hold each other in almost mythical high regard and this can lead to perceived elites and hierarchies within the subsets of progressive legal practice. Any exploration of identity should take account of how identity shifts and the changing accounts that people give of themselves. This is, in part, due to the distinction between the real and imagined self.[38] In particular, loyalties that individuals may feel to others can be subject to change but *imagined* loyalties might also exist. These changes potentially influence power relations in both practical and theoretical terms, hence the adoption of an interactive and adaptable research methodology that accommodates shifting experiences and vantage points.

[37] Edgar S Cahn and Jean C Cahn, 'Power to the People or the Profession? The Public Interest in Public Interest Law' (1970) 79 *Yale Law Journal* 1005.

[38] See Anthony Kronman, *The Lost Lawyer: Failing Ideals and the Legal Profession*, 6th edn (Harvard University Press, 2001). Kronman explores the gap between the legal professional ideal and reality, in particular the fall of the historical notion of 'hero figures' in law in the US as indicative of the way in which lawyers wished to see themselves: 'The lawyer-statesman – possessed of great practical wisdom and exceptional persuasive powers, devoted to the public good but keenly aware of limitations of human beings and their political arrangements …' (at 12).

IDENTIFYING AREAS OF PRACTICE

As I outlined in the preface to the book, I was called to the Bar of England and Wales in 2007 and moved to UCL Faculty of Laws in 2010 to set up a clinical legal education programme. My focus in this programme was to facilitate experiential learning opportunities for students alongside theoretical engagement in access to justice issues. This involved a partnership model developing casework together with lawyers in external charities, NGOs and law centres in areas including social welfare, human rights and youth justice. My work teaching and in pro bono programme development has allowed me to maintain my own legal network for more than a decade in a way that uniquely spans legal education and practice, as well as the legal aid and not-for-profit legal sectors and different types of legal work including both high volume casework and strategic litigation.[39]

My experience over many years facilitated the identification of progressive areas of practice for the study and the social network that underpins the research in this book. I draw upon McLean's definition of a social network as a set of relations between objects, which includes both people and organisations.[40] Importantly, my concern is to identify lawyers working within and across the social network of progressive legal practice. The research investigates different subsets of legal practice that I have delineated as 'sites' throughout the book but they might also be thought of as network 'nodes' connected by different sets of relations and ties.[41] Within these sites, or nodes, of practice lie other network ties that are flexible and interactive. As McLean outlines, these network ties might be social relationships, shared memberships of groups, a flow of resources or geographic proximity. Within each of these ties lie connections that facilitate progressive legal work: 'humans are exceptionally adept at stitching different types of ties together, across different domains, to forge connections'.[42]

To identify areas of practice, I conducted an initial analysis of online biographical details of a sample of well-known progressive practitioners in the UK, which confirmed a parity of movement through and towards places of employment. It seemed possible that early political networks and experiences

[39] Jacqueline Kinghan, 'Teaching Access to Justice: Cause Lawyering and Strategic Litigation in Clinical Context' in Chris Ashford and Paul McKeown (eds), *Social Justice and Legal Education* (Cambridge Scholars, 2018); Jacqueline Kinghan and Rachel Knowles, 'Striking a Balance in Clinical Legal Education: Reimagining the Role of the teaching Practitioner in Casework Partnerships' in Linden Thomas et al (eds), *Reimagining Clinical Legal Education* (Hart, 2018); Lisa Vanhala and Jacqueline Kinghan, *Using the Law for Social Change, A Landscape Review* (The Baring Foundation, 2018); Lisa Vanhala and Jacqueline Kinghan, *Using the Law to Address Unfair Systems: A case study of the Personal Independence Payments Legal Challenge* (The Baring Foundation, 2019).

[40] Kadushin (n 7) 3.

[41] McLean (n 7).

[42] ibid 36.

opened up new opportunities and lend weight to professional progressive credentials. I observed in my work how experience in law centres and charities or NGOs and then into legal aid practice (and back again) is common, especially with the aim of career advancement and progression, or simply striving to make positive change while also developing network ties. There are connecting experiences and achievements in early professional life that act as progressive rites of passage, for example: (historically) a Reprieve death penalty internship, volunteering at a local law centre, Tribunal representation with FRU, working for a Labour or Lib Dem MP, paralegal work in a legal aid firm, a legal or policy officer post at organisations such as the UN, Liberty or JUSTICE and, more recently (and UK wide) holding a Legal Education Foundation Justice First Fellowship. Likewise, membership of organisations forms an integral part of the network, for example: The Haldane Society for Socialist Lawyers, The Young Legal Aid Lawyers Association, Legal Aid Practitioners Group, The Human Rights Lawyers Association or The Association of Labour Lawyers (to name a few). I note that while I qualified into legal practice in England and Wales I did my undergraduate law degree in Scotland and come from Northern Ireland. Many of my classmates qualified into human rights practice in Scotland and Northern Ireland, and I utilised these networks to identify practitioners outside of England and Wales. Relevant organisations to which these lawyers belong include the Scottish Human Rights Consortium, RebLaw Scotland and the Northern Ireland Human Rights Consortium.

To further identify areas of practice I consulted reports from bodies that seek to support and encourage the legal profession in their access to justice activities such as Law Works, The Law Society, PILNET and The Bar Association.[43] Literature by the Legal Aid Practitioners Group (LAPG) was particularly informative in delineating the historical overlap between different types of work. Abel also endorses the term 'progressive' and points to its appropriateness precisely because of the diffusion it captures across different types of activity:

> I use the euphemism 'progressive' deliberately. All these lawyers are on the 'left' … that left is a very diffuse category, including trade unionists, Marxists, feminists, populists, anti-imperialists, environmentalists, anti-racists, the movement against nuclear weapons, etc. Although these movements have not been able to unite under a single ideology, political party, or association, they recognize each other as actual or potential allies, and so do the lawyers who serve them.[44]

Abel highlights here the ease with which lawyers recognise one another as 'actual or potential allies' on the left across a broad spectrum. My identification

[43] See, eg, Justice, *To Assist the Court: Third Party Interventions in the Public Interest* (Justice/Freshfields, 2016); *The LawWorks Clinics Network Reports* (Lawworks, 2015–2018), *The Law Society of England and Wales Pro Bono Manual: A Practical Guide and Toolkit for Lawyers* (The Law Society, 2010); *Justice: A Precious Asset, Bar Council Party Conference Briefing 2015* (The Bar Council, 2015).

[44] Richard Abel, 'Lawyers and the Power to Change' (1985) 7 *Law and Policy* 15.

of progressive network nodes and individuals working within them also rests on lawyers' perceptions of their own politics. They each self-identify as being 'on the left' and recognise one another to be so, despite the disparate and broad ranging political perspectives this might encompass. This ranges from participants who describe themselves as centre-left to those who self-identify as communists or socialists.[45] The differentiation of left lawyers can therefore be said to encompass both radicals and reformers.[46] With this in mind, I traced work across different subject areas with the common thread being those lawyers who worked within, or were members of, network nodes that were perceived to be broadly on the left and delineated the types of work outlined below.

Finally, is important to note that the field of human rights has developed considerably over the time period of the study. Many practitioners doing human rights work in the past did not identify it in those terms whereas there is now an interplay between broad social welfare work and human rights, often termed 'public law' (that is to say legal work that broadly concerns regulating government use of power). I intended to capture both the 'grassroots' social welfare work as well as public law practice and therefore selected both the general spectrum of social welfare law (for example, housing, family, debt, benefits, mental health) and human rights within the remit of the study (for example, equality rights, prisoners' rights or privacy rights). Finally, I have limited the study to those lawyers primarily working on domestic issues in the UK but acknowledge their work may be informed by and connected to international human rights legal practice.

In light of the above considerations I delineated the following types of activity for the study:

Legal Aid Casework

As outlined in the previous chapter, legal aid has been considerably curtailed over the time period of the study since the 1970s. At present (in England and Wales), it includes lawyers working on family law matters only if there is risk of serious abuse or harm, for criminal matters or if clients face prison or detention, if clients are at risk of becoming homeless, have been discriminated against

[45] I note that the broad 'left' spectrum also accommodates changes over time. Several participants in the study described themselves as holding communist or socialist values in the early years of their legal practice (particularly in the 1980s and 1990s) but now simply self-identified as being 'on the left' or 'left-wing'. Only a minority of participants in the study reference their politics with reference to association with political parties.

[46] Kate Nash, *The Political Sociology of Human Rights* (Cambridge University Press, 2015) 172. The concept of the 'tempered radical' is also relevant in this context: Debra Meyerson and Maureen Scully, 'Tempered Radicalism and the Politics of Ambivalence and Change' (1995) 6(5) *Organization Science* 585.

or the case involves human rights matters.[47] The scope is slightly broader in Northern Ireland and Scotland.[48] Historically legal aid was available for a much wider range of social welfare matters and at earlier stages in the development of legal problems. It is important to acknowledge that not all lawyers who work on legal aid do so exclusively and the study also includes practitioners who work on some legal aid matters in addition to other types of casework (private work, philanthropically or crowdfunded funded casework in charities, law centre practice, pro bono or law school clinics). It also important to recognise, as historically outlined in chapter two, that legal aid work exists across each of the different practice sites and indeed the study is designed to capture this fluidity (see further below).

Campaigning

Lawyers campaign around their casework to varying degrees and in different forums. Activism and campaigning are particularly common for lawyers working in house in charities and NGOs[49] (for example charity/NGO Directors, legal officers or caseworkers) but is also conducted by barristers instructed by those organisations and for law centre or legal aid solicitors on matters related to, for example, social welfare and rights entitlements.

Policy Advocacy

This is again common for in-house lawyers who play a role in connecting their litigation to broader policy goals (eg, by way of strategic litigation). There are obvious overlaps between campaigning and policy advocacy but this activity better describes the subtle creation of dialogue conducted by lawyers, often through negotiation and establishing persuasive networks, as a means of drawing attention to particular policies and encouraging evidence-based change from a legal perspective.

Strategic Litigation

As described in chapter two, this term refers to high impact casework that seeks to change a law, policy or practice by carefully selecting the issues and

[47] Changes implemented in England and Wales by the Legal Aid, Sentencing and Punishment of Offenders Act 2012.

[48] For a comparison of civil legal aid across the UK see, Yohanna Sakkberg and Benjamin Politowski, *Civil Legal Aid: England & Wales, Scotland and Northern Ireland Compared* (House of Commons Library Briefing Paper No 7603, 9 June 2016).

[49] I define this widely for the purposes of the study to include not-for-profit organisations that use the law in the public interest; and do so independently of the state.

litigants at the heart of the case. Strategic litigation can potentially involve all three of the activities described above in that it might be, for example, a legally aided judicial review of government decision making with associated policy reform matters and campaign issues.[50] Another route to lawyers becoming involved in strategic litigation is by way of third party interventions.[51] Since the mid-1990s this procedure allows public bodies, individuals or NGOs to make submissions that assist the court by adding value on matters of fact or law within their expertise. Charities and NGOs use it in cases that might further their goals or objectives or are likely to impact those whom they support.

These activities overlap and lawyers may engage in some or all to varying degrees. In identifying study participants, I sought to find lawyers who had engaged in at least two of the four activities and coded their involvement, aiming to achieve a broad cross-section and overlap between each of the four categories (see appendix one for table of interviews). Informed by my wider ethnographic fieldwork, I then connected these activities to subsets of practice comprising five practice-sites, which form the network nodes of the study:

Barrister-Campaigner

This subset describes those barristers working predominantly in human rights or legally aided casework (for example child law, inquests, mental health, community care or criminal law) who also engage in campaigns either directly or indirectly related to their cases. These might include, for example, general campaigns related to the abolition of the Human Rights Act or cuts to legal aid or, more specifically, a miscarriage of justice in an individual case or lobbying for law reform with respect to particular group/s. Barrister-campaigners may also be instructed in strategic litigation, either on behalf of a claimant or an intervener (usually a charity or NGO). Although not exclusively so, barristers-campaigners tend to work from what are perceived to be left-wing sets of Chambers and are sometimes referred to (or self-identify) as members of the 'radical Bar'. I note that where barristers (in England and Wales) work in-house in law centres, legal aid law firms or NGOs they would be captured by one of the practice sites below. As such, for the purposes of this study, barrister-campaigner refers to those barristers or advocates practising at the independent Bar rather than 'in-house'.

[50] I note that the number of crowd funded strategic legal cases significantly increased during the course of the research. See, Joe Tomlinson, 'Crowdfunding and the changing dynamics of public interest judicial review' in *Justice in the Digital State: Assessing the Next Revolution in Digital Justice* (Policy Press, 2019) 19–36.

[51] Deana Smith et al, *Third Party Interventions in Judicial Review: An action research study* (The Public Law Project, 2001); Harriet Samuels, 'Feminist Activism, Third Party Interventions and the Courts' (2005) 13 *Feminist Legal Studies* 15.

Legal Aid Lawyer

These solicitors work in legal aid practice on legally aided casework as described above. For the purposes of the study, this subset of practitioners specifically delineates and captures those lawyers working in legal aid law firms rather than law centre solicitors who might also conduct legal aid casework (see below). While legal aid solicitors may also accept private cases in discrete areas of law in addition to legally aided work, solicitors selected for participation in the study have a practice that is either *exclusively or predominantly* comprised of legal aid work.

Law Centre Lawyer

Law centres are not-for-profit legal practices historically intended to provide representation for the most disadvantaged in society (modelled on the US 'neighbourhood law offices' as described in chapter two). These practitioners are solicitors who work in a law centres in areas of civil law[52] usually funded by some combination of legal aid, local authority funding, grant funding and corporate donations. Legally aided areas of advice have significantly changed over the time period of the study and can vary depending on location and specialism. In the 1970s through to the early 1990s solicitors worked in 'collectives' and were often said to be part of a much wider law centre movement (again, to a greater or lesser extent depending on location). These solicitors tend to work to alleviate the root causes of poverty and inequality in addition to their casework. This might include pursuing strategic litigation and engaging in public legal education[53] initiatives.

Charity/NGO Lawyer

This subset of practitioners describes lawyers, qualified as either solicitors or barristers, working in the wider charity or NGO sector. They often hold positions of leadership and play an important role influencing the direction of the organisation and managing legal programmes. Their work might also include campaigns, directing or conducting individual and/or strategic casework and policy advocacy. While they have legal knowledge and expertise they are required to work across government and civil society. They do not usually have the same financial targets as lawyers working in private practice, although their ability to

[52] Civil law is distinguishable from criminal law. While some practitioners in the 'legal aid solicitors' subset may work in criminal law, law centre solicitors tend to work in areas of civil law. This includes housing, debt, discrimination, family, community care, employment, immigration and asylum, mental health and welfare benefits.

[53] Public legal education is a term used to describe the education of members of the public in order that they can better understand and enforce their rights and more effectively participate in the resolution of their legal problems.

pursue successful campaigns and strategic or test case litigation may be linked to grant funding or philanthropic support. From a regulatory perspective in England and Wales, barristers who work in this way are often considered to be 'employed' rather than 'self-employed' at the Bar.[54]

Law School Clinic Lawyer

These lawyers direct and supervise pro bono projects across social welfare and human rights and/or provide legal representation in free advice clinics based in law schools. For the purposes of the study, this subset refers to lawyers whose clinical work takes a 'social justice' rather than a pure legal skills development approach: they seek to both engender greater social justice awareness in legal education while making a positive community impact with their work.[55] The work they supervise might be on either a curricular or extra-curricular basis or both.

The network nodes assist in ensuring a sampling of practitioners engaging in the different types of activity (described above) and facilitate comparison between them. Aside from the distinction of being a solicitor *or* barrister (or, alternatively, a solicitor who also engages in advocacy by having obtained higher rights of audience) I have observed that there is considerable movement within and across the network. For example, it is common for a barrister in progressive practice to take pro bono work on behalf of an NGO or to work as an in-house lawyer for a charity or on secondment.[56] Legal aid solicitors might also work in an in-house capacity at charities or volunteer at local CABs or law centres (time permitting) in addition to their private practice. Notwithstanding this fluidity, by eliciting narratives across these network nodes common themes can be found and analysed in order to address similarities and differences in experiences of practice and to facilitate an understanding of the reconstruction of experience in relation to others and to the social world. As McLean outlines, it is important to address how people interact, and how their identities are shaped by, the networks to which they belong. This includes interrogating 'the faces they present, the goals they pursue and the interests they develop.'[57] I am also concerned with sustaining the network and how the identities of those lawyers within it might help the network itself to evolve. The book therefore seeks to locate common threads across the individual narratives in each of the

[54] I note that barristers called before the year 2000 who worked in law centres were subject to special provisions under the previous Code of Conduct (6th Edition).

[55] Donald Nicolson, 'Education, Education, Education: Legal, Moral and Clinical' (2008) 42(2) *Law Teacher* 145–72.

[56] I note that this practice is confined to England and Wales. In fact, the Faculty of Advocates in Scotland do not permit employed (rather than self-employed) practice for advocates (barristers) in Scotland such that any 'in-house' working in charities or NGOs is uncommon unless in a pro bono capacity.

[57] McLean (n 7) 18.

practice sites above in order to delineate collective stories that are indicative of the cultural settings in which they occur. I draw on wider ethnography and, within it, in depth narrative fieldwork interviews in order to do so.

ETHNOGRAPHY

I outlined above how my ethnographic experience working in the field facilitated identification of participants for narrative interviews. While these interviews form much of the in depth analysis of the book they are informed by other ethnographic encounters as I continued to work part-time in my University law clinic role and engage in wider projects. The participant observation therefore extends to immersive encounters with law students, other lawyers, academics (clinical legal education, human rights, political science) and other representatives of voluntary sector organisations (ie, project managers, fundraisers, policy researchers) throughout the fieldwork period. Eighteen of these were formal interviews but many others were naturally occurring conversations.[58] I kept a fieldwork diary throughout and drew upon this in my analysis. My fieldwork observations also comprised formal events such as panel events, conferences and workshops on subjects relevant to the study including legal education, legal aid and the use of law for social change.

FIELDWORK INTERVIEWS: RESEARCH PARTICIPANT SELECTION

Having identified progressive legal practice activities and practice sites I began to identify individuals working across them to select for narrative interviews. I started with my own network in the pilot phase and thereafter continued to draw upon my own network ties and then used a snowball method to identify further practitioners for the study. A majority of participants were identified by other participants in the study (frequently a participant would say after interview 'you really should speak to [x] because he/she has done some brilliant work on [y]' and might also offer an introduction). To that extent, a significant factor in the sample set of practitioners has purposefully been the impact and significance of work that lawyers engage in as *perceived* both by myself (through analysis of involvement of activities outlined above) and by other lawyers in the study. In addition to being esteemed by colleagues generally, many lawyers have received accolades from the profession itself (Legal Aid Lawyer of the Year Award, Law Society Excellent Awards or similar) for their work. These traits

[58] Charlotte Selleck, 'Ethnographic chats: A best of both method for ethnography' (2017) 30 *SKY Journal of Linguistics* 151; Silvia Kunitz and Numa Markee, 'Understanding the Fuzzy Borders of Context in Conversation Analysis and Ethnography' in Stanton Wortham et al (eds), *Discourse and Education. Encyclopedia of Language and Education*, 3rd edn (Springer, 2016).

have formed part of the generic profile of participants in the study and support the conceptual framework of the research as a whole.[59] There has therefore been a purposive element to the sampling of the study and this bears relevance to the reflexive nature of the research. As Emmel states:

> [I]n using theoretical or purposive sampling, researchers do more than act reflectively through engaging in deep and careful thought. They are reflexive. They recognise the presence of researchers in what is being investigated and they actively shape their research in a messy social world, including making ongoing decisions about sampling in their research.[60]

The sampling was a continuous, interactive process that required adaptation as the research progressed and sampling decisions were made. It was important for the purposes of the research that participants were not only perceived to participate in progressive networks (as identified by activities and practice sites outlined above) but that they also perceived themselves to be a participant of one of the network nodes of the study. I made sure to explore and clarify participants' perceptions of their own network ties where possible in my initial contact (where conversationally in person) and during interviews. Finally, my selection was also influenced by the need to achieve balance across the network nodes of the study as well as geographic location, gender, ethnicity and age or number of years in practice. All participants were anonymised and allocated a pseudonym (see appendix one). In order to preserve anonymity a 'process-orientated' approach was also adopted with some details changed in the write-up phase as necessary where there might be a risk of identification.[61]

OTHER DATA SOURCES AND DATA ANALYSIS

Aside from the primary data collection from interview and ethnographic observation, secondary sources have been collected in relation to practitioners' work where relevant. I include these in my conceptualisation of narrative as part of the study where they enhance or explain the storytelling of participants. They include an initial analysis of biographic information available on employment web profiles or on Linked In, social media (including Twitter content analysis), newspaper articles relevant to casework or campaigns, written articles or blog posts, research reports, policy documents, case reports, casework manuals and guidance documents (where available). I analysed press articles and professional legal journals from across the decades of the study as well as more recent social

[59] Brian Alleyne, *Narrative Networks: Storied Approaches in a Digital Age* (Sage, 2015) 43.

[60] Nick Emmel, *Sampling and Choosing Cases in Qualitative Research: A Realist Approach* (Sage, 2013) 46.

[61] Benjamin Saunders et al, 'Anonymising interview data: challenges and compromise in practice' (2015) 15(5) *Qualitative Research* 616.

media analysis from both individuals and organisations across the network nodes identified above. I also juxtaposed the narratives in the study with those described in biographical texts of leading progressive lawyers.[62] Taken as a whole, these secondary materials were used as background information in order to guide the interview as appropriate and are later included in my analysis where relevant. Complementary data collection took place in the form of a written field diary, collecting observations from each of the interviews both before and after they took place and from my wider ethnography (outlined above).

Interviews were transcribed verbatim and uploaded to the qualitative data analysis programme NVivo (see interview question guide at appendix two). Following a review of underlying theory, a coding tree was developed with 23 major codes and more than 50 minor codes. Illustrative major codes included motivation, networks, memorable cases, legal aid changes, ethical conflicts, organisational culture and critical events. After the pilot phase of interviews in August 2016, the coding themes were further refined alongside some additional questions. The codes were created inductively and NVivo coding was used as a starting point for further analysis. I found it necessary to frequently return manually to full transcripts in order to capture the nuance of stories and research encounters alongside more static coding. In narrative research a degree of categorisation, selection and omission is to be expected. However, I sought to minimise the extent to which stories were fragmented or mistakenly interpreted out of context by using manual and NVivo coding interchangeably and keeping a detailed fieldwork diary. I also found it helpful to listen again to interviews (often very many times) in order to revisit the experience of the research encounter and ensure I was adequately capturing the texture as well as the content of the data.

In my analysis, I sought to analyse and explore individual and collective identity *through* the stories rather than seeking to objectively explain why particular events might come about. As a lawyer, I have often had to remind myself of this distinction and that ethnography is concerned with interpretation and not causal analysis.[63] Through the use of interchangeable analytic processes, I sought to overcome the risk of coded phrases losing emotional value and meaning when 'disembodied' from their story as a whole. In this context too I acknowledge that the process of writing up became an additional tool: 'in narrative analysis, writing itself is itself a methodology'.[64]

[62] For example, Helena Kennedy, *Just Law: The Changing Face of Justice – and Why it Matters to Us All* (Random House, 2011); Michael Mansfield, *Memoirs of a Radical Lawyer* (Bloomsbury, 2009); Geoffrey Robertson, *The Justice Game* (Vintage, 1999); Geoffrey Bindman, 'What Made me a Legal Aid Lawyer?' (2002) 29(3) *Journal of Law and Society* 510.

[63] John Flood, 'Socio-legal ethnography' in Reza Banaker and Max Travers (eds), *Theory and Method in Socio-Legal Research* (Hart, 2005) 47.

[64] Steven Maynard-Moody and Michael Musheno, *Cops, Teachers and Counselors: Stories from the Front lines of Public Service* (University of Michigan Press, 2003) 176–77.

CONTESTED LABELLING OF PROGRESSIVE LEGAL IDENTITY

This section sets out research findings that outline the challenge of identifying progressive lawyers, as well as the fluidity of identity formation outlined in the methodology of the study. As I explore in the next chapter, while self-categorisation, identification and comparison outside of corporate law is clear, an easily identifiable label for the network to which participants subscribe less so. As discussed in the last chapter, the term 'cause lawyer' is significant to the study but applies to both the political left and right and is not widely accepted or understood by practitioners in the UK.[65] I selected the term 'progressive lawyer' because I understood it to capture the element of social advancement in lawyers' work; as well as the interplay between legal aid and other not-for-profit work. As detailed in the first chapter, the term 'public interest lawyer' is prevalent in the US and other jurisdictions but has not been widely adopted in the UK. Professor Sandy Fredman, whose research has addressed public interest lawyering and international human rights, commented that this is precisely because of the existence of the UK legal aid system and the strong professional identity of legal aid lawyers.[66] This is borne out in my research to some extent: I found that those in the 'legal aid lawyer' sub-set did not struggle as much as other participants with self-identifying what they do and with their own intra-group categorisation. I also found that those who work exclusively in legal aid are more easily *identifiable* and have an influential professional network through the Legal Aid Practitioners Group (LAPG) and, more recently, the Young Legal Aid Lawyers (YLAL). However, in terms of categorisation the label fails to adequately capture the range of activities being undertaken by lawyers in the wider not-for-profit field.

I note that while participants in the study view their work as making a social contribution in order to achieve change and also holding the government to account, only a minority appeared to accept the label 'progressive lawyer'. I outline in chapter four how lawyers see themselves as being part of a network of other lawyers who are *like them*. They express with clarity whomever they perceive to be 'in' or 'out' but there is a lack of consensus as to what *lawyers like us* actually means. There may be mutual identification within and across network nodes but terms are problematic and no wider label for their collective identity has been negotiated and agreed upon. To be clear, they seem to have internal recognition and intuitively identify 'us' and 'them' (ie, 'other' lawyers) but external labelling is contested. The following interview extracts highlight some tensions for participants around both individual and collective identity

[65] Andrew Boon, 'Cause Lawyers and the Alternate Ethical Paradigm' (2004) 7 *Legal Ethics* 250.
[66] Fieldwork interview with Professor Sandy Fredman, 11 December 2017.

especially in light of contextual and structural change over time. Let us begin with Kenneth who qualified in the 1960s:

> Jacqueline: So did you identify as a human rights lawyer?
>
> Kenneth: Well, I don't think I did. I don't think anybody did. In some ways maybe I was one of the first human rights lawyers because such a thing didn't really exist.

He then went on to describe how he found it 'rather funny' that people referred to him as a 'left wing lawyer'. His discomfort lies to some extent in the particularities of the changing context and the ways in which professional legal identities developed over time, especially for example in the years after the passage of the Human Rights Act 1998. Ben, for example, qualified as a lawyer in the early 1990s before the Act came into force:

> I suppose one of the things that I find a bit alien to me is the concept of human rights lawyers and public lawyers … we thought of ourselves as legal aid lawyers doing civil liberties work as we described it then. It was obviously pre Human Rights Act (Ben).

For solicitors and barristers in the study the term 'public lawyer' tends to refer to those lawyers advising on and engaged in judicial review casework and potentially encompasses those lawyers who work for, as well as against the government, on those cases. There tends to be some elitism in the field of public law, confirmed by participants in the study, who commented that it was related to the assumption that it is more intellectually rigorous than other areas of law, perhaps especially so at the Bar (see further discussion on constructions of 'excellence' in chapter eight). For Ben, he says: 'I've never been convinced by the idea of pure public lawyers or pure human rights lawyers.' He finds that both of these terms are misleading because you have to, he explains, attach public law to other areas of law and they are simply a part of a package of substantive legal tools you might use on behalf of your client. He picked up on the elitism point with public law barristers in particular when we discussed further:

> Jacqueline: So there's a cultural and legal professional problem there?
>
> Ben: I think the Bar is really to blame for this. Because barristers, a certain type of barrister, will call themselves a 'public law barrister'. It's just ridiculous. You get … there's a whole raft of human rights barristers because they act for the Government opposing human rights claims. In what Universe does that make you a human rights lawyer?

Ben also highlights here the political value judgements at the root of the identification problem. The term 'human rights lawyer' has obvious connotations of working on the left to defend human rights *against* government interference. Ben becomes quite exasperated therefore that someone acting *for* the government might use this term to identify themselves and their work. He prefers the term 'civil liberties' which was more prevalent in the 1980s and 90s than it is today. He continues by describing the difficulty with the widely used term 'public lawyer':

> I know for barristers it's slightly different, but I don't think for solicitors in particular you can be competent if you don't understand your field. And if you're saying you're

> a public lawyer, you can never really get to the root of a public law challenge ... if someone comes to me with a planning law thing I could probably come up with an answer but I wouldn't really be any better than a student doing it (Ben).

He reflects on public law being pervasive across all areas of law and finds that it is misleading for lawyers to self-identify as 'public lawyers' without describing the substantive area of law (for example, housing, community care, immigration, planning or prison law) underpinning the public law remedies they aim to provide. These are all quite distinct fields and it can be difficult both for clients and for other professionals to determine the nature of professional legal expertise.

This preference for 'civil liberties' is not however confined to the 1980s. Tim, a recently qualified charity sector lawyer, also preferred the term civil liberties and described human rights as 'constricting' terminology. This resonates with the judicial turn to common law in relation to access to justice issues.[67] Tim explained: 'a lot of our cases are about enforcing other rights against public bodies ... such as housing, benefits, school exclusion'. These do not necessarily engage the Human Rights Act but rest in entitlements either in other legislation such as child law or housing law, backed up by general public law principles that dictate decisions about allocation of entitlements should be made lawfully and fairly. Tim makes clear that it is about a basic process of 'making sure rules have been followed properly'. In fact, Tim found it hard to settle on any one term. While his approach might fall more neatly into traditional social welfare law Tim also struggled with the term 'social welfare lawyer' and commented: 'I'm not a huge fan of the word welfare because it's picked up negative connotations'. Even though his clients experience severe disadvantage in the work he does he thought the term 'social welfare' made them even more so, and risked associating legal advice and representation with paternalism. Another participant, Eve, conversely refers to social welfare as a positive label precisely because of how it has connotations of being able to 'just go and sort shit out for people':

> Jacqueline: So what do you think of the term social welfare lawyer?
>
> Eve: I think that's really good and better than human rights lawyer. Cause I think human rights law has taken on quite a privileged place and I think it takes you away from working with people and social justice. It's overly legalistic. Social welfare is actually like just go and sort out shit for people.

Another term adopted intermittently over the last five decades is 'activist lawyer'. It was used by the Home Office in a social media video in 2020 to refer to lawyers pursuing immigration challenges.[68] While the video was later removed, it stated

[67] The case of R *(UNISON) v Lord Chancellor* [2017] UKSC 51 declared Employment Tribunal fees unlawful on general common law access to justice grounds. For further discussion of common law framing of human rights arguments, see Adam Straw, 'Future Proofing: Running Human Rights Arguments under the Common Law' (2015) 20(4) *Judicial Review* 193.

[68] Adam Wagner, 'It's not "activist lawyers" this government hates but the laws themselves' (*New Statesman*, 28 August 2020).

that the current regulations were 'open to abuse' and that activist lawyers were responsible for delaying and disrupting the return of migrants, stating that this would no longer be possible when the UK is not bound by EU laws.[69] As outlined in chapter one, the 'activist lawyer' identity was in fact assumed and embraced by some lawyers in response to comments made by Prime Minister Theresa May in 2016. The Director of Liberty (National Council for Civil Liberties), Martha Spurrier, made the following response to her criticism:

> I am an activist human rights lawyer. We are watching Theresa May and Amber Rudd and Liz Truss and Michael Fallon, and politicians across the spectrum. We will not be cowed by your cuts, nor your spin, nor your cumbersome computer systems. If you put a toe out of line, we will come down on you like a ton of bricks, because we are activist human rights lawyers, and that is what we do.[70]

Spurrier is making a clear connection here between activism, human rights and the use of public law remedies. The coming down 'like a ton of bricks' is a direct reference to the lawyers' ability to hold government to account by way of judicial review and makes an appeal to their collective identity as human rights lawyers ('we are activist human rights lawyers, and that is what we do'). For some participants in the study this framing is accepted, for example, when I asked Kenneth if he would ever have identified himself as an activist lawyer over the course of his career he replied positively: 'Oh yes, yes, I think I would'. I also describe in chapter four how another participant, Eve, embraces an activist identity with lawyers because she sees it as subversive, however, with other activists, she perceives the term to be alienating because 'lawyer' holds too much privilege. An NGO lawyer in the study expressed some hesitation in adopting the dual identity of an activist and a lawyer. Ankita's work is directly related to campaigning on policy issues and she expresses discomfort with the terminology because of the negative influence it might potentially have:

> Jacqueline: Would you define yourself as an activist lawyer or campaigning lawyer?
>
> Ankita: I think the term is now so loaded and that's the problem … I wouldn't choose to do so but that is because of the negative influence in some of the spheres in which I work … And so, if I was to accept that label, then I'd find myself perhaps struggling sometimes to communicate with people who I need to influence … but that's not to say there's something inherently wrong with being a campaigner.

Ankita goes on to say that she perceives the 'activist' identity as putting her in a 'small niche box' and has concerns that it limits her ability to reach across boundaries in her work. She twice stresses 'there's nothing inherently wrong with' the term but this only serves to demonstrate the sense of conflict she feels. She hints

[69] May Bulman, 'Misleading and dangerous: Home office condemned for describing solicitors representing migrants as activist lawyers' (*The Independent*, 29 August 2020).

[70] Martha Spurrier, Keynote Address, Legal Aid Practitioners Group Conference, 16 October 2016. See, Fiona Bawdon, 'In praise of activist human rights lawyers' (*Legal Voice*, 18 October 2016).

at a broader term being preferable ('lawyer for social justice or something') while also illustrating the lack of clarity in alternative identities available. She prefers the term 'human rights lawyer', and self-identifies as such to an extent, seeing it as a contrast to 'activism' while still acknowledging the negative attention human rights receives in the UK as opposed to within international forums:

> Jacqueline: Do you think there's a problem with the terminology of the human rights lawyer?
>
> Ankita: I'm less bothered by that. I think, I think that shouldn't particularly be … and that's … it's a contrast, isn't it? I mean, I don't think human rights is as toxic a phrase as a lot of people would say it will be. I think certainly, outside of the UK it's not and whenever we're talking to Government about what happens outside of our borders, human rights is a very positive term and they're very enthusiastic about it. So I don't think it's as hopeless for those of us who call ourselves human rights lawyers.

When I explored the same issue together with Gail, a barrister campaigner, she gave the following explanation for how she perceives her own legal practice and campaigning:

> Jacqueline: If we think of you as a lawyer in that context, where would you say the law begins and ends and campaigning starts – how to you view the policy and campaign issues?
>
> Gail: It's kind of seamless, I don't really see a distinction between law and campaigning as a human rights lawyer because you're always trying to use the human rights framework to ultimately achieve a better society for a wider group of people. So there's always a campaign. Even if it's an individual case at the heart of it, you're always trying to improve the law.

This approach is less hesitant than Ankita's, despite the similarity of their work in human rights law and policy. While Ankita is reluctant to stress her campaigns, Gail is clear that there is 'always' a campaign when using a human rights framework. It is pertinent too that Gail wants to set herself *apart* from other non-lawyer human rights campaigners by stressing because of the 'legitimacy' that law gives:

> Jacqueline: And if someone described you as a 'campaigner' are you happy with that terminology?
>
> Gail: Yeah, I'd rather 'lawyer and campaigner' but again it's about saying that the law provides that structure and that legitimacy that I really like. Because you look at campaigns in other areas they can sometimes be a bit flabby and like, where's the rigour?

Both Ankita and Gail studied law not long after the Human Rights Act 1998 came into force and developed their professional legal identities just as those rights were 'being brought home' in a domestic sense. Kenneth, who qualified some four decades previously, was keen to point out that the Act simply brought a new *framework* with which to resolve disputes and access rights and entitlements for clients; but those rights already existed in law. As lawyers argued within that framework 'over and over again' he said it brought about 'serious change' in terms of particular provisions being applied but he notes that the problems themselves never changed: 'we were getting the same issues coming up'. Ankita and Gail are more comfortable with the identity of human rights lawyering than Ben and Kenneth before them. For Tim, starting his legal career in the shadow of Brexit and at a time when 'rights talk' is contested,[71] he suggests that relying on traditional common law remedies resting in access to justice and the rule of law holds more promise and expresses a desire to re-label his work as being about civil liberties.

The responses to the 'activist lawyer' Home Office controversy in 2020 discussed above perhaps exemplify the contestation as to labelling of progressive legal work: on the one hand, the Law Society and Bar Council issued responses in strong terms stating that immigration lawyers are simply performing the functions of their role as professionals:

> Legal professionals who apply the law and follow parliament's express intention, are not 'activists'. They are merely doing their jobs, enabling people to exercise their statutory rights and defend themselves against those in power. Without those lawyers, our system would crumble.[72]

On the other hand, some lawyers again embraced the term 'activist lawyer' and were quick to present themselves in that way (for example, changing twitter handles to include the term).[73] There are obvious challenges in capturing the range of work that progressive lawyers do and navigating the professional, social and political implications of the terminology used to describe that work. As this study also makes clear, identity shifts over time and context; and how a lawyer perceives themselves may not be how they are perceived by others. The methodology in this study therefore aims to take account of this complexity by reaching across boundaries and capturing both similarity and difference in order to locate the shared framing of progressive lawyering identity.

CONCLUSIONS

This book is concerned with how lawyers understand and experience their role as practitioners within their network of practice, and the extent to which that

[71] Philip Alston, 'The Populist Challenge to Human Rights' (2017) 9(1) *Journal of Human Rights Practice* 1–15; Alan Greene, 'The Human Rights Act in a Culture of Control' in Claire-Michelle Smyth and Richard Lang (eds), *The Future of Human Rights in the UK* (Cambridge Scholars, 2017) 4–26.

[72] Amanda Pinto QC, 'Bar Council condemns misleading communication by government' (*Bar Council Press Release*, 27 August 2020), available at www.barcouncil.org.uk/resource/bar-council-condemns-misleading-communication-by-government.html.

[73] Aishah Hussain, 'Legal Twitterati outrage over Home Office's activist lawyer tweet' (*Legal Cheek*, 27 August 2020), available at www.legalcheek.com/2020/08/legal-twitterati-outrage-over-home-offices-activist-lawyer-tweet/.

network might be considered a progressive lawyering movement. As the narratives in this study reveal, it is perhaps in the times of uncertainty and change, in the contingencies and contradictions that the social and cultural value of progressive legal practice will be made known. The law does not operate in a vacuum but is subject to its time, place and every instance of its application. The lived experience of the law is central to revealing what law in the social world means to those who choose to invoke it; and the relationship between that invocation and lawyers as individuals and as a collective.

The research methodology captures individual experience but ensures that it rests within its broader social and historical context:

> The challenge is to craft methods of analysis that are inclusive rather than exclusive; that go beyond the particular and idiosyncratic but are wary of universalities; that locate and define the interplay between institutional power and the daily, lived experience of that power.[74]

There are obvious contradictions between the construction of events as *both* personal experience and phenomena and between the law itself as a static institution and the lawyers who act as agents of change within it. The law is of course about politics and power but 'people control power; politics is about people making things happen, shifting the course of events and rewriting history as it happens'.[75]

The underlying ethnography, coupled with reflexivity and narrative analysis, captures and explores the interactive network nodes of progressive legal practice. Notwithstanding contestation as to labelling, my aim is to interrogate the ways in which the ties that exist both within and across the progressive legal network facilitate interaction on the basis of a shared collective identity such as to comprise a progressive lawyering movement.[76] In the next chapter I will outline the ways in which study participants' narratives reveal constructions of shared political values, motivations and turning points towards progressive legal practice that demonstrate a collective identity, which underpins progressive lawyers' relationships with one another, with 'other' lawyers and with the state itself.

[74] Kitty Calavita and Carroll Seron, 'Postmoderism and Protest: Recovering the Sociological Imagination' (1992) *Law and Society Review* 765, 769–70.

[75] ibid 770.

[76] Mario Diani, 'The Concept of a Social Movement' (1992) 40(1) *Sociological Review* 13.

4

Pathways to Law

> The law is just really interesting .... it raises interesting questions. At their heart, they're political questions. I always think law is another way of doing politics. Politics is another way of doing law. You know they're very symbiotic in that sense. And so if you are interested in the world around you, why wouldn't you want to know more about the rules and be able to shape those rules yourself? (Gail)

THE NARRATIVES IN this book reveal professional and personal lives that are richly interwoven and underpinned by deeply instilled values that influence and shape the causes and cases that progressive lawyers pursue. Consistent with the approaches identified in cause lawyering and legal mobilisation studies outlined in chapter two, some lawyers in the study seek to shape the rules of society, while others hope to subvert the relationships of power upon which society rests. Some lawyers daily use the law to secure rights and entitlements for clients, while others campaign in order to raise consciousness of that very process. For *all* lawyers who have participated in the research, there is a compelling desire to achieve transformative results through the work they do and a clear conception of justice underpinned by commonly held values. Particularly striking is the way in which lawyers collectively connect the formation of their professional selves to these values and how their personal histories shape decision-making at important turning points in their lives.

This chapter considers whether a collective identity for progressive lawyers exists by analysing how participants construct stories of their beginnings, in particular, their shared pathways to law and the values that underpin their work. It first sets out a selection of narratives that detail early motivations to pursue progressive work in order to outline how participants delineate their pathways to legal practice. In this context I identify in particular the boundary of social class for participants in the study in terms of entry to the profession. In the next section, narratives from across different practice sites and historical contexts are introduced in order to interrogate in more detail how progressive lawyers negotiate and frame their collective identity throughout their careers. The analysis illustrates a framing of identity where progressive lawyers differentiate themselves and other lawyers within their networks as being 'one of us'. This differentiation is constructed as first, being less motivated by financial incentives and, secondly, recognising the power imbalance in society: 'our job is to represent people without power' (Stefan). There is a clear turning point where participants describe a moment where they realised they didn't want to, or no longer wanted to, work in more commercial fields of legal practice.[1] This turn is strikingly common across all sub-sets of practice and decades of the study. I argue that these shared narratives demonstrate a collective identity for progressive lawyers across their networks of practice notwithstanding other divergent factors such as class background and the contested labelling of progressive legal identity.

THE LEGAL PROFESSION AND SOCIAL CLASS

Social mobility has been a longstanding challenge for the legal profession. The legal profession has one of the lowest levels of widening access of all the professions and this is even more pressing for lawyers wanting to pursue careers in legal aid, social welfare and human rights where financial support for education and training is not as comprehensive as in the corporate sector and success can be contingent upon (often unpaid) work experience.[2] A 2016 study showed that nearly three quarters of High Court and Court of Appeal judges went to independent schools and 74 per cent went to Oxbridge. For leading QCs the findings were 71 per cent and 78 per cent respectively such that leading barristers and judges are ten times more likely to have had a private education than the population as a whole.[3] For both barristers and solicitors, on the whole they 'disproportionately herald from the same schools and universities'.[4] Therefore, while motivational factors are often held in common for progressive lawyers their formative context diverges dependent on, most notably, class background. Other divergent themes such as gender and race have arisen in the study and intersect with class issues.[5] However, the analysis here concentrates on class given that, first, it has been the most prevalent common barrier described over the five decades of the study and secondly, other experiences of exclusion, or discrimination, tended to be related first through an exploration of class background. With some participants, these experiences of exclusion were conveyed in highly emotive terms during interview encounters and I also observed urgent attention

[1] Narrative turning points might also be referred to as 'critical junctures' which are often used to help people create meaning out of difficult choices and decisions. See further Jerome Bruner, 'The narrative creation of self' in LA Angus and J McLeod (eds), *The Handbook of Narrative and Psychotherapy* (Sage, 2004) 3–14.

[2] *Young Legal Aid Lawyers: Social Mobility in a Time of Austerity* (Young Legal Aid Lawyers, 2018).

[3] Philip Kirby, *Leading People: The educational background of the UK professional elite* (The Sutton Trust, 2016) 2.

[4] ibid.

[5] Jennifer Tomlinson et al, 'Privileges and Penalties in the legal profession: an intersectional analysis of career progression' (2019) 70(3) *The British Journal of Sociology* 1043.

being drawn to the issue in my wider work in University widening participation, as well as in events, workshops and related social media communications that I analysed as part of the study.

An early 2018 social media Twitter trend is particularly relevant in this context. When a legal academic at Exeter University who works on the Pathways to Law Programme[6] asked his Twitter following to tell their own pathways to law stories the response was quite overwhelming. More than 200 lawyers engaged with the 'mypathtolaw' hashtag with tales of overcoming adversity to study and qualify as lawyers. The vast majority described coming from working class backgrounds. The stories spanned all areas of law but I replicate below a small illustrative sample of lawyers who outlined their experiences and fit the typology of the study:

> Council estate kid from Glasgow. Hated that folk were frightened by authority & thought 'the rules' were something that happened to them. First in family to go to Uni. Never shut up. First Saturday job hawking on a stall at the Barras Market. Barras to the bar. #mypathtolaw.[7]

> Brought up in Leeds by strong single mum who felt the stigma of 'broken home'; taught me about equality. First jobs in fish and chip shop & as legal secretary. £al suppt frm @TheInnerTemple. Inspired by @helenakennedyqc, @HenryBrooke1 and all at @DoughtyStPublic #mypathtolaw.[8]

> #mypathtolaw council estate, state education, supportive teacher, polytechnic, full grant, another polytechnic, full grant for post grad, articles, job offer doing crime on back of advocacy competition, legal Aid crime for 24 years, HCA for 12 … Fortunate it was affordable![9]

Themes of poverty, education, exclusion (from family or community), discrimination and prejudice are common. Likewise, the stories repeatedly reference the help and support – from peers and educators and, most significantly, by way of grants and other funding rather than family ties to the profession – received along the way. With the aim of the exercise being to encourage students to fulfil their own pathways to law despite the hurdles and difficulties related to access to the profession, it is not unsurprising that the responses from more privileged pathways were very few (less than 2 per cent). Of those who did participate and acknowledged that background, they tended to work in legal aid or other progressive subsets of practice rather than corporate law. Again, similar to the narratives in the study that I discuss in this chapter, there is interplay between

[6] The term 'pathways to law' is the name of The Sutton Trust widening access to the legal profession programme. The programme aims to inspire and support students from widening access background to pursue a career in the law. See further www.suttontrust.com/our-programmes/pathways-to-law/.

[7] Twitter, @Angela_Patrick, 19 January 2018.

[8] ibid @henrietta_hill, 19 January 2019.

[9] ibid @tired_lawyer, 21 January 2018.

'privilege' and 'working hard' for progressive lawyers. This connection gives lawyers a shared collective space to voice their experience regardless of class background:

> Aspiring lawyers please do read the #mypathtolaw hashtag. I'm from a relatively privileged background but it has taken a huge amount of hard work and many setbacks to get where I am today. Others you will read about are twice as talented as I am but had to work twice as hard.[10]

Social media platforms permit information that might otherwise be private to be made public and for users to even narrate themselves as if they were characters in a story. We are presented with an example here of how public narratives can be inspiring and motivating. While there is a clear performance in lawyers' stories generally, studies have also shown a heightened level of performance to twitter hashtag participation and the 'mypathtolaw' trending exercise reinforces the autobiographical performance of lawyers in collective storytelling.[11] Similar to participants in the study, the narratives also demonstrate how lawyers who come from privilege relate and connect underpinning motivational factors in ways that seek to find common ground across their networks.

SHARED BEGINNINGS

This section explores the ways in which lawyers construct shared beginnings despite otherwise divergent personal histories. For those participants who come from working class backgrounds there is a distinctive depth of experience to their pathways to the profession. They were more likely to describe their desire to pursue progressive legal practice as being experientially informed by: (i) an experience of working hard to get to where they are; (ii) a formative experience related to injustice (often related to family members); and / or (iii) work experience that led to their career in law.

Lena described her working class background and the experience of not being able to pursue her preferred choice of an apprenticeship in her hometown in Scotland:

> I became a lawyer by complete accident, I was meant to work in my local factory. I'm from a very working class background and I wanted to do an apprenticeship at 16 but my name wasn't picked out. So I ended up staying on at school after my O Levels … there were no jobs so I was the first in my family to go to University (Lena).

[10] ibid (anon), 21 January 2018.
[11] Zizi Papacharissi, 'Without You I'm Nothing: Performances of Self on Twitter' (2012) 6 *International Journal of Communication* 1989.

She goes on to relate her experience working in social welfare advice after University alongside her work in politics and having a realisation that it was a job she *could* do:

> I set up an advice bureau advising homeless people … so I started doing representation, mainly social security … then I realised at that point, I was doing a lot of work with lawyers and I thought, god I could do what you're doing (Lena).

A memory of experientially informed decision-making is especially common for participants from working class backgrounds. One barrister in the study described having started his career in a commercial set of Chambers in the 1980s. Dominic knew the work wasn't what he wanted to do and said that to 'ease his soul' he undertook voluntary work in law centres in the evenings. He worked in four different law centres until through one he met a barrister from a progressive set of Chambers who later invited him to become a member. As Dominic puts it, he joined and 'never looked back'. Here too we see the importance of experience in providing opportunities and exposing early career lawyers to types of work they want to do while giving them a glimpse of a collective professional network that might embrace them. By stark contrast, Dominic reflected about his time in the commercial set of Chambers: 'I hated it, I don't reckon they liked me very much'. When I asked him why he responded:

> Uh, I was just working class and I didn't accept all the shit they used to throw at me. I used to say why do I have to make you tea? Why do I have to drive your car? (Dominic)

Dominic reflected further that the injustice of this experience made him 'more progressive' such that he sought out a place of work that was 'completely egalitarian'. In Dominic's story he relates that in this new environment he developed a shared understanding of 'fighting the cause of the small person, taking on the cause of the state, collectivism and protest' that strongly influenced his practice and stayed with him throughout the following decades of his career. The importance of collectively held values for Dominic was one of the clearest in the study in light of his prior experience in a workplace where he didn't feel at any sense of collective identity and where he felt, on the contrary, wholly excluded by virtue of his class background.

Such experiences of injustice are common for participants in the study and emotionally laden stories of injustice featured strongly in interviews for working class participants in particular. For Ruth, she described an employment experience of her own:

> Because the reason I got into law was because I had employment problems with an agency while working with [redacted]. I think I was so furious that people could get treated like that as agency workers that I went to the CAB for advice and then just kind of thought this is exactly where I want to be (Ruth).

Through helping herself and her fellow co-workers in an employment dispute Ruth realised, like Lena, she was capable of doing legal work and decided to train as a lawyer. In Ruth's story she quite clearly connected her own experience to being able to empathise with others in similar situations. Another participant, Lee, describes getting an eviction order when she was homeless and squatting in London:

> The first time it happened to me I got an eviction order through. So I went to the Advisory Service for Squatters saying what do I do? And this guy said well I'll show you how to do it yourself. So I probably spent about five hours with him, you know, on one of those first computers, the Amstrad? Creating a defence. And he was just teaching it to me. And I thought this was amazing (Lee).

As with both Ruth and Lena, Lee saw that she could do similar work on behalf of other people and began to do so:

> Jacqueline: So you realised you could get results for people?
>
> Lee: Yeah, well for yourself because I was living in squats. So I was doing it for me and for my friends.

For other participants, there is an exposure to injustice most often linked to class and a desire to 'fight back' to redress the imbalance of power:

> My Grandad was a miner and went through the miners' strikes, I was taught to hate Maggie Thatcher [laughter] … that was the injustice that I saw. Normal working class people being taken advantage of and not being able to fight back against the government. So yeah … it sort of went on from there (Emily).

Dominic also described the fierce competition for places in the profession generally and the need for work experience that is often unpaid and how hard it is to compete with people who have the resource to fund it: 'it's affecting the numbers, people think twice'. For those participants from privileged backgrounds who had family members in the law or related professions and/or were privately educated, I noted the comparative ease with which a career at the Bar in particular seemed to be available to them. Likewise, prior formative experiences featured less strongly in their narratives. The sense of having options available or 'luck' in finding work experience is quite striking:

> After University I sort of tumbled unexpectedly into the world of speech writing and politics (Martin).
>
> I decided I wanted to be a lawyer … it had always been something I could have been because I went to a posh school and I can remember having a school careers day thing when a barrister came to speak and I thought 'uh, that sounds alright' but, you know, it was just one of a range of careers (Gail).

There is a clear contrast between these experiences and both Gail and Martin seemed at pains to stress that they had chosen their careers in order to make a social contribution. Similar to the pathways to law trending exercise, they seek to frame themselves and their work by appealing to common values and motivations but this can present challenges. For example, a 1993 newspaper article follows the pupillage (trainee barrister) interviews for Bethnal Green Chambers, a radical set in East London committed to social welfare and open about only recruiting left-wing candidates. The writer describes how one candidate with work experience in legal aid and helping the homeless didn't get through the selection panel. One barrister on the panel lamented: '[It's a] Florence Nightingale application, a privileged background stepping down to help the poor … This is someone who has the resources, but not the feeling'.[12] It is pertinent that the requirement is one of 'feeling': the theme of emotion and passion for social justice is prevalent in the study and how to construct and evidence this, as discussed further in chapter eight, has the potential to create tension. For this barrister, he perceived coming from a privileged background as a less authentic story than an *experience* of injustice. A participant in the study from a privileged background also raised this as a tension. Having attended a working group on social mobility in the legal profession Wendy talked about how 'awkward' she felt about her own class background. She explained that while she didn't go to private school she came from a family of professionals and went to a good University with no debt to carry into her career: 'I just sensed so much resentment for people like me'. The public narrative of an experience of injustice or poverty leads to solidarity for some lawyers, and those who come from privilege are well aware of their 'public narrative' being less able to connect to experiences of injustice and they seek to overcome this by negotiating and framing shared common values and motivations.

SHARED LEFT VALUES

I began most interviews with an open question asking participants to think back to the time when they 'decided to become a lawyer'. When I asked about motivating values participants quite naturally began describing their political backgrounds. A majority of participants in the study connected their chosen career paths to their liberal politics. They predominantly reflected on family-based formation of political values and tended to naturally link these to their decision to pursue a career in the law: 'I mean I'm very left wing. My family are old East End Jewish Communists. So I've always been quite political' (Ben). Several participants valued an opportunity to delve into their own family histories, outlining political values going back generations and thereafter connecting them to their own work or that of their parents:

> Martin: My fifteenth birthday present was membership of the Labour party.
>
> Jacqueline: Were your parents Labour?

[12] Marianne Macdonald, 'Jobseekers put to test in chambers challenge: Trainee barristers seeking entry to one of Britain's most radical practices face a rigorous examination' *The Independent* (19 April 1989).

> Martin: Yeah … big time, big time.
>
> I grew up, my Uncle was in [redacted] … the communist party, my parents were very much, saw the left as being the voice of social justice and equality and that was very much where I always put myself. Absolutely, I still do (Ankita).
>
> I mean I come from a working class background … My grandmother in particular, my paternal grandmother was very active in the social-democratic party, you know, trade unions, she was on the executive of a trade union (Rodrigo).
>
> I think actually my Mother has always been a very active opponent of the death penalty … She was quite an active [redacted left wing party] and she had canvassed and campaigned a bit for them and I think at some points had thought about going into politics herself (Gail).

For participants who saw family members in political roles and experienced liberal values their narratives connect those roots and experiences to their professional lives. Many participants describe a cause and their family members' connection to it: 'she was on the executive of a trade union', '[she was] a very active opponent of the death penalty' (Gail), '[my parents] saw the left as being the voice of social justice and equality' (Ankita).

Yet family political background obviously cannot *solely* account for this decision-making: children may of course grow up in a household of one political persuasion and grow into another. Other structural factors and choices must be at play (and are explored in more detail below). One legal aid lawyer reflected on this distinction in relation to her brother. Ruth is a legal aid lawyer with considerable experience working in law centres and legal aid. When we talked about the underpinning motivations in her work she said that she often jokes that she sees her job as 'pointing at something and saying "that's just wrong" or "that's not fair"'. She has a clear sense of right and wrong that guides her decision-making day to day. When I asked Ruth where this sense of fairness came from she directly linked it her 'upbringing' and said that her 'whole family' were 'fairly left wing' and her Dad's side of the family were 'all at Greenham Common and were members of the Labour Party'. While reflecting further on this background she paused however and noted: 'Although … my brother isn't really that into it … he's married to someone with a Trust Fund and doesn't really work'. The light heartedness of the exchange seemed to dissipate a little at this point and her hesitation indicated some unravelling of her own narrative: it is so common for progressive lawyers to relate stories of family based liberal identity yet for her own sibling the experience had simply not been formative. This was a loose thread she wasn't sure how to connect back to her own story and she moved quickly onto another aspect of her work.

Nonetheless political values are prevalent and nearly all participants made the assumption that when I asked broadly about values I was referring to their left wing politics. In fact, I was prepared for this question to lead in other directions but it rarely did. The majority of participants moved with ease between their values and a desire to pursue a career that they perceived to be worthwhile:

> Neither of my parents are lawyers but they're both pretty left wing. I was brought up in a household which was quite political and a lot of discussion, a lot of reflection on the need to do the right thing and make a contribution (Andrea).

Participants commonly constructed a narrative that connected 'doing the right thing' and 'making a contribution' to their left political values. Consistent with Marshall Ganz's work on public narrative a public 'story of self' is evident. For Ganz, a narrative is not simply a form of self-expression but 'an exercise in leadership by motivating others to join you in action on behalf of a shared purpose'.[13] He argues that when a 'story of self' becomes a 'story of us' it is a public narrative that is a call for action, outlining shared motivating values and experiences that will inspire others. This public narrative is clear, for example, in the twitter hashtag trend on pathways to law explored at the beginning of this chapter. I was intrigued to note during my fieldwork that the Justice First Fellows[14] I interviewed were being introduced to Ganz's 'story of self' framework in the communications training offered by the Legal Education Foundation as part of the JFF programme. Across the network, collective stories of motivating values are therefore both consciously and unconsciously narrated by progressive lawyers and more privileged lawyers use this to transcend class divides. As explored further in chapter eight, newly trained lawyers narrate a strong desire for change and being attuned to the importance of a public narrative in the current socio-political climate and the challenges ahead for the profession.

The public and collective framing of a personal narrative comes with hesitation for some participants. For example, when Tim and I explored his decision to pursue progressive legal work he said: 'it's a bit tricky for me because of the way I've remembered that process'. He explained further: 'I've got it into my head that there was a clear narrative for me anchored in the [law school] clinic.' He seemed to be stumbling a little over what he remembered as his own experience and what he had adopted as the narrative of that experience such that there was some hesitation around how to frame it. Likewise, while Lena was clear in her own mind about the connection between her politics (the 'only reason' for

[13] Marshall Ganz, *What is Public Narrative: Self, Us & Now* (Working Paper, 2009) 2, available at https://dash.harvard.edu/handle/1/30760283.

[14] The Justice First Fellowship Programme is funded by the Legal Education Foundation and was established in 2014. Trainee solicitors (and a very limited number of barristers) are selected to work in the field of social welfare in organisations including law centres, NGOs and legal aid law firms and funded through to qualification. In 2020 there were 88 fellows so far in the programme (81 solicitor and 7 barrister fellows). See further https://jff.thelegaleducationfoundation.org/the-fellowship/overview/.

her work) and her desire to pursue social change, there was still some verbal hesitation as she outlined her political background. It seemed that this was not due to any lack of commitment to her politics but rather a hesitation about the acceptability of the extent to which it guides her work and awareness of how other people 'judge' it:

> Jacqueline: Can you tell me a bit about the motivation for doing that sort of work?
>
> Lena: Political. It was political. I mean the only reason I'm doing it now is political.
>
> Jacqueline: Can you flesh that out for me?
>
> Lena: Um, I think ... you know I'm a socialist. And I ... I ... I think you know as its base I think you know socialists ultimately want to change society but as part of changing society you want to assist people. Um ... and kind of, you know, fight the man if you like. And I suppose that's always informed all my work. And I suppose, um, it's for other people to judge whether it's good, bad or indifferent but that informs my work.

Lena's acknowledgement that 'it's for other people to judge' is consistent with the contestation identified as to the labelling of progressive collective identity. There is a tension, for some but not all participants, between the politics of their work and how they frame it both within and outside their networks. For one participant in the study he expressed regret that his radical politics had been curbed by his time in practice:

> Ben: To be honest, the one thing that's I'd say has probably disappointed me in my professional life the most is the extent to which I feel that I've had to be less political in my personal life. Before I became a lawyer I was very active politically sort of party based ...
>
> Jacqueline: What party?
>
> Ben: Well, I was in the Communist party when I was young. I don't know what party I would have been in, if any.

Ben went on to say that when he started in his career he made the decision that because he was working with people who were 'very much in the public eye' that they didn't need the person representing them 'to cause detriment to their case by being overtly political'. Ben explained that this meant he had 'not had any sort of party political involvement for two decades'. In fact, this is a considerable point of divergence in the study: some participants campaign more overtly than others, some hold links to political parties while others work in broader progressive politics without overt association with any political party at all. In Scotland, one participant, Eve, said that she describes herself as a political activist within legal circles precisely because of how conservative the Scottish legal profession is and the greater need to self-identify as an 'activist'. She saw an assertion of politics within professional circles in Scotland as something that is rarely done in comparison to England and Wales but something that could help lead to positive change. Conversely, when I asked Eve about whether she would use the term 'lawyer-activist' she laughed and said:

> That makes me squirm a wee bit. If I was out with activist friends I wouldn't ever say that. There's way too much privilege in the term lawyer (Eve).

Eve's view of herself is fluid dependent on her social interactions. She is aware of the power attached to the term 'lawyer' outside of her professional life and perceives it to be exclusionary in her interactions with other activists. Nonetheless, participants generally felt able to speak openly about their political affiliations in fieldwork interactions and the confidence with which they express the values underpinning their work to each other was, for the most part, abundantly clear. Those affiliations across the study of course differed, as did the means of expressing them and the extent to which participants' navigate and negotiate their interactions with their clients and with activists or other types of lawyers.

In terms of law's interaction with politics I note that several participants in the study described turning to law precisely because of the abstraction of politics. Gail, for example, describes her motivation as follows:

> But then when I really wanted to become a lawyer was because of an interest in politics and the way in which politics intersects with actual human experience rather than as a kind of abstract phenomenon (Gail).

She reflects back on working as a caseworker for an MP and seeing people with 'really serious immigration and housing problems'. She said that she saw two solutions to their problems, 'if there were any solutions at all' and described them as:

> It was either the brute force of the MP ringing up, you know, Heathrow and saying please don't deport my constituent and getting them off the plane. Or, having a good lawyer. And I figured it was better to have a good lawyer than to have an MP begging someone (Gail).

The way in which Gail frames the lawyer's role here is highly relevant to the study. The reference to being able to do *more* with the law than with 'abstract' politics because of the underlying framework that permits enforcement of rights and access to entitlements features strongly for participants and is key to how cause lawyers distinguish themselves from other lawyers. Gail wants to get results: she describes how you're not just 'begging someone' with the law and there is the potential for tangible outcomes. Here, Gail presents herself as fitting into Hilbink's typology of the elite/vanguard cause lawyer outlined in the first chapter.[15] While linked to politics, Gail sees the law as a superior form of politics and has an ultimate belief that the law itself might be used to bring about change for individuals.

[15] Thomas Hilbink, 'You Know the Type: Categories of Cause Lawyering' (2004) 19 *Law & Social Inquiry* 657.

Martin, another barrister-campaigner, also presents as an elite/vanguard cause lawyer. He describes working as an aide to an MP and seeing the limits of advice surgeries in the resolution of problems:

> Even as a policymaker and speechwriter I was there in the advice surgeries every weekend just as an extra body. Every week, taking instructions from people. It felt like being a solicitor. We were referring cases onto solicitors (Martin).

Martin goes on to describe the 'dynamic, exciting' environment of working at Westminster and, while he was 'really loving it', he also found the abstraction 'incredibly frustrating'. He elaborates:

> Martin: It was lots of right we will get x hundred thousand people into work or we will move x billion off the public finances into x billion of you know infrastructure and that sort of thing. And you know for someone in their 20's coming into it and really understanding the method of politics, the combination of it being at a high level, almost unimaginably big numbers of money and numbers of people being moved around ... [pause].
>
> Jacqueline: You wanted to see ... ?
>
> Martin: Well, you couldn't really see anything. You couldn't see any tangible change ... Ever.

I found Martin's comment that you just 'couldn't really see anything' striking in light of his personal history. It was only on revisiting his narrative several times during analysis that I began to see the recurring theme of a perceived familial expectation to contribute. The intangibility of other career options – while still within the public service realm – is salient in the context of the deeply rooted social contribution ethos in Martin's family coming from 'generations of public servants'. Both at the beginning and towards the end of the interview he refers to being 'under quite a lot of pressure to do something useful':

> You know my parents were the sort of people who always drilled into us that you're privileged you help people. Use your skills, use your intellect, use your experience to kind of help people. I really mean that .... it never occurred to me to do anything else (Martin).

A motivating desire to drive social change is particularly strong for Martin and, like Gail, he constructs a narrative of leaving the general abstraction politics and coming to law from a privileged background in order to use that privilege to help others. This construction is one that has been identified and negotiated in light of other prevailing narratives, most notably the turn away from corporate law and its associated financial rewards, in order to pursue progressive work.

SHARED TURNING POINTS

Political values and a related determination to make a social contribution underpin the process of categorisation and lead to a collective turning away from other types of legal practice. This decision-making process is often articulated in strong terms:

> One friend said to me- 'you know shuffling other people's money in the City, it's just not for us is it?' It's always struck me … I'm not sort of denigrating. I have a respect for those in the profession who engage themselves in commerce and business and contracts and things. But shuffling money never felt like – in any respect … law, commerce, banking – it never really felt like what I was destined for (Martin).

I note the ease with which Martin relays what his friend said about shuffling money not being 'for us'. Here again we see distinctions being drawn about who is in or out of the networks of lawyers pursuing social change. There is an appeal, and an assumption, that they are connected by virtue of their collective desire to do more than – indeed 'destined' to – simply practising commercial law. Others in the study express similar sentiments:

> It was in the City … I didn't like it, it was awful … basically it was just about preserving capital. Moving money around. Didn't get to see any clients. I wasn't interested in the subject matter. It was just about how to make money and preserve money (Stefan).

> They were really keen on me joining them [commercial law firm], doing my articles, as they then were then, to the point that they, they sort of lobbied me to join them and I said, you know what, I don't really fancy this commercial stuff, um, I just felt, being a lackey for commercial ventures with no morality. You just got paid good money, so you just jumped around for them and facilitated their lives (Phil).

> Jacqueline: What were the underlying for reasons for making the jump [from commercial law]?

> Rodrigo: Well, all I thought, at that point, yes, I did make it a sort of, principled choice. I mean, I thought it was much more important to be doing stuff for people, helping people, um, and particularly legal aid work rather than you know, working for companies to improve their profits or whatever.

Consistent with the differentiation articulated in cause lawyering literature, lawyers in the study set themselves apart from corporate lawyers from early stages in their legal studies or careers. In fact, it would seem that across the network nodes some participants even appear to reject any alternative version of lawyering distinct from their own, and the lawyers that do it, in strong terms. One participant, Rodrigo, illustrates well how progressive lawyers define their work as being distinct from the rest of the legal profession. He describes at several points in his story not wanting to be like what he perceives as the *other* type of lawyer ('… the thought of spending my life with them wasn't too good' [referencing fellow law students], 'I didn't want to be like her, I didn't want to have her kind of practice which was very much, rich people' [referencing a commercial law firm partner]). Similar to Dominic's experience described above, with the turning away from corporate practice comes a turn towards, and identification with, others doing work consistent with his values. For example, Rodrigo describes the contextual political factors that facilitated the move towards work he wanted to do. Looking back, the political change connected him to a network of lawyers he could identify with and whose political values he shared (working in law centres and legal aid):

> Well, things started to happen actually, we got to 1968, the politics kind of changed in 1968, there are actually ways of doing things that you want to and they're actually possible. At the same time, you have the start of the law centres movement (Rodrigo).

This turn facilitates interactions where lawyers are introduced to lawyers 'like them' and begin to develop the same common features, especially around constructions of motivation.

Kenneth, for example, qualified in the 1960s and describes the privilege in which he grew up but his exposure to poverty giving him a sense of unease about wealth:

> Other people in my family were motivated by money, by business and so on. I grew up when [sic] you know we lived a reasonably comfortable life but a lot of my childhood was spent visiting rather flashy relatives who had flash cars and very big houses. I was put off by it, I didn't like it. I eventually began to feel contempt for people whose lives are motivated by making money (Kenneth).

The uneasy relationship with wealth that Kenneth describes is a common theme. In fact, the absence of money as a motivating factor in the narratives of lawyers in the study as a whole is striking. It is either simply not mentioned or, on the contrary, participants describe turning away from corporate law because they did not want to work for and with 'rich people'. This of course does not necessarily lead to a conclusion that remuneration is *never* a motivating factor. However, it is significant that money is never *described* or identified as a motivating factor by lawyers in the study. I sense that it is important for participants to construct their narrative in this way and, in fact, I noticed that some are almost eager to do so. In general, participants are quick to highlight they were not drawn to the salaries attached to corporate legal practice and the majority of participants acknowledge that they could be earning considerably more doing other types of work. This seems to be the case regardless of class background and all participants, across the different sub-sets of practice, were likely to outline social contribution as a key motivating factor in their work.

Both Rodrigo and Kenneth describe a turning point towards working together with those with commonly held values. Participants generally highlighted their networks, which includes formal membership of professional organisations but also more informal ties to other progressive practitioners, as being instrumental to their work. Work experience relates also to processes of exclusion in view of its central importance to accessing opportunities but also to collective identity.[16] Andrea, for example, describes working as a paralegal for

[16] Andrew Francis and Hilary Sommerlad, 'Access to Legal Work Experience and its role in the (re)production of legal professional identity' (2009) 16(1) *International Journal of the Legal Profession* 63.

two female practitioners at the start of her career: 'an incredible lesson in how you can be effective, intelligent female lawyers whilst being campaigners, whilst being nice. They were a very good lesson for me'. Rihana also tells a story of the motivational role played by the senior partner in her firm who she repeatedly describes as 'all about fighting for justice' and Ruth describes finding a law firm where she once worked: '… it had like Martin Luther King quotes and all this stuff and I thought how brilliant, this is exactly the kind of place I want to work'. Eve describes a charity she worked with in effusive terms: 'they're amazing, really outcome focussed – they find a way to use the law to improve housing conditions but the outcome comes first. They speak truth to power'. The motivational influence of these key, inspirational people and places of work appears to facilitate a circular process of *motivation* and *expectation* across the network of progressive practice. This process is experienced by individual practitioners but is collectively shared.

Across divergent themes, it is clear therefore that dynamic interactions facilitate the formation of the professional self and are instrumental to collective identity. In their journeys towards becoming lawyers, participants' moments of interaction contribute to their view of themselves, their work and their relationships with others.[17] We see here that boundary making is an important part of the social process where classifications as to being 'in or out' are integral to the formation of networks of interaction based on shared beliefs and solidarity that Diani identifies in his unifying conception of a social movement.[18] As Bourdieu observed:

> What is at stake in the struggles about the meaning of the social world is power over the classificatory schemes and systems which are the basis for the representation of groups and therefore their mobilization and demobilization.[19]

The construction of common experiences, values and motivations is central to the classificatory scheme that Bourdieu describes and to the capacity of progressive lawyers to mobilise to achieve change. There are of course legal professional boundaries; but perhaps even more striking is the further classification of progressive personal values and the related pursuit of social justice by those considered 'in' progressive networks. The literature illustrates some overlap between the development of collective professional identity and social identity theory and it is useful to consider this approach in order to reveal the interplay between the individual sense of self and perceived roles within and across wider network nodes.[20] Tajfel and Turner identify the three stages of social identity as

[17] Kim Adams et al, 'Investigating the Factors Influencing the Professional Identity of First-Year Health and Social Care Students' (2006) 5(2) *Learning in Health and Social Care* 55.

[18] Mario Diani, 'The Concept of a Social Movement' (1992) 40(1) *Sociological Review* 1.

[19] Pierre Bourdieu, *Distinctions: A Social Critique of the Judgement of Taste*, translated by Richard Nice (Harvard University Press, 1984) 479.

[20] For an exploration in the context of medical professional identity see Paivi Niemi, 'Medical students' Professional Identity: Self-Reflection in the Pre-Clinical Years' (1997) 31 *Medical Education* 408.

social categorisation, *social identification* and *social comparison*.[21] They describe how social actors first assign people to categories to both identify themselves and others and then, secondly, adopt the identity of the group and may begin to exhibit the norms and behaviour of that group. Once identification with a particular group has been made it is possible to begin to make comparisons with other groups, which is the final stage of the social identification process. These stages take place at a number of levels for lawyers in the study and serve to strengthen collective identity. As outlined above, perhaps the clearest example of categorisation, identification and comparison comes from the distinction made between corporate and non-corporate lawyers and the turning point this represents. Consistent with research that shows the process of involvement in social movement organisations at turning points such as adolescence, study participants reveal a clear turning point away from corporate work at similar times in the life course, either during or shortly after legal education and training.[22] The narratives explored in this chapter reveal a process of in-group identification for lawyers as a whole in terms of the framing of their shared progressive values.

Sociological work has further focussed on the fluid quality of identity construction where personal values are negotiated into the framing of the professional self and are even at times a powerful defence against any critique of professional practice.[23] Consistent with cause lawyering theory, narratives in the study reveal a similar fluid and nuanced presentation of self, such that participants' roles as lawyers are so deeply connected to their personal identities that clear lines of selfhood cannot easily be drawn. As I explore in chapter seven, this leads to circular ethical tensions where a 'defence' of values driven legal professional decision-making itself rests on the personal values that underpin those decisions.

COLLECTIVE IDENTITY: CONCLUSIONS

In this chapter I have sought to outline the connecting features of progressive lawyers' work across their networks, especially across class boundaries. I have described the importance of constructions of underlying progressive political values and how they relate to the pursuit of social change as an important

[21] Henri Tajfel and John Turner, 'A integrative theory of intergroup conflict' in William Austin and Stephen Worchel (eds), *The Psychology of Intergroup Relations* (Brooks/Cole, 1979).

[22] Florence Passy and Marco Giugni, 'Life-Spheres, Networks, and Sustained Participation in Social Movements: A Phenomenological Approach to Political Commitment' (2000) 15(1) *Sociological Forum* 117.

[23] See, eg, Janice McLaughlin, 'Risky Professional Boundaries: Articulations of the Personal Self by Antenatal Screening Professionals' (2003) 17(4) *Journal of Health Organization Management* 264.

feature of collective identity. Without exception, lawyers in the study describe a turn away from corporate and commercial legal practice and 'other' practitioners working in those settings.[24] They are thereafter connected by virtue of their motivation to pursue progressive legal work, across all sub-sets of practice and periods of time. To summarise, the following points in relation to shared motivating features can be distilled:

- Across a broad spectrum, liberal political values underpin professional life.
- Money is never *described* as a motivating factor.
- Lawyers describe in various ways a motivating desire to make a social contribution.
- Lawyers describe or intimate anger at injustice, or the desire to pursue justice, as a motivating factor.
- For lawyers from working class backgrounds their pursuit of justice is related as being informed by experiences of injustice.
- Constructions of motivation are linked to an ethical approach focused on representing those experiencing vulnerability and disadvantage in society.
- Lawyers describe motivations that rest on an idealistic vision of how society should function, where vulnerable and disempowered society actors achieve access to justice.

Notwithstanding points of divergence, especially in relation to class and access to the profession, there is an overwhelming expression of shared values and collective belonging within each of the subsets of practice in the study. Participants are keen to express their shared values, which tend to reveal a strong sense of solidarity:

> We were a collective in every sense of the word (Stefan, referring to Law Centre).
>
> There's a real camaraderie. They're critical. And they keep you going when you're feeling like you don't have enough work or you've got a difficult problem. You know some of my closest friends are now my colleagues in Chambers and they are an absolute source of sustenance (Gail, referring to Chambers).
>
> They've always taken a 'there must be something we can do to help' approach. It's one of the freeing things about working for them. They never just stop … they're ballsier than some other organisations (Jessica, referring to Charity).

[24] I note that this does not necessarily mean those 'other' lawyers do not pursue progressive legal work. Many commercial lawyers engage in pro bono activities that touch upon the progressive subsets of practice and work together with progressive practitioners (eg, where a city law firm supports an NGO in a strategic third-party intervention or delivers free legal advice sessions in a local law centre). The key consideration here is how the progressive lawyering movement perceives commercial lawyers and it appears that pro bono work (perhaps with some limited exceptions and dependent upon the extent of engagement and collaboration) does not necessarily enable those lawyers to be perceived as 'one of us' rather than 'other'.

In their stories, participants also frame their collective identity *back*, both temporally in the narrative itself and also in their own biographies, to shared politics:

> Martin: It helps that there's a fostering environment at the radical Bar, the left Bar, of we're all in this together. … we're all driven by the same basic things. There is a kind of burning sense of injustice.
>
> Jacqueline: And [those values] are driven by?
>
> Martin: Well, I think it's driven by a radical current of politics which runs through this Chambers which you pretty much have to demonstrate to get through the door. You certainly have to demonstrate a commitment to social justice, which goes hand in hand with that politics to get here.
>
> As a firm or partnership there's a commitment to access to justice, a real commitment to legal aid (Phil, referring to legal aid law firm).

For lawyers in the study the subsets of progressive practice themselves lend weight to their progressive credentials and also relate to the status and prestige they afford one another. Participants describe experiences and achievements in early professional life that act as progressive rites of passage and each of these experiences provide a valuable, reliable network of support that both motivates and sustains them. The features are reminiscent of Etienne's study of criminal defence cause lawyers outlined in chapter two. Etienne identified common traits including a shared ideology combined with scepticism of government action and shared group identity.[25] For participants in this study these features are also clear and are accompanied, indeed manifested by, a shared turning away from corporate legal practice. This turn is consistent with a differentiation process that serves to strengthen the solidarity of their networks by virtue of shared collective identity as well as a shared motivational frame for action against injustice.[26] Participants delineate and present this identity as a shared set of values, attitudes and commitments which distinguishes them from 'other' lawyers and intimates that they are engaged in a *collective* political and cultural conflict.

[25] Margareth Etienne, 'The Ethics of Cause Lawyering: An Empirical Examination of Criminal Defense Lawyers as Cause Lawyers' (2005) 95 *Journal of Criminal Law and Criminology* 1209.

[26] Robert Benford and David Snow, 'Framing Processes and Social Movements: An Overview and Assessment' (2000) 26 *Annual Review of Sociology* 611, 617–19.

5

Tools for Change

THE AIM OF this chapter is to outline the difference that collective identity might make to how participants conceptualise the tools they use to achieve social change. Socio-legal scholars in the UK have traditionally conducted ethnographic studies of discrete areas of legal aid practice[1] such that we have limited understanding of the connectivity and collaboration between lawyers working in different subsets of progressive legal practice and their perspectives on how the tools they use interact. This chapter interrogates the extent to which the constructions of tools for change across the network nodes might impact upon the choices that lawyers make and perceptions of how these have changed over time.

The tools participants in the study use broadly relate to the activities that formed the basis of the data collection strategy for this study. As outlined in chapter three, each participant engages in at least two of the following types of activity: legal aid funded client representation, policy work, campaigns or strategic litigation. My focus is on the perceived tension between providing individual advice and representation to clients at grassroots level and conducting high impact strategic litigation or related policy work and campaigning at the, so-called, 'grasstops'.[2] The former seeks to impact high numbers of people through volume casework while the latter aims to impact high numbers of people through a case or campaign that might have far reaching consequences for law and policy. Within progressive lawyering networks, and especially in law centres in the 1980s and 1990s, there has been some debate around which of these tools should be used and for what purpose.[3] Often, those lawyers favouring high

[1] See, eg, Daniel Newman, *Legal Aid Lawyers and the Quest for Justice* (Hart, 2013).

[2] Effie Fokas, 'Directions in Religious Pluralism in Europe: Mobilizations in the Shadow of the European Court of Human Rights Religious Freedoms Jurisprudence' (2015) 4 *Oxford Journal of Law and Religion* 54.

[3] Philip Leask, 'Law Centres in England and Wales' (1985) 7(1) *Law and Policy* 61, 62; Roger Smith, 'Human Rights and Access to Justice' (2007) 14(3) *The International Journal of the Legal Profession* 261. The debate relates to what Cappelletti and Garth identify as three 'waves' in the access to justice movement: legal aid for the indigent, public interest law for diffuse interests and the provision of alternative forms of dispute resolution to formal court processes. See, Cappelletti and Garth, 'Access to Justice and the Welfare State: An Introduction' in Mauro Cappelletti, *Access to Justice and the Welfare State* (Springer, 1981) 1, 4.

volume casework tend to view the law as a means of resolving injustices and obtaining outcomes for clients on the ground. Some who engage in strategic litigation however have argued that it is futile resolving those legal problems without challenging the structural problems that cause them and assert that, under the right conditions, litigation has the potential to achieve systemic (rather than symptomatic) change.[4] This corresponds with the perspective that for social movements turning to the legal opportunity structure holds promise especially when political opportunities have closed down.[5] These debates have historically raised questions about the extent to which legally aided casework should be used to achieve social change at all;[6] while others argue that individual client needs may need to be sacrificed as a 'tragic but essential trade-off' in the interests of a wider 'mobilisation effort'.[7] I have observed that for many lawyers in the study these distinctions and related tensions are prevalent in narratives throughout the 1990s and 2000s but that the frame of the debate has somewhat altered in light of resource constraints in recent years.

As discussed in chapter two, the interplay between the activities at the heart of the study often makes it challenging to assign lawyers to a particular cause lawyering type. Likewise, lawyers might self-identify as using a particular tool for change but be perceived as using different tools by others; or be using different tools at different times.[8] Cummings and NeJaime outline in their 2010 study on lawyering for marriage equality the many levels upon which lawyers engage and interact: 'advocacy across different domains (courts, legislatures, media), spanning different levels (federal, state, local), and deploying different tactics (litigation, legislative advocacy, public education)'.[9] They highlight the ways in which US lawyers have moved towards alternative understandings of their roles such that they see themselves as broader agents of social change working together with other activists and campaigners across these levels rather than preserving a traditional lawyer-client model.

Another US study further demonstrates how lawyers think strategically using 'multiple approaches' and argues that while high impact cases are still important, they are undertaken 'with a more realistic vision of how they

[4] Charles Epp, 'Law as an Instrument of Social Reform' in Keith Whittington et al (eds), *The Oxford Handbook of Law and Politics* (Oxford University Press, 2008); Carol Harlow and Richard Rawlings, *Pressure Through Law* (Routledge, 1992).

[5] Chris Hilson, 'New Social Movements: The Role of Legal Opportunity', (2002) 9(2) *Journal of European Public Policy* 238.

[6] Richard Abel, 'Law Without Politics: Legal Aid Under Advanced Capitalism' (1985) 32 *UCLA Law Review* 474, 491.

[7] Paul Tremblay, 'Acting "A Very Moral Type of God": Triage Among Poor Clients' (1999) *Fordham Law Review* 2475, 2532.

[8] Andrew Francis, *The Edge of Law: Emergent and Divergent Models of Legal Professionalism* (Routledge, 2011) 94.

[9] Scott Cummings and Douglas NeJaime, 'Lawyering for Marriage Equality' (2010) *UCLA Law Review* 1235, 1242.

will service long-term goals'.[10] As discussed in chapter two, Scheingold has drawn attention to the importance of lawyers seeing the limitations, as well as the possibilities, of legal action and to envisage legal strategies in combination with other forms of political action.[11] This study adopts a wide and multi-level analysis that takes an encompassing view of political and social action. Similar to these previous studies, I identify that progressive lawyers in the UK might not solely rest at particular ends of Hilbink's cause lawyering spectrum[12] (such as grassroots or elite) but that we can increasingly identify lawyers working 'strategically' across it, facilitated by their networked interactions. This is, I suggest, because the more recent access to justice crisis in the UK has facilitated a blurring of separate but related types of cause lawyering activity. For example, as outlined in chapter two, the proposed abolition of the Human Rights Act 1998 saw lawyers speaking out and campaigning around their own cases, with the help of social media, in a broad public space.[13] Reminiscent of Sommerlad's contention that UK cause lawyers are motivated by a 'master ideal of access to justice',[14] one might say that a new cause lawyer has emerged in recent years: a practice at the edges of human rights, although not committed to it exclusively, with a focus on the cause of access to justice for all.

I also note in this context that for present day practitioners cuts to legal aid in England and Wales represent a dominant austerity narrative against which other narratives are constructed in the study. When I refer to 'cuts' I mean predominantly those changes enacted by LASPO 2012 in the civil law context but also, for the small number of criminal practitioners in the study, through changes to criminal legal aid contracting and fixed fee arrangements in England and Wales.[15] I observed early in my fieldwork that the most recent cuts, and the perceived crisis in the justice system more generally, tended to form a story within which other stories were framed. The use of an austerity narrative was a form of sense making for participants, either by looking back and placing other stories in a temporal sense 'before' and 'after' the reforms or by

[10] Deborah Rhode, 'Public Interest Law: The Movement at Midlife' (2008) *Stanford Law Review* 2027, 2046.

[11] Stuart Scheingold, *The Politics of Rights: Lawyers, Public Policy and Political Change* (University of Michigan Press, 2004) 5.

[12] Thomas Hilbink, 'You Know the Type: Categories of Cause Lawyering' (2004) 19 *Law & Social Inquiry* 657.

[13] See, eg, James Farrell, 'Social Media for Social Change Lawyers: An Australian Housing Rights Lawyer's Experience' (2013) 20(2) *International Journal of the Legal Profession* 209.

[14] Hilary Sommerlad, 'Reflections on the Reconfiguration of Access to Justice' (2008) 15(3) *International Journal of the Legal Profession* 179, 180.

[15] Most participants in the study work in England and Wales and are thus impacted by these cuts. However, even for participants in Scotland and Northern Ireland the cuts in England and Wales were prevalent in their narratives by way of comparison. Likewise, for those Northern Irish and Scottish participants resource issues still tended to dominate their narratives notwithstanding government cuts to legal service not being as comprehensive as in England and Wales.

telling stories about clients and the tools they use to resolve their legal issues, directly against the backdrop of cuts to legal aid. These forms of narrative sense making have been studied in a variety of cultural contexts including for medical practitioners[16] and especially when remembering emotional or traumatic events.[17] For lawyers exploring emotive issues around vulnerable clients and legal service provision attempts at sense making around a background austerity narrative is similarly common.

In this chapter I interrogate lawyers' own experience of legal aid casework, strategic litigation and related campaigning in order to better understand their roles within and across progressive lawyering networks nodes. Perceptions on working conditions across subsets of practice are outlined in order to analyse the ways in which the tools that lawyers use shift in light of perceptions on resource constraints and other socio-political factors. The questions posed by Southworth's study of right-wing cause lawyers are pertinent in this chapter: (1) what strategies did [these] lawyers pursue? (2) what did they *believe* they were accomplishing?[18] My fieldwork has shown that present day practitioners relate that funding restrictions, both in terms of remuneration and for the justice system more widely, inhibits their ability to achieve client benefits in day to day legal service provision. As such, by drawing on the networks that exist to support their activities many participants turn to an alternative vision of lawyering, which I characterise as both strategic and collaborative, to achieve their goals. I analyse present day narratives alongside those of practitioners in preceding decades to draw out contrasting perspectives over time. Further, lawyers' collective beliefs about the strategies they adopt lead to a more nuanced understanding of the relationship between the different tactics they use and the collaborations that exist to support their activities. The connection between lawyers' methods and their own positioning within and across progressive lawyering networks is important. Progressive lawyers construct narratives of progress and change from early on in their professional lives that both connect them in the work they do. In the same way that scholars have explored how networked interactions lead to involvement in social movements;[19] interactions around legal tools for change within progressive lawyering networks provides texture and insight into the strategies lawyers adopt for social change.

[16] Kathryn Hunter, 'Narrative Literature and the Clinical Exercise of Practical Reason' (1996) 21 *The Journal of Medicine and Philosophy* 303.

[17] Avril Thorne and Kate McLean, 'Telling Traumatic Events in Adolescence: A Study of Master Narrative Positioning' in Robyn Fivush and C Haden (eds), *Connecting Culture and Memory: The Development of an Autobiographical Self* (Lawrence Erlbaum, 2003) 169.

[18] Ann Southworth, 'Lawyers and the Myth of Rights in Civil Rights and Poverty Practice' (1999) 8 *Boston University Public Interest Law Journal* 473.

[19] John Lofland, *Social Movement Organizations: Guide to Research on Insurgent* Realities (Aldine de Gruyter, 1996).

LEGAL ADVICE AND REPRESENTATION

> The cuts have changed the environment in which everyone does law. (Gail)

I described in chapter two the background to legal aid in the UK and the upheaval across the legal aid and not-for-profit legal sectors brought about by LASPO 2012 in England and Wales and resource constraints in other jurisdictions. I sought to highlight in particular the link between legal aid and strategic litigation by virtue of legal aid funding being used to facilitate strategic impactful casework.[20] It is worthwhile considering further the historic interplay between legal casework and broader social change even before the establishment of legal aid in the 1940s. While we might assume that an alternative vision of legal service provision originated in the 1970s, in fact we can trace it to the turn of the century. In the early 1900s the 'Poor Man's Lawyer' scheme developed to provide voluntary legal services to hundreds of unrepresented litigants in London. It was an ad hoc, voluntary scheme that sought to meet the legal needs of some of the most vulnerable people in society. One of the most influential service providers, which still exists to this day, was the early Settlement at Toynbee Hall. The history has been well documented: its co-founder, Samuel Barnett, was a cleric and social reformer who was firm in his belief that 'no lasting solution to the social problems of the day would be found by dealing with the individual in abstraction from the social structure'.[21] For Barnett, 'the solution to social problems lay in a judicious mixture of individual reform, effective access to the means of securing existing legal rights and the extension of those rights through social and political action'.[22] Barnett set up a University settlement at Toynbee Hall where students lived in local communities and worked to try and improve individual welfare through the provision of advice and community engagement. This powerful blend of legal service provision and influential social action is perhaps the earliest example of a holistic and progressive type of lawyering in the UK, and also perhaps the first University law clinic. Barnett also provided an early understanding of strategic practice with the following observation about his casework altering the 'character of legislation':

> It will alter the character of legislation, which, often adopted with intention to remove some grievance or establish some good, remains a dead letter for want of knowledge of the conditions in which the law will be administered.[23]

[20] Richard Abel, 'Lawyers and the Power to Change' (1985) 7 *Law and Policy* 5; Hilary Sommerlad and Peter Sanderson, 'Social Justice on the Margins: The Future of the Not for Profit Legal Sector as Providers of Legal Advice in England and Wales' (2013) 35(3) *Journal of Social Welfare and Family Law* 305.

[21] Samuel Barnett and Henrietta Barnett, *Towards Social Reform* (T Fisher Unwin, 1909) 170.

[22] ibid 171.

[23] ibid.

Throughout the early 1900s the Poor Man's Lawyer scheme expanded across the UK with Toynbee Hall as the leading example. The key to its success was a collaborative model of social, political and legal action.[24] Importantly, the infrastructure of the scheme laid the foundations for the modern legal aid system in that the pressure on voluntary lawyers, including geographical disparity and scare resources, helped facilitate a series of investigations and reports by successive governments into the adequacy of civil legal advice provision. These investigations demonstrated the necessity of equal access to law and judicial processes:

> But in the complicated structure we call law it goes without saying that equal protection of the law must assume an equal opportunity to receive the advice and guidance of the expert in the law, the lawyer, and an equal opportunity to enter the halls of justice without danger of eviction for want of cash to pay court costs, out-of-pocket expenses, and living expenses while the judicial process unfolds.[25]

The need to adequately remunerate lawyers for their services underpinned the scheme implemented by the Legal Advice and Assistance Act 1949. Notably, this was also at a time of post war austerity and pressing social need[26] when people were said to 'believe in public service'.[27] In contrast to the more recent media narratives outlined in chapter one, the free legal services provided by Settlement lawyers and others was recognised in the corridors of power; and in the public sphere by the 1940s. The Director of Public Prosecutions, Theobold Matthew, commenting on the report of the Rushcliffe Committee in 1945, highly commended lawyers noting:

> I have especially in mind those persons who, for no reward, spend a full evening one or more times a week after a busy day, on a hard chair, in an ugly room, in an inaccessible neighbourhood, listening to stories of everyday tragedies and follies and bringing relief to harassed minds by their sympathy and kindness.[28]

With equal opportunity *to* the law came increased opportunity *for* the law. As legal aid expanded between the 1950s and the 1980s so did the opportunities to use that funding strategically as a means of providing pressure through law and challenge to state power.[29] Similar to the US neighbourhood law centres that

[24] I note there is some divergence of opinion as to whether the Poor Man's Lawyer scheme as a whole replicated the social change model of Toynbee Hall. See Tamara Goriely, 'Law for the Poor, The Relationship Between Advice Agencies and Solicitors in the Development of Poverty Law' (1996) 3 *International Journal of the Legal Profession* 215.

[25] Elson, 'The Rushcliffe Report' (1946) 13(2) *The University of Chicago Law Review* 131.

[26] Douglas Johnson, *Imagine any MP today supporting legal aid lawyers being paid 85 per cent of assessed standard costs*, Legal Action Group (September 2020).

[27] Tamara Goriely, 'Rushcliffe Fifty Years On: The Changing Role of Civil Legal Aid Within the Welfare State' (1994) 21(4) *Journal of Law and Society* 545, 547.

[28] Theobold Mathew, 'Legal Aid and Legal Advice in England and Wales, The Rushcliffe Committee Report' (1946) 7(1) *The Howard Journal of Criminal Justice* 39.

[29] Harlow and Rawlings (n 4). See also *Justice for All* (Society of Labour Lawyers, 1968).

emerged in the 1970s with a strategic vision for creating environments where lawyers could pursue positive social change,[30] some UK law centres used legal aid funding to pursue more strategic casework or to otherwise fund pro bono work in other areas of strategic importance.[31] During this time a greater number of single-issue pressure groups also emerged and challenged more traditional notions of the welfare provision. As Goriely notes, 'a wave of left-wing critics castigated welfare providers for being out of touch with their clients, putting their own interests first, and pursuing essentially bureaucratic agendas'.[32] Legal Action Group (LAG) was also founded in 1971 to encourage lawyers to use the law to help alleviate the needs of those living in poverty and began to lobby for greater recognition of legal rights enforceable by individuals.[33] As I outlined in chapter two, the historic development of these challenges to state power in practice, similar to US congressional restrictions imposed in the 1990s, has been met with increasing conservative backlash over time. For example, most recently, LASPO 2012 and the Criminal Justice and Courts Act 2015 in England and Wales have placed restrictions on the areas of law for which legal challenges could be funded as well as access to judicial review by charities and NGOs.[34] For many participants in the study therefore, resource needs feature strongly in their narratives. This is especially so for law centre and legal aid lawyers, where a lack of resource particularly influences their choice of tools for change. I will outline the contrasting narratives of these lawyers and explore how, similar to the early strategic and collaborative model of Barnett's Settlement lawyers, a lack of resource coupled with the perceived injustice of current social conditions has collectively incentivised lawyers to consider more deeply the interplay between models of individual advice and representation and other strategic tools for social change.

I begin by exploring the story of Stefan who was a law centre lawyer for nearly two decades, and described well the interplay between resource considerations and the *perceived* impact of his casework as a means of justifying the legal tools he uses day to day. He outlined from the outset of the interview that his motivation in the 1990s lay in doing individual housing advice and representation because of the results he could achieve: 'You know, somebody walked in who was homeless and going to be on the street and wanted to stop that happening and I'm doing it. I can actually do it.' He repeatedly pointed to the real 'impact' of the law being helping individuals 'deal with and overcome absolutely

[30] Louise Trubeck, 'Public Interest Law: Facing The Problems of Maturity' (2011) 33 *University of Arkansas Law Review* 417, 418.

[31] Leask (n 3).

[32] Goriely (n 27) 553. Goriely argues that the challenge to the 'public service' underpinnings of legal aid came from both the left and the right between the 1970s and 1980s (p 555).

[33] ibid 554.

[34] The Bingham Centre et al, *Judicial Review and The Rule of Law: An Introduction to the Criminal Justice and Courts Act 2015, Part 4* (The Bingham Centre, 2015).

awful … potentially life threatening situations' because 'all the impact flows from [the advice]'. When I asked him what his most memorable case was he again highlighted the importance of 'volume' as a tool for change while also referencing debates within the law centre movement throughout the 1990s:

> Jacqueline: For you what would you say in those early years was your most memorable case or cases?
>
> Stefan: Yeah, that's interesting because this is where I think I depart from some people in the law centre movement … We saw our most important role, well I certainly did, as casework. As volume casework. We were always on the lookout for strategic cases and for policy work. We wanted to do that work and it became harder and harder to do because of a squeeze on funding. My best highlights were, the cases, and I think literally hundreds … thousands of cases, which were evictions, someone comes in, they're about to be evicted and you can make an application to the court to prevent that eviction. I would do those on a weekly basis.

Stefan was acutely self-aware of the distinction between his approach and that of other more strategic law centres more readily pursuing judicial review and appellate level casework. He describes this several times as the 'debate' within the law centre movement about divergent approaches. For Stefan, he said the 'squeeze on funding' made it difficult to pursue more strategic work as a priority, however he was also quick to point out that some of the housing and employment discrimination cases he took nonetheless had a strategic impact through appeals pursued, including to the European Court of Human Rights. For Stefan, even those cases had to be bottom up and began with individual clients on the ground: 'So what I would say is, look, we did this amazing strategic case that impacted the whole country and what did it come out of? It came out of doing high volume casework. You do both.'

At Stefan's law centre during the early 1990s resource came both from the local authority and from legal aid contracts ('about fifty fifty') and Stefan reflected on how much the local authority gave them then compared to more recent times: 'it was a progressive local authority … they said well you're a bunch of crazy hippies suing us all the time but that's fine, here, have the money!' He remarks on how the rise in contracting and more restrictive local authority funding meant there was 'even less time to think about policy work and to strategise'. Stefan's narrative is therefore somewhat conflicted: on the one hand he argues that he is motivated by individual casework, which is the type of work, in his view, law centres should be doing as a starting point which might then lead to strategic cases. On the other, he suggests that he would have pursued more strategic work in law and policy but didn't because of funding pressures. In any event, it is clear that for Stefan resolving client issues on the ground was his first priority and this related to what funding was available for him and his colleagues.[35]

[35] While outside the remit of this study the role that funding itself plays in culturally creating and shaping legal strategies is important. See Alan Chen and Scott Cummings, *Public Interest Lawyering: A Contemporary Perspective* (Wolters Kluwer, 2014).

The distinction is pertinent and in analysing Stefan's narrative I noticed his tendency to *justify* his volume casework approach even when we were not touching upon it at that point in his story or I had not asked him directly about it. He conveyed the pressure of the perceived preference for high impact litigation by some within progressive lawyering networks. It seemed that Stefan was acutely aware of how he, and the law centre where he worked, were perceived by other law centres as less effective than those at the more elite end of the cause lawyering spectrum doing strategic work. When we discussed the collective structure of the law centre he again turned to a justification of their tactical choices by looking back and describing conversations he recalled:

> Jacqueline: And what happened? Did they keep the collective structure?
>
> Stefan: We kept it. Right through the 2000s. It was really interesting because I think in the 90s people would have characterised [our] law centre as a bit lame. They said you know we were too much a part of the system. That we were propping up the system. That we weren't doing the really important work. They said to us what's the difference between you and [legal aid] solicitors if you don't do the fancy strategic work? They would be having a go at us for that. On the other hand, we were a die-hard collective, equal pay right through that time.

I sensed some frustration at this point in the interview: having done 'thousands' of housing cases and maintained a collective law centre model, Stefan still felt perceived as 'a bit lame' for not doing 'fancy strategic work'. At another point in Stefan's story he describes going on a march to oppose cuts to public sector funding in the 2000s and being challenged by another demonstrator: 'I remember getting into a conversation about what I do … and someone there said to me but you're part of the problem by saving people who are living miserable lives because of the structures in place.' Stefan was acutely aware, amidst the prevalent debates at the time, that by helping people at risk of eviction there was a view that he was preserving the unfair systems in place and that, linked to this, other progressive lawyers thought his work was somehow less valuable.[36] He repeatedly expressed however that *he* valued the volume casework approach and connected it to the values of his law centre, which was embedded in the local community and strictly upheld the collective model of working.[37]

It would seem that recent restrictions in funding have collapsed the debate that Stefan describes to some extent; or at least altered the frame in which it occurs. While (in England and Wales) a law centre housing lawyer can still hold a legal aid contract to provide advice in certain discrete areas (prospective eviction resulting in homelessness, for example, would still be in scope for funding where other eligibility requirements are met) the rates of pay are comparatively

[36] See, eg, Stephen Wexler, 'Practicing Law for Poor People' (1970) 79 Yale Law Journal 1049.

[37] For discussion of legal aid advice provision as a means of politically mobilising groups see Abel (n 6) 496.

poor and early stage advice is not as readily available. As such, getting the client outcomes and 'impact' comparable to that seen in the 1970s, 1980s and early 1990s, which Stefan describes, through high volume casework may not be possible despite the sheer importance of this type of casework provision. This is especially so given that, at the time of writing, many parts of the UK are experiencing a crisis in the availability of social housing.[38] Another law centre lawyer, Sue, makes clear that the social welfare reforms also make *meaningful* advice in order to achieve the outcomes that Stefan describes difficult and laments: 'LASPO has just led to terrible things'. She describes her weekly duty housing list at court and summarises the adverse impact on clients of being evicted because there is no longer legal available for social welfare benefits advice:

> The silos we work in and the inability to be able to refer out for things. So I go to court on a Friday and you know mainly it's benefits issues that mean that a person has been evicted. And unless I've got someone to refer the benefits issues to because it's out of scope, how does it get resolved in between the next four weeks when it comes back to court? (Sue)

I note that Sue's narrative as a whole centred around the cuts to legal aid and other social welfare reforms. She frequently expressed exasperation, as illustrated in the extract above, at not being able to help clients using the tools she historically used in the provision of housing advice and representation because of the gap in social welfare legal advice provision. For Sue, trying to make sense of the cuts during the interview itself was exasperating and she often used them as a frame to consider the related judgement placed on her clients and her own work by others: 'People aren't bad or good. People on benefits aren't scroungers. You know we've had so much of that really … I see so many people facing eviction and at a crisis point and other people don't see that.' Sue turns to austerity funding cuts several times and expresses futility at the current context of legal service provision: 'Well, it's just there are holes that people fall down and they can't get back up again. And it's just too hard you know?' Many participants describe funding constraints in similarly emotive terms conveying frustration, exasperation or anger: 'It's just devastated our clients to be honest. And it's frustrating as a lawyer …' (Ruth), '… it has been horrible, since 2013. It has been horrible …' (Rihana), 'And they [The Legal Aid Agency] sold us that, it was a big lie that it would be cost neutral … it wasn't cost neutral!' (Phil). The frustration and exasperation of lawyers is acute and collectively experienced: for a majority of participants in the study the tools they historically used to achieve positive outcomes for clients, and broader social change, are either no longer available or more difficult to deploy.

[38] Owen Bowcott, 'Thousands left homeless by shortage of legal aid lawyers, say charities' (*The Guardian*, 18 December 2016); Andy Winter, 'There is a financial case for reversing legal aid cuts – as well as a human one' (*Inside Housing*, 12 February 2020).

The prevalence of legal aid cuts impacting the provision of advice and representation consistently featured in the narratives of participants whether they were newly qualified or had qualified in the 1970s, 1980s or 1990s. In fact, for more senior practitioners resource issues tended to dominate in the present by way of contrast to their legal practice in the past in terms of the adequacy of results they could achieve on behalf of clients. Those participants look back in particular to those three decades ago and see legal aid advice and representation, as it then was, as an adequate tool for change. One participant, Phil, made a comparison to legal aid practice in the 90s being similar to working as a GP: '[you] were a general practitioner on the frontline, protecting people who had absolutely no chance of protecting themselves' and that 'effectively, most people could get legal aid'. Another legal aid law firm solicitor, Ben, describing the 1990s said 'the sort of conditions of work were immeasurably better than now' because 'legal aid was available for any matter of English law and not just in restricted areas'. Similar to Stefan, Ben described the lack of bureaucracy compared to present legal aid practice: 'when you got [legal aid] certificates they were limitless'. For Aidan, who came to legal practice in the 1980s, he notes how the legal aid rates in the past meant that lawyers could pursue more pro bono work. For him, that pro bono work was 'strategic' where he worked to change the law in a particular field:

> The fact is my generation had it pretty good. You could earn a reasonable living on legal aid. At the higher levels, a very very good living. That left one with enough financial freedom to do other cases. There was a different atmosphere then (Aidan).

All participants who describe their work in the 1980s and 1990s portrayed both a less pressurised internal working culture and a public realm where they felt more valued than in the present day. Stefan describes the funding for the law centre where he worked with ease compared to now: 'Well, the thing is we had some legal aid funding. But almost all the funding came from the local authority, with no pressure. No real targets.' Stefan's description of law centre practice in the 1990s is sharply at odds with Emily's description of working in law centres since the mid-2000s. Emily related working through several funding upheavals in her story; but when she came to the most recent cuts her narrative turned:

> And you know … it was a bit like the Titanic to be honest. You could see the iceberg, you knew it was coming but it was that reactionary thing … it pretty much hit us full on. I was on maternity leave and I got a risk of redundancy notice through the post. It continued for several years. It became a real reality that we were struggling as an organisation (Emily).

Her use of catastrophic imagery conveys the impact of the cuts on both her professional and personal life. In fact, in Emily's narrative in particular there was a tendency to use the dialogue of the interview itself to clarify the meaning of events in the past and make sense of them in the present with 'before and after' reflection.[39] Emily goes on to describe how many members of staff made salary sacrifices during that time of re-structure. While they are now on a solid footing she describes the funding environment as challenging and 'more competitive than it's ever been' with 'more organisations trying to get the same pots of money'. Further, just as the Poor Man's Lawyer Scheme developed to expose geographic disparity in advice provision, research has shown that one of the effects of restrictions in legal aid funding has been advice deserts in some parts of the UK where service providers no longer hold legal aid contracts in certain areas of law,[40] as well as regional disparity in access to judicial review.[41] Emily touched upon this issue:

> The opportunities here are very different from what they are in say London or Manchester. Particularly since the courts have moved and decentralised outside of London as well because [redacted City] has been left behind a little bit. ... it's a different climate completely. Leeds seems to have taken a lot of the kudos for, well, it's a growing legal community whereas I think ... you know ... it's all had an impact certainly (Emily).

I highlight these narratives in order to contextualise the recent constrained landscape of legal advice provision. For many lawyers within progressive lawyering networks as a result of resource constraints, and related activism and campaigning by lawyers on the fact of those constraints, the context in which tools are deployed has drastically altered in recent years. Interestingly, this view was echoed in Scotland regardless of legal aid not being curtailed to the same extent: 'the quality of work that you can do on legal aid alone is too low' (Kimberley).

Ankita, a barrister-campaigner, also described her perspective on the background to the cuts to legal aid and linked it to lawyers' perspectives of themselves. She talked about her own litigation as 'wiping the floor with the government a lot of the time' because 'the decision making is so bad' and then described the response of the government as follows:

> So the government is being like, well, we can't win in court because we're losing these cases, so what do we do about that? Well, you restrict access to the court. And how do we do that? We cut legal aid. We cut down on judicial review by raising a tax, by chipping away at fees, everything, and what else do we do? We attack the lawyers because this is the way to stigmatise this kind of work and make it difficult (Ankita).

[39] Michael Agar and Jerry Hobbs, 'Interpreting Discourse: Coherence and the Analysis of Ethnographic Interviews' (1982) 5 *Discourse Processes* 1.

[40] Monidipa Fouzder, 'Legal Aid Cuts Creating New Advice Deserts', *The Law Society Gazette* (18 April 2016).

[41] Sarah Nason and Maurice Sunkin, 'The Regionalisation of Judicial Review: Constitutional Authority, Access to Justice and Specialisation of Services in Public Law' (2013) 76(2) *Modern Law Review* 223; Sarah Nason, 'Justice Outside London? An Update on 'Regional' Judicial Review' (*Constitutional Law Blog*, 2016).

The interplay between what participants describe as the government's perception of progressive lawyer's work, and their perception of themselves is striking. As Gail comments, resource issues have quite simply 'changed the environment in which everyone does law'. She explains further:

> I think it's made law much more political. In some ways it's brought home to the legal profession the importance of rights of access to the court and so of their role as defenders of people's access to justice … in a way I think that perhaps we'd become a bit lazy about that kind of thing before. So I think people feel that more keenly (Gail).

We can contrast this context with what Stefan described about his work: his priority had been high volume advice casework and while, at times, there was considerable pressure on resource for the most part some form of legal aid and/or local authority funding was available to pursue it in the 1990s. However, more recent restrictions imposed on access to justice makes the provision of advice difficult (in some areas of law impossible) to deliver. This has differentiated progressive lawyers within their networks to a 'much more political' way of doing law resting on a desire to uphold the 'rights of access to the courts'. Participants reveal a desire to use the limited legal aid funding that remains, alongside *other* tools such as campaigning, lobbying or pursuing strategic casework to focus their attention on more strategically achieving social change.

STRATEGIC LITIGATION

> You just need to push towards change (Eve).

In this section I explore the ways in which some participants in the study perceive and conceptualise strategic litigation as a tool for achieving social change. The analysis rests not only in narrative interviews but also in broader ethnographic fieldwork encounters with lawyers and campaigners. As outlined in the first chapter, a strategic case is one that seeks to make a broader impact in terms of changing law and policy and when an organisation looks to the courts to achieve its aims that action can usually be characterised as strategic.[42] From a practical perspective, it might seek to clarify a legal point which is unclear, or 'to challenge a state of affairs which has persisted for some time and which has seemed immune to ordinary challenges by ad hoc litigation or campaigns'.[43] A recent study of strategic litigation activities confirms its versatility as a concept and suggests that 'it is not attached to a particular cause, but rather it is a method by

[42] Lisa Vanhala, *Making Rights a Reality? Disability Rights Activists and Legal Mobilization* (Cambridge University Press, 2011) 7.

[43] Charlotte Kilroy QC, 'Strategic Litigation: What is it? When and How to Use It'. Speech to the IPLA conference (19 November 2019, Doughty Street Chambers).

which the objectives of a cause can be achieved'.[44] There are studies in the US[45] and elsewhere[46] of the ways in which lawyers work with activists and campaigners by turning to the courts; and an emerging body of work in the UK based on individual strategic case studies.[47] I am especially interested here in the networks that facilitate strategic litigation as a desired tool for change within the current landscape by contrast to other decades in the study. The construction of the theme of change is perhaps most explicit in the context of strategic litigation. Participants in the study talk for example of 'pushing towards change' (Eve), 'identifying an issue … and taking it forward' (Lena) and of 'making new law' (Aidan) when describing their roles in strategic casework. These constructions go some way in explaining the justifications that Stefan tended towards in his own narrative by way of comparison; and arguably aligns with the literature on how litigation might serve to overwhelm and distract from other tools for social change.

I note that the shortcomings of litigation as a strategy illustrate the complex social practices that underpin how rights are construed and negotiated. These include how litigation may in fact inhibit grassroots action,[48] that it can divert scarce resources from more productive strategies[49] and assist or empower opposition groups.[50] Gerald Rosenberg goes so far as to question whether courts can *ever* actually produce meaningful social reform.[51] The assertion generally is that by emphasising litigation lawyers steer movements and activists away from other, possibly more successful, political actions or overwhelm them with their

[44] Michael Ramsden and Chris Gledhill, 'Defining Strategic Litigation' (2019) 38(4) *Civil Justice Quarterly* 407.

[45] Michael McCann, *Rights at Work: Pay Equity Reform and the Politics of Legal Mobilization* (Chicago University Press, 1994) 8; Ann Southworth, *Lawyers of the Right: Professionalizing the Conservative Coalition* (University of Chicago Press, 2008).

[46] Pieter Bouwen and Margaret McCown, 'Lobbying Versus Litigation: Political and Legal Strategies of Interest in the European Union' (2007) 14(3) *Journal of European Public Policy* 422; Kieran McEvoy and Rachel Rebouche, 'Mobilizing the Professions: Lawyers, Politics and the Collective Legal Conscience' in John Morison et al (eds), *Judges, Transition and Human Rights* (Oxford University Press, 2007).

[47] Lisa Vanhala et al, '"Let Us Learn": Legal Mobilization for the Rights of Young Migrants to Access Student Loans in the UK' (2018) 10(3) *Journal of Human Rights Practice* 439; Leila Baker and Miranda Lewis, *Detained Fast Track Litigation Case Study: Detention Action Using the Law for Social Change* (Institute for Voluntary Action Research, 2017); Lisa Vanhala and Jacqueline Kinghan, *Using the Law to Address Unfair Systems: A Case Study of the Personal Independence Payments Legal Challenge* (The Public Law Project, 2019).

[48] Michael McCann, *Taking Reform Seriously: Perspectives on Public Interest Liberalism* (Cornell University Press, 1986).

[49] Michael McCann and Silverstein, 'Rethinking Law's "Allurements": A Relational Analysis of Social Movement Lawyers in the US' in Austin Sarat and Stuart Scheingold, *Cause Lawyering: Political Commitments and Professional Responsibilities* (Oxford University Press, 1998).

[50] Gerald Rosenberg, *The Hollow Hope: Can Courts Bring About Social Change?* (Chicago University Press, 2008); Michael Klarman, 'Brown and Laurence (*and* Goodridge)' (2005) 104 *Michigan Law Review* 431.

[51] ibid 341.

legal tactics.[52] On the other hand, Southworth asserts that such an analysis is reductive and 'does not consider how litigation might complement rather than displace other strategies and how activists might use litigation to influence other processes'.[53] A more recent analysis of cause lawyers further illustrates how a loss in court can still lead to important precedent setting on issues.[54] This is especially the case where a series of incremental changes can build towards more significant legal change over time such that cause lawyers might use a series of smaller wins as a tool for wider social change.[55]

One example of the complementary potential of strategic litigation lies in the use of third-party interventions, as outlined in chapter two. These provide a way for charities to become involved in a case, and to inform the court about the potential impact on the groups they represent, without the pressure of conducting the litigation. The change across time periods of the study with respect to strategic litigation and third-party interventions is well illustrated by Kenneth's story. He describes the process of undertaking an intervention on behalf of an NGO in the House of Lords (as it then was) in the 1990s:

> I rang up the House of Lords Judicial Office and said I want to apply to intervene on behalf of [redacted NGO]. But no one had ever done that before! It was I think the first time this had ever been done … The funny thing was that I said to the person in the Judicial Office you know, what do I have to do? [laughter]. He said oh well, he said ah, just give me half an hour and I'll see what I can find out … (Kenneth).

Kenneth describes here an unfamiliar procedure that neither he, nor the court, were clear about because the procedural directions of the court had not seemingly caught up the newly established practice. He goes on to say it was all done 'very informally' and commented that in a 'matter of half an hour we were in' because the person at the end of the phone spoke to one of the Law Lords directly. Kenneth reflected that even then the application had to be decided by three judges saying 'I never knew whether that happened or not'. These procedures have now been formalised by Part Two of the Supreme Court Rules 2009.

I attended several events related to strategic litigation during my fieldwork and observed in particular the connections between collective values and assumptions underpinning progressive legal practice; and a preference towards undertaking strategic challenges in different forums. One event held at Doughty Street Chambers was particularly explicit about strategic casework

[52] McCann and Silverstein (n 49).
[53] Southworth (n 18) 478.
[54] Scott Baker and Gary Biglaiser, 'A Model of Cause Lawyering' (2014) 43(1) *Journal of Legal Studies* 37, 38.
[55] ibid 60.

as a tool for social change.[56] Helena Kennedy QC made the following introductory remarks:

> I would imagine there isn't anyone in the room who didn't go into law to improve the lives of people and help them access their rights through the law ... you came into law because you wanted to make a difference in the lives of people, to challenge abuses of power. To help people who couldn't make use of the law themselves (Helena Kennedy).

Kennedy's appeal to the lawyers in the room extends the analysis in the preceding chapter by explicitly reinforcing the 'us and them' narrative. There is an assumption that these are lawyers who try to 'improve the lives of people' and help them 'access their rights' through legal challenge to state power. The lawyers at the event comprised representatives of law centres, legal aid law firms, NGOs, charities and progressive sets of Chambers. Throughout the introduction, and in the contributions of panel members that followed, there were repeated references to how 'we' can 'use' the law to 'challenge power'.[57] Amidst a landscape of threats to fundamental rights and freedoms during Brexit uncertainty, hostility to 'rights talk' and socio-economic upheaval in the aftermath of the austerity agenda, the construction of litigation as a means of empowerment is particularly prevalent.[58]

I make two observations from this event: first, the lawyer is presented as an agent of social change by other lawyers but is also differentiated within progressive networks such to present her or himself in that way. This occurs at diverse sites of legal education and practice and also through intra-network events I have described.[59] Secondly, the context of austerity and other social welfare reforms has raised legal consciousness[60] and further incentivised progressive lawyering networks to pursue change. For some participants strategic litigation is an obvious means of achieving that change ('to challenge abuses of power') and its recent importance as a tool for progressive lawyers is evidenced, first, by the high number of strategic litigation events and workshops during the fieldwork period of the study between 2016 and 2018 that I have drawn upon in this section; secondly, related literature on the use of litigation across different areas of law by civil society organisations in the UK;[61] and, finally, the use of

[56] Doughty Street Chambers, 'Using the Law as A Tool for Social Change' (17 May 2018).

[57] See, eg, Shayne Misselbrook, 'Political Litigation and the Politics of Litigation' (2016) 22 *Auckland University Law Review* 341.

[58] Lisa Vanhala and Jacqueline Kinghan, *Using the Law for Social Change: A Landscape Review* (The Baring Foundation, 2018).

[59] Other examples include conferences, panel events and training held by organisations such as the Young Legal Aid Lawyers Association, Haldane Society of Socialist Lawyers and the Law Centres Network.

[60] See, eg, Simon Halliday, 'After Hegemony? The Varieties of Legal Consciousness Research' (2019) 28(6) *Social and Legal Studies* 859.

[61] Lisa Vanhala, *Framework for Better Use of Law by Voluntary Sector Organisations* (The Baring Foundation, 2016); Lisa Vanhala, *Successful Use of Strategic Litigation on Issues Related*

judicial review to challenge perceived unlawfulness relevant to access to justice issues.[62] Scholars have further hypothesised that the recent increased interest in the use of the term 'strategic litigation' by civil society organisations reflects a move away from the 'unwanted political baggage' of other terms (such as public interest litigation) as well as, in view of the connection between the local and the global, a 'contemporary trend towards transnational legal activist movements'.[63]

My observation is also that strategic litigation and related campaigns are not so much confined to barrister-campaigners, NGOs or the more radical law centres. Roger Smith commented in 2003 that:

> The legal NGOs that have been active in the legal [strategic litigation] field have seen themselves as somewhat separate from law centres and as more attached to the lobby and campaigning groups of which they are part than the law centre movement from which many of their lawyers individually have come.[64]

In fact, during the fieldwork period of the study there were several successful challenges to the legal aid regime pursued by law centres. In one case the Law Centres Network successfully challenged Ministry of Justice proposals to restrict the provision of the housing possession court duty scheme providing legal advice in court to those who are at risk of eviction.[65] The mood was encapsulated by Julie Bishop, Director of the Law Centres Network, who said: '[w]e are dedicated to giving legal assistance to people in need, and are sick and tired of watching vital services be degraded'.[66] Another successful judicial review challenging the lack of availability of legal aid for unaccompanied asylum seeking children resulted in an almost immediate reinstatement after a five-year legal battle.[67] This case demonstrated successful collaborative working between The Children's Society, The Public Law Project, Islington Law Centre and several other charities, which all provided evidence on the impact of the loss of legal

to Discrimination and Disadvantage (The Baring Foundation, 2016); Harriet Samuels, 'Public Interest Litigation and the Civil Society Factor' (2018) *Legal Studies* 1; Erika Dailey, 'Implementation of Judgments: Practical Insights from Civil Society' (2020) 12(1) *Journal of Human Rights Practice* 224.

[62] Alison Pickup, *Top Legal Aid and Access to Justice Cases of Recent Years* (The Public Law Project, 2018), available at https://publiclawproject.org.uk/wp-content/uploads/2018/08/Top-legal-aid-and-access-to-justice-cases-of-recent-years.pdf.

[63] Ramsden and Gledhill (n 44) 426.

[64] Roger Smith, *Experience in England and Wales: Test Case Strategies, Public Interest Litigation, The Human Rights Act and Legal NGOs* (Essex Human Rights Centre, 2013) 1.

[65] *Law Centres Federation Limited v The Lord Chancellor* [2018] EWHC 1588 (Admin).

[66] *Law Centres Network Challenges Government on Legal Aid to Prevent Homelessness* (Law Centres Network, 18 May 2018), available at www.lawcentres.org.uk/policy/news/news/press-release-lcn-challenges-government-on-legal-aid-to-prevent-homelessness.

[67] An amendment to LASPO 2012 was proposed by way of written statement from the Parliamentary Under Secretary of State for Justice) to both the House of Commons and the House of Lords. See www.parliament.uk/business/publications/written-questions-answers-statements/written-statement/Commons/2018-07-12/HCWS853/.

aid on separated and unaccompanied migrant children with whom they worked. The fluid interactions and collaborations between law centres, NGOs and legal aid law firms serve to provide a clear example of how progressive lawyers are networked to identify issues and areas of change. Ben provides an example of the distinctions between lawyer and client led strategic casework, a point that Stefan also touched upon:

> Jacqueline: So in that strategic litigation, what way around does it come for you, do you see the issue first and then the clients or do the clients come to you with the issues?
>
> Ben: I think it's a mixture of both. Um, I think there have been times when new legislation has passed and I've looked at it with my colleagues and thought this is likely to be a real problem … and you then try and speak to clients who might be affected by it and see if they are affected. And then there are other times that people just come to you with a really mundane, or what seems like a really mundane problem, and then when we've investigated it has a much wider impact. So then it's completely just casework driven.

I asked Ben whether in the former example he still worked together with lawyers in the charity where he used to work on identifying issues (despite now being in a legal aid law firm). He responded:

> Yeah and we do try and see things together … I don't think we view our work as competitive. It's completely collaborative. I still supervise the lawyers at [redacted charity]. I have done since I left (Ben).

There are 'collaborative' approaches across networks nodes therefore, often based on experience in previous places of employment that connect lawyers in the tools they use. In this lawyer led approach, Martha Spurrier, while speaking at a 2018 panel event gave another example of how strategic litigation might work in practice. She reflected back on successful challenges made to legal aid cuts and highlights the necessity of early attention to the LASPO Bill itself as it passed through Parliament in order to be in a strong position to challenge provisions:

> When the Act was moving through Parliament the lawyers [at The Public Law Project] were working through it line by line. They were learning how to quickly construct really powerful cases to dismantle the system. This work would not have been done without the homework being done when it was a draft Bill moving through Parliament.[68]

Aidan, a barrister campaigner who began his legal practice in the late 1970s, describes litigation around a particular area of human rights advocacy in an

[68] Martha Spurrier, 'Using the Law as A Tool for Social Change', public event held at Doughty Street Chambers, 17 May 2018.

approach that could also be characterised as lawyer led. When I asked him what was strategic about the work he described the process of collaboration:

> Yes, I mean we would have meetings with all the lawyers … doing this kind of work where we would actually brainstorm about how one could attack the system. About what we would do, how we would attack the fact that decisions were not reviewable. I mean it was a discussion of ideas um but there was an um, you obviously couldn't rule out that the wrong case might get there first. But we had a broad strategy and we followed it (Aidan).

While some even progressive legal organisations may not want to conduct litigation due to risk ('… I think they had reached the view that while they had been comfortable giving advice they didn't want a full blown litigation attached to themselves' (Ben)) there have been some recent attempts to facilitate greater interaction within progressive legal networks to support non-legal charities with litigation strategies. In the UK, there has been an increase in models of collaboration where expert legal organisations work with frontline organisations to develop understanding of public law and their ability to challenge unfair systems.[69] Cummings has studied similar models in the US context and describes an 'integrated', or collaborative, approach that is designed 'to support strategic collaboration with non-lawyer activists and encourage analysis about the potential consequences – intended and unintended – of legal interventions'.[70] Many of the legal aid and social welfare challenges referenced in chapter two involved a range of charity sector interveners including, for example, the housing charity Shelter, Child Poverty Action Group and Inclusion London (a charity that works to promote equality for deaf and disabled people).[71] Aidan talked about the value of 'getting lawyers together around a good cause' that he experienced in the 1970s and 1980s and the importance of an iterative process of 'cooperation and discussion'. Similar to Aidan's construction of these causes in the past, some of the collaborations remain lawyer led. They form an alternative vision of lawyering, to an extent, because solidarity across progressive lawyering networks has been strengthened of late by the common crisis in access to justice and the lawyer's potential role in collaboratively working to resolve it.

The relationship here to resource issues cannot be underestimated, as highlighted by many participants in the study. For example, having related the impact of cuts to legal aid on the law centre where she works, Emily explained how she hoped her law centre would now get a legal aid public law contract

[69] Jacqueline Kinghan and Lisa Vanhala, *Supporting Systems Changers Through the Use of Collaborative Legal Approaches* (The Public Law Project, 2020).

[70] Scott Cummings, 'Movement Lawyering' (2017) *University of Illinois Law Review* 1653.

[71] Alison Pickup, *Top Legal Aid and Access to Justice Cases of Recent Years* (The Public Law Project, 2018), available at https://publiclawproject.org.uk/wp-content/uploads/2018/08/Top-legal-aid-and-access-to-justice-cases-of-recent-years.pdf.

specifically in order to enable them to do strategic casework:[72] 'we're looking at public law with a view to going back and doing [strategic casework] again … the only thing that achieves policy change is strategic litigation'. In fact, several participants revealed the practical reality of the constrained funding climate as a clear incentive for strategic litigation. As Emily stresses however, the legal aid contract would be 'an add-on rather than [our] main source of income'. The other sources of income to which Emily refers are trusts, foundations and other grant-making bodies who are 'interested' in strategic work. This same sentiment about diversity of resource is echoed by another lawyer in the study who does legal aid work within a charitable organisation:

> We don't rely solely on legal aid income. We're not even able to rely on most of the legal aid income [sic] the quality of work that you can do on legal aid alone is too low. It's inexcusably low. I think it's unethical really … in terms of how effective we can be its important that we do strategic work (Kimberley).

Another newly qualified participant, Tim, who has experience in strategic litigation expressed a strong desire to continue working in that area when I asked him about next steps: 'The short answer is I want to stay … I just want to stay in strategic litigation now.' When I asked him why, he talked about wanting to overturn unjust policies and the necessity of litigation challenges in his particular field: 'some of the [strategic] work we're doing at the moment, you just want to shout at people how is this still an issue? How have we not reached the point as a society where we say this isn't acceptable?'

Here Tim is connecting the value of strategic litigation to a related access to justice problem in the criminal justice sphere. Ben, who has worked in criminal justice for nearly three decades, expressed similar preference for litigation as a means of effecting change over simply doing policy work and explained his move back to that area of work:

> I did really like the policy side but I didn't like it at the expense of litigation. And particularly litigation that wider implications, that was the frustrating thing, it was litigation that would affect large numbers of people (Ben).

This study is not directly concerned with measuring the success or failure of the tools that lawyers use, rather, it hopes to better understand lawyers' perceptions of that success or failure in terms of achieving change; and in turn how that influences their decision-making around which tools to adopt. I note with interest here that while Stefan and Ben describe a preference for different tools (volume casework and litigation), they are both motivated by the same thing

[72] In the absence of other funding (such as crowdfunding) legal aid contracts for judicial review are often necessary to ensure costs protection is in place in the event of losing a case. For discussion see, *Public Law in Clinical Legal Environments* (The Public Law Project, 2018), available at https://publiclawproject.org.uk/resources/public-law-and-clinical-legal-environments/.

and each describe a desire to pursue cases that will 'affect large numbers of people'. Another participant, Ankita, described moving from litigation to also doing policy work because 'on a personal level, [litigation] wasn't enough for me … I needed to be in an issue, seeing that issue through, over a longer period'. She intimated that policy work, alongside litigation, would make that litigation more impactful and long lasting. Despite their different approaches, the same motivating desire for widespread change is collectively held. In the many events and practitioner led conferences on this issue, it seems that lawyers view strategic litigation as a means of challenging the policy that has resulted in restrictions on access to justice and of achieving the change required to realise rights entitlements. A strategic approach is also seen as necessary for opening up closed institutions and this has been the case for some time:

> [I]t's funny because when I first started there were a couple of issues that we thought were the key to unlocking the whole system because the system was closed in every way. In the years I was at [redacted charity] effectively all these secret systems were challenged through the courts. They became proper fair procedures. At the time I thought once we'd done that there would be nothing left to do. I did find it amazing that sort of fifteen, twenty years on from that there are still issues (Ben).

For different practitioners of course litigation is less dominant in their narratives. For some, like Tim, it features strongly and for others they value it as a tool but also perceive it to rest alongside other tools available:

> I think strategic litigation is just one part of the toolbox. Most situations require political change. If strategic litigation pushes towards that you don't even need to win. You just need to push towards change (Eve).

In any event the restrictions on access to justice pervade narratives around the 'tools' that lawyers use and has collectively politicised lawyers towards challenging the status quo such that there has been raised rights consciousness in recent times. While in previous decades described in the study there were isolated pockets of campaigning (for example, miscarriages of justice, gender discrimination or children's rights) senior practitioners reflect that the context of advice provision, and the future of the profession, never felt under threat to the same extent as in the current landscape. This common experience across different areas of human rights has galvanised lawyers across at both ends of the cause lawyering spectrum and the network ties between them are strong: lawyers working on individual client casework are increasingly engaged in policy matters due to the social welfare issues faced by clients in light of a political austerity climate. Likewise, lawyers who might have traditionally worked on strategic litigation are more engaged in challenging the cuts to legal aid and other austerity reforms, therefore working to help facilitate individual advice and representation at grassroots level. Each of these tools relates to the final tool of campaigning and related policy work described by participants in the study.

POLICY WORK AND CAMPAIGNING

> I don't really see a distinction between law and campaigning. (Gail)

I have illustrated how the current context of restrictions on access to justice has facilitated a strategic mind-set among participants across several subsets of practice. In this section I discuss the interplay between that strategic casework and campaigning as explored by participants in the study. The 'Act for the Act' campaign outlined in chapter two provides an example of strategic casework being used more broadly in the public realm to gain support for a related human rights issue (in this case, opposing the proposed abolition of the Human Rights Act 1998). Other key examples during the fieldwork phase of this study include the 'Let Us Learn' campaign which ran alongside the *Tigere* UK Supreme Court case about access to student loan funding for migrant young people,[73] casework in the Scottish context on sibling contact for children in care in collaboration with the 'Stand up for Siblings' campaign,[74] disability rights campaigns on reform to Personal Independence Payments[75] and pro-choice campaigning alongside the Northern Irish Supreme Court case on facilitating access to abortion.[76] As these examples illustrate, campaigning for progressive lawyers often relates to litigation or potential litigation and is rarely in isolation from the law or upholding human rights. As Lena neatly describes:

> It's about identifying an issue and a client and building a campaign and taking it forward (Lena).

There was considerable interplay between litigation and campaigning for lawyers in the study. Of 35 participants, 20 had been involved in strategic litigation at one or more points in their legal careers.[77] Of these 20, nine had ongoing involvement in a strategic case at the time of interview. The first recorded time for the pursuit of strategic casework for any lawyer in the study was by way of one of the earliest interventions in the UK in the late 1990s, with the majority of cases being in the last seven years.[78]

Cause lawyers have historically combined legal and political mobilisation and their tendency to use these strategies rests on how they are perceived by

[73] Vanhala et al (n 47).

[74] Later leading to the UK Supreme Court decision of *ABC (AP) v Principal Reporter and Another* [2020] UKSC 26.

[75] *RF v Secretary of State for Work and Pensions* [2017] EWHC 3375 (Admin).

[76] *In the Matter of an application by the Northern Ireland Human Rights Commission for Judicial Review (Northern Ireland)* [2018] UKSC 27.

[77] By 'involvement' I mean either being instructed to act on behalf of a claimant in a case, conducting legal work on a third-party intervention either on behalf of an organisation where the lawyer works in an 'in-house' capacity or (for self-employed barristers) by being instructed by an organisation on a case or, thirdly, through involvement in a campaign related to a strategic case.

[78] The first recorded intervention was in the case of *R v Khan* [1996] 1 WLR 962, a surveillance case in which Liberty intervened. See further, Justice, *To Assist the Court: Third Party Interventions in the Public Interest* (Justice/Freshfields, 2016) 4.

activists, campaigners and more widely in the public realm. This broader public perception is shaped by social, political and economic factors but also by other 'cultural products'.[79] In this respect, media analysis shows that the participants in the study engaged in on-going strategic casework also tended to be more active in tweeting, blogging, wider press engagement (writing for or being interviewed by broadsheets or political magazines), lecturing and debating around issues relevant to strategic cases. Of the 20 participants involved in strategic casework, eight could be described as being active in the public realm.[80] While not all lawyers in the study are involved in campaigning, those eight participants described above who are more active in the public realm, obviously portrayed a more acute awareness of its importance. Gail, for example, takes the view that in the practice of human rights law there is 'always' a campaign:

> Jacqueline: How do you view the policy and campaign issues?
>
> Gail: It's kind of seamless, I don't really see a distinction between law and campaigning as a human rights lawyer because you're always trying to use the human rights framework to ultimately achieve a better society for a wider group of people. So there's always a campaign. Even if it's an individual case at the heart of it, you're always trying to improve the law.

Gail's approach here can be contrasted with another participant, Eve, and they perhaps demonstrate two separate but related types of cause lawyering. Gail takes a law centric approach in her description of campaigning and outlines how 'you're always trying to improve the law' through a campaign. For Eve, campaigning rests within a personal history of activism and is related to grassroots work. Her story as a whole reveals connection to causes *outside* of purely legal frames such that she contests the professional label: 'there's way too much privilege in the term lawyer'. Of the 35 participants only Eve and Lena overtly stressed that law is 'just one part of the toolbox' for social change. Again, like Lena, Eve is disapproving of the profession itself and her observations relate to the critique that lawyers disempower grassroots organisations through their use of litigation.[81] Eve seems particularly cognisant of the need to be aware of the limits of law:

> My ears prick up when someone says we're here for the rule of law and I'm like no we're not! I've always been quite sceptical of anything that shows too much respect for law (Eve).

[79] Austin Sarat and Stuart Scheingold, 'Bringing Cultural Analysis to the Study of Cause Lawyers: An Introduction' in Austin Sarat and Stuart Scheingold (eds), *The Cultural Lives of Cause Lawyers* (Cambridge University Press, 2008) 3.

[80] By the term 'active' I refer to repeat, rather than ad hoc, engagement using two or more of the methods described above. Of these eight participants who were active in the public realm all had on-going strategic cases.

[81] Rosenberg (n 50).

When describing litigation as a means of achieving political change she stresses that it would be preferable 'to get the politicians to change [the law] before they get a big embarrassing law suit'. She continues:

> I'm not madly keen on the idea that change is brought about by causing economic damage to public services … you just want to get [the case] far enough to make the political change. But of course if you admitted that as a lawyer you'd completely undermine litigation. People would be like, hang on, that lawyer doesn't think they're here to win (Eve).

Eve describes here the longstanding issue of strategic litigation diverting scarce resources in a constrained funding environment, as well as touching upon the related issue of the problem of the expense and time-consuming nature of litigation. Eve articulates discomfort at having to present herself as being in litigation 'to win'. She understands that a win in court is not always a political win and, conversely, to lose in court might nonetheless be a win. For example, even a dismissed appeal might raise awareness of an issue such as to nonetheless inform policy change, create a dissenting judgment that develops into a new line of decision making in subsequent cases or mobilise a campaign.[82] The unintended consequences of litigation therefore have the potential to raise consciousness around important human rights issues. This understanding of the role of litigation in a broader social space is aligned with Eve's perspective that the law is only one part of the toolbox and that related campaigns can be just as powerful, if not more powerful, a tool for achieving change.

Lena also refers to the importance of building up and taking a campaign forward to 'generalise' an issue. While doing so, she importantly touches upon a professional controversy explored in the literature in chapter one. The controversy lies where the claimant at the heart of the case may not wish to be involved in a campaign, or where it might not be in their best interests to receive media exposure due to, for example, their youth or mental and/or physical vulnerabilities. Several participants were acutely aware of this tension such that they related instances where they had pulled back from using litigation as a tool because clients did not feel able or willing to participate. As Lena describes, there might be 'a friction between the client wanting the case to go forward but not wanting publicity'. Lena comments that you have a 'professional duty' to respect what the client wants and that it's important when you want to 'broaden things out' to make sure you 'keep the client on board'. Having a separate campaign that is only broadly linked to the legal case but doesn't, for example, identify or draw attention to the client at the heart of the case can assist in overcoming these tensions and facilitate greater use of campaigning.

Eve and Lena were the most campaign orientated of the study and also both aligned to the 'grassroots' cause lawyering type. Eve referenced several times

[82] Shauneen Lambe and Caoilfhionn Gallagher, *How To Be Strategic About Strategic Litigation* (The Public Law Project, 2013).

the need to 'push towards change' and, like Len, stressed the reluctance of the legal profession on the whole towards doing so. In the context of being based in Scotland, she commented:

> There's just not a great amount of activism or lawyers willing to challenge the status quo or even able to (Eve).

They express the view that lawyers in the UK have inhibitions about campaigning, which are of course often linked to ethical constraints as explored in chapter six. Lena and Eve both intimated that most lawyers even within progressive lawyering networks in the UK were conservative in their approach. The former Advocacy Director for Liberty, a US trained lawyer, made the similar observations at the Doughty Street event I described above:

> In the US we take for granted a whole community of lawyers who advance a social movement through a case … There is willingness to take more risk in the legal culture as a whole in the US. The legal profession in the UK is prone to thinking about the way things have always been done. They are seen as givens when often they are part of what has to change (Corey Stoughton, former Advocacy Director, Liberty (UK).

While the campaigns outlined above demonstrate a tendency for strategic litigation to be accompanied by campaigning, there are divergent perspectives amongst participants about the particular role that campaigning might play. For many lawyers, they see campaigns as being too overtly political and feel constrained by their professional status as lawyers such that they refrain from using it as a tool for change. For others, they criticise such constraint as being overly conservative and resting in a legal culture that is reluctant to 'take risk'. As Eve alludes to, many progressive lawyers simply don't feel 'able to' engage in activism. The constrained funding climate has put legal jobs at risk and also puts lawyers under considerable pressure day to day. Not all lawyers therefore, as reflected by the narratives in the study, feel in a position to be able to engage in public facing campaigns. Others, for example, might prefer to engage in professional lobbying (for example with the Bar Council or Law Society) or to work to change government policy (for example, by feeding into the Ministry of Justice review on legal aid or other legislative consultations) or legislation (working to table amendments to proposed legislation). Across these different types of campaigning and policy work however, collaboration and communication through professional networks to alleviate the access to justice crisis or advocate on particular causes has been a preoccupying feature of lawyer's stories in recent times.[83] The underlying motivations of ensuring access to advice and representation and upholding human rights, and challenging the government in one form or another to achieve it, are collectively shared: 'It's about using the law as a tool to achieve social justice. And social justice isn't just using the law. Sometimes

[83] See, eg, Maria Lee and Carolyn Abbot, *Environmental Groups and Legal Expertise: Shaping the Brexit Process* (UCL Press, 2021).

cases are about the statement … sometimes it's worth fighting for just to send a message' (Dominic).

CONCLUSIONS

Abel wrote that we should be interested in progressive lawyers at the fringe of the profession 'for much the same reason that the "fringe" often is the most interesting part of arts festivals … these lawyers have sought, and attained, the "power to change" to an unusual degree'.[84] Rather than perceiving themselves to be at the fringe, participants in the study view their own approach to be centrally important to upholding justice, fairness and adherence to human rights. Despite using different tools of legal advice and representation, strategic litigation, policy work and campaigning; they collectively perceive them to be separate but related. One barrister-campaigner, interviewed as part of wider ethnographic fieldwork, described the value of lawyer's self-perception and motivation in this way:

> Some lawyers want to change the law on a grand scale and others want to provide direct and intense support but there's no right answer on which to choose … they're both equally good … when as a lawyer you're faced with the question of using different tools the answer often depends on who you are (Molly).

In their legal careers some participants move towards strategic approaches while others towards 'direct' and 'intense' casework, and as Stefan and Ben described: 'you need both'. The narratives from the 1970s, 1980s and 1990s reveal that collective identity facilitates collaboration across progressive networks: such collaboration is not new and was common in the 1970s and 1980s in distinct areas of practice. However, they expose the value judgements placed on particular seemingly opposite strategies that perhaps fail to capture the nuance of how they interact. Leask commented in his analysis of law centres in the mid-1980s, that the 'proactive' and 'reactive' dichotomy was entirely misleading: 'what from one point of view seems to be a passive, defensive approach – waiting for individual tenants or defendants to come in – from another point of view is an aggressive, consistent counterattack on landlords and the police'.[85] Nonetheless shared collective identity and solidarity around austerity reforms has facilitated a growing awareness of proactive approaches, as well as lobbying and campaigning. The interactions between lawyers in this heightened climate have perhaps narrowed the frame of the debate between volume casework and strategic litigation and highlighted the complementary nature of both in recent times. I will turn later in the book to the urgent question of whether the conditions, and resource, will be available to continue to use these tools in future.

[84] Abel (n 20) 6.
[85] Leask (n 3) 64.

6

Educating Progressive Lawyers

> In all Western societies law schools are typically caught in a tug of war between three aspirations: to be accepted as full members of the community of higher learning; to be relatively detached, but nonetheless engaged, critics and censors of law in society; and to be service-institutions for a profession which is itself caught between noble ideals, lucrative service of powerful interests and unromantic cleaning up of society's messes.[1]

IN THIS CHAPTER I consider the relationship between progressive legal practice and legal education. I build upon my analysis of the networked interactions and early constructions of collective identity for progressive lawyers as they are shared in relation to experiences at law school. The aim is to draw out how lawyers present *themselves* in relation to their educational experience while also being mindful of ambiguity and silence in their stories. The chapter analyses narratives in light of one of the professional controversies outlined in chapter two, focussing on the tension of progressive lawyers being both within and outside the legal profession as a whole[2] as illustrated by the sense of social alienation they describe.[3] I am concerned with how legal education might serve to create progressive lawyering identity. The 'tug of war' Twining outlines is relevant: progressive students want to be the critics of law in society, serving the law's 'noble ideals' and even 'cleaning up society's messes' rather than providing service to powerful corporate interests.[4] As outlined in chapter four, their turning away from corporate legal practice is expressed in clear and strong terms that often serves to collectively reinforce socio-political values. Yet, progressive law students tend to learn the law in social spaces that train lawyers in *both* the noble ideals and lucrative service to corporate power. Legal education has long had a role to play 'in the production and reproduction of social hierarchies and the conceptions and categorisations of professionals'.[5]

[1] William Twining, *Blackstone's Tower: The English Law School* (Sweet and Maxwell, 1994) 2. Reproduced by permission of Thomson Reuters and The Hamlyn Foundation.

[2] Richard Abel, 'Lawyers and the Power to Change' (1985) 7 *Law and Policy* 5.

[3] Melvin Seeman, 'On the Meaning of Alienation' (1959) 24(6) *American Sociological Review* 783; Melvin Seeman, 'Alienation Studies' (1975) 1 *Annual Review of Sociology* 91.

[4] Twining (n 1).

[5] Hilary Sommerlad and Ole Hammerslev, 'Lawyers in a New Geopolitical Conjuncture: Continuity and Change' in *Lawyers in 21st-Century Societies: Volume 1 National Reports* (Hart, 2020) 28.

In order to explore these tensions, I begin by drawing on my own experience perceiving the social alienation of students while setting up a clinical legal education programme in a UK law school. I then explore the different ways in which participants in the study similarly experience social alienation in their legal education, as well as the ways in which they overcome it. In this chapter I focus in depth on a small sample of stories drawn from my fieldwork interviews and wider ethnography. They include a legal aid lawyer who studied in the early 1990s and described considerable alienation during his time at law school in the UK, a barrister-campaigner who experienced a transformative educational experience in the US in the mid-2000s and a law centre solicitor who had a similar transformative experience in the UK in the early 1980s. Through these stories I will outline related experiences from other participants in the study and describe how collective values, or a quest to find them, framed their future roles as lawyers in society.

AN AUTOETHNOGRAPHIC PERSPECTIVE ON LEGAL EDUCATION

> It made me think about how I could make a difference and why it is important that I should (Isabelle).

In the autumn of 2010 I took up a post as a teaching fellow and pro bono coordinator at UCL Faculty of Laws. Still typical of traditional law schools in the UK at the time, there were few pro bono or work based learning opportunities for students. Having been heavily influenced by my own experience of clinical legal education in the US and Canada, I was drawn to the role as an opportunity to develop a transformative approach to legal education in the Faculty. I was tasked with setting up the first accredited undergraduate clinical law course at UCL in partnership with local charities and NGOs and to establish a Centre for Access to Justice to accommodate pro bono activities and in time a freestanding legal advice clinic.

The theoretical underpinnings of the clinical programme lay in the Faculty strengths in empirical legal studies[6] and a desire to expose students experientially to *law in context*. I designed and launched an accredited undergraduate Access to Justice and Community Engagement course (AJCE) in 2011. Students undertook immersive casework with NGOs and charities working in areas including social welfare, human rights and child law and were given reflective learning opportunities alongside their experience.[7] By drawing on empirical work on access to justice, legal ethics and professional legal identity they were

[6] Hazel Genn, *Paths to Justice* (Oxford University Press, 1998); Pleasence et al, *Causes of Action: Civil Law and Social Justice* (Legal Services Commission, 2006).

[7] This was facilitated through reflective tutorials and also by diversifying assessment methods to include journal entry writing and oral presentations. See, eg, Jeff Giddings, *Promoting Justice Thorough Clinical Legal Education* (Justice Press, 2013).

encouraged to reflect on their own role in clients' cases but also on the social role of the lawyer: do lawyers have a duty to facilitate access to justice in society? Does the government have a duty to provide legal aid, if so to whom? How can the law be used as a tool for social change? Who are the lawyers doing public interest legal work and what motivates them?

As I have outlined in the preface to this book, I became aware that I was teaching in a sociological vacuum. While there was much ethnographic work on public interest lawyers in the US to draw upon, UK examples were comparatively few. As I grappled with a sense of academic isolation in this field, what struck me most was a similar sense of isolation for some of my students. A small number would relate feeling isolated and powerless, and such feelings could be exacerbated by 'micro-level experiences' in daily interactions.[8] I sensed palpable *relief* from several students on the course that an alternative path was now available in their final year of study. While still very much in the minority, it presented an opportunity to talk about a treadmill towards corporate practice,[9] a sense of frustration at a lack of interest in human rights or legal aid practice and comparatively little careers advice, at the time, for working in the third or public sector. Especially amidst cuts to legal aid, students perceived a malaise towards careers in the public interest such that they feared losing sight of how they might simply use the law to help vulnerable people resolve everyday problems. This formed a stark contrast to the wealth of interest and support for careers in corporate law. As one of my students put it, until the course they had become lost and disconnected from why they had wanted to study law in the first place:

> Many of us come here having written personal statements about how we want to study law because we are interested in human rights and using law to make a difference, yet somewhere between the property II course and the visits to the big shiny corporate law offices, we sometimes forget that law is still a hugely important part of individual justice, and I'll admit that part of me was starting to forget it too. It wasn't until I took AJCE that I really realised the significance of how the law, or the lack thereof has an impact on individuals and their daily lives (Shiva).

Another student, Charlotte, noted that the critical engagement on the course allowed her to see that she had to be 'part of the dialogue of change, not just an apathetic observer'. I began to see the transformative power of a *situated* approach to legal learning and how students' own sense of professional self might be shaped by contextual exposure to lawyers pursuing work legal work they found valuable:

> When I did the Access to Justice course, that's when I found out what legal aid was exactly and from then on I only ever wanted to work in a legal aid firm. It was an

[8] Bradford Barnhardt and Paul Ginns, 'An Alienation-Based Framework for Student Experience in Higher Education: New Interpretations of Past Observations in Student Learning Theory' (2014) 68 *Higher Education* 789.

[9] Jean Francois Lyotard, *The Postmodern Condition: A Report on Knowledge* (Manchester University Press, 1984) 51.

> amazing opportunity and [redacted] was really inspirational … I thought woah, I want to be like her … she just seemed really passionate. She'd dedicated her life to trying to help people … the placement was perfect for me. It got me excited (Ellie).
>
> Not only did I gain a deeper understanding of social justice, it made me think about how I could make a difference and why it was important that I should (Isabelle).

While clinical legal education and work-based learning opportunities were novel to UCL in 2011, they had been well established in vocational law schools and in many newer universities[10] for some time. Developments in the US were key: the establishment of clinics there led to an interest in setting up similar programmes in the UK in the early 1970s.[11] The simultaneous emergence of the socio-legal studies movement in the UK and the newly established Centre for Socio-Legal Studies in 1972 supported a law in context approach to legal education.[12] Law as a discipline of study also experienced a boom around this time. Clinics were first established in Universities such as Warwick and Kent, tending to offer advice to fellow students and operating mostly on an extracurricular basis. Over the next two decades further programmes developed, most notably perhaps in Northumbria and Strathclyde and in the vocational law schools teaching solicitors Legal Practice and Bar Vocational Courses. However, for the most part, the programmes developed in an ad hoc fashion with little coherence and tended, in some law schools, to launch but lack the commitment or funding needed for long-term sustainability.[13] When I started my post at UCL in 2010, highly ranked law schools such as Oxford, Cambridge, Kings, LSE and UCL still had no integrated or curricular clinical opportunities to speak of. Since then, UCL's clinical programme has become an embedded part of the Faculty and is now home to a freestanding legal advice clinic in East London and associated access to justice research activities. Kings Law School launched their legal advice clinic in 2017 and, while Oxford and Cambridge have yet to follow suit in embedding clinic in a curricular capacity, the establishment of the Bonavero Human Rights Institute at the University of Oxford represents a step forward in integrating research *and* practice into their law degree programmes.[14]

[10] The term 'new' University in the UK historically refers to Universities established in the 1960s in response to the Robbins report on higher education or, more typically, to former colleges of higher education or polytechnics that were given University status under the Further and Higher Education Act 1992, or have been given such status since then.

[11] Kevin Kerrigan and Victoria Murray, *A Student Guide to Clinical Legal Education and Pro Bono* (Palgrave, 2010) 10. See also, Richard Wilson, *The Global Evolution of Clinical Legal Education* (Cambridge University Press, 2017).

[12] William Twining, 'Remembering 1972: The Oxford Centre in the Context of Developments in Higher Education and the Discipline of Law' (1995) 22(1) *Journal of Law and Society* 35.

[13] Kerrigan and Murray (n 11).

[14] I note however that research shows that students in such *pre* 1992 law schools are significantly more likely to have access to *informal* work experience through family and other ties, which, has been shown to exacerbate social exclusion: Andrew Francis, 'Legal Education, Social Mobility, and Employability: Possible Selves, Curriculum Intervention and the Role of Legal Work Experience' (2015) (42) *Journal of Law and Society* 173, 186.

What led to this educational shift? At UCL, the newly appointed Dean at the time Professor Dame Hazel Genn QC had spent many years working in access to justice and wanted to establish a comprehensive and ambitious programme of clinical legal education in the Faculty.[15] Secondly, and more generally, the climate of cuts to legal aid drew stark attention to access to justice needs in the communities local to universities. Thirdly, a renewed focus on responding to student feedback and enhancing student experience as a result of the increase in student fees highlighted the need for more diverse law degree programmes.[16] As Wilson contends, many legal academics previously had no interest in what lawyers actually *do*[17] but arguably a greater connection between theory and practice was driven in part by *student* engagement in that concern. This is reminiscent of the 1970s where developments in socio-legal studies and clinical legal education were a reflection in part of the 'relevance' demands made by students.[18]

For participants across the different time periods of this study, they relate a similar sense of alienation and a feeling of being set apart from their peers. For many, this was formative in driving them towards finding alternative opportunities in their fields of interest *outside* law school. What is most striking however are the *silences* in narratives of formal educational experiences in the UK. For most participants in this study, legal education appears to have done little more than incentivised a move away from corporate law. However, the exceptions to the silences resonate by way of contrast. For those few participants who have had some form of experiential learning in the UK or, importantly, an opportunity to study in the US their connections and turning points are narrated with animation, key individuals who inspired them are fondly described and formative moments of interaction for collective progressive identity are revealed. I draw out these contrasting narratives in this chapter.[19]

SOCIAL ALIENATION AT LAW SCHOOL

> I was absolutely shocked by what I found there. (Phil)

Participants' stories about law school either featured quite strongly when we spoke, or not at all. I noted early in my fieldwork that those with undergraduate

[15] Jacqueline Kinghan and Rachel Knowles, 'Striking a Balance in Clinical Legal Education: Reimagining the Role of the teaching Practitioner in Casework Partnerships' in Linden Thomas et al (eds), *Reimagining Clinical Legal Education* (Hart, 2018).

[16] John Morgan, 'Are practical law degrees the future?' (*The Times*, 24 May 2012).

[17] Richard Wilson, 'The Role of Practice in Legal Education' (2010) 15, available at SSRN http://ssrn.com/abstract=1695618.

[18] Stephen Murgatroyd and William Rees, 'The Radical Estate? A Response to Bankowski and Mungham's Critique of Curriculum Developments in Legal Education' (1977) *The Law Teacher* 151.

[19] The research sampling for this study limits deeper exploration of educational stratification in the UK. Participants have qualified as lawyers and the vast majority are engaged in fulfilling careers. They therefore tend not to describe a sense of limitation in terms of educational *disadvantage* per se,

law degrees tended to delve into more reflective detail about their experience than those who did a graduate law conversion course. The latter skipped over that time in their life history without much detail about the experience of education itself:

> So I got a grant to do the CPE. A two-year grant from the local authority so I was really lucky and I came to the College of Law in London. I mean when I studied I really wanted to work in a legal aid practice and so I got a job in a High Street firm in East Ham. It was a proper old-fashioned High Street firm … (Ben).
>
> I decided to do law part time at the College of Law … I had to do my GDL. I wanted to do my GDL and see what I was interested in … The reason I got into law was because I had employment problems with an agency while working … (Ruth)

This is understandable given the condensed nature of the graduate conversion course predominantly taught in the UK.[20] When asked about the conversion course, participants were more likely to relate the part-time work they had been doing at the time or the internships or volunteering they pursued outside of law school and were clearly focused on ensuring employment at the end of the course. Ankita described a complete lack of engagement with the course at all ('I hated it, I hated every minute of it') and instead went into detail about working part-time at a human rights law firm while studying: 'If I hadn't had that, I think I would have jacked it in … I found the subject matter [of the course] incredibly dull … and I didn't enjoy the style of teaching'. Despite probing, for most participants their conversion studies weren't a memorable or formative educational experience and they viewed the course as a means to the end of legal qualification. Their undergraduate degrees in other subjects were more likely to provide the formative basis for the approach they took to the law:

> Jacqueline: Where did you do your undergraduate degree?
>
> Stefan: At Birkbeck, social science … I had an inspirational teacher and it was a joint degree. Loads of stuff about Marxist theory, structuralism and all that kind of stuff …
>
> Jacqueline: And then you did the CPE?
>
> Stefan: Yes. And then I did a training contract at a city firm … that was the refugee thing, get yourself a profession, be secure, earn money. I did a training contract and they paid for the CPE and all that sort of thing.

This contrasts with students who studied law at undergraduate level. Participants who studied undergraduate law presented *themselves* within their

beyond reflections on overcoming barriers on their paths to law. Data continues to show that 'poorer and ethnically diverse students are concentrated in low status schools' and that social hierarchies are reproduced by national University league tables: Sommerlad and Hammerslev (n 5) 32.

[20] Some institutions, for example the accelerated LLB programme in Scotland, teach a two-year law conversion course but all participants in the study who had not done an undergraduate law degree had experience of one-year postgraduate law conversion courses. These will change in future in England and Wales for solicitors with the introduction of the Solicitors Qualifying Examination.

narratives and more frequently situated their own experience in relation to other students. This is true both of students who studied recently and those who studied in the 1970s, 1980s and 1990s, many of whom described it as an alienating experience. They related an awakening during law school where they began to frame themselves as set apart by virtue of the type of law they valued. They expressed a desire to find people who saw the law the way they did:

> Well, I decided to become a lawyer when I was um, in the very last month of my law degree. I found my law degree extremely boring and I didn't like most of the people who were studying with me. The thought of spending my life with them wasn't too good (Rodrigo).
>
> It was a real shock whenever I got to University to suddenly have people talk about vacation schemes and things like that. I'd literally never heard of them and never even considered commercial law (Tim).
>
> Jacqueline: So how do you think those other students viewed you?
>
> Ellie: I mean I really only had a few people. I think there were only a couple of people in the whole year who were interested in legal aid. Amaya would argue a point in class and I'd be like, yeah I agree with that [laughs]. (Ellie)

One participant who reflected considerably on the isolating experience of legal education was Phil. What struck me when I met him was that this seemed quite at odds with his confidence and outgoing personality. I arranged to interview Phil early one morning before court. He had been working in legal aid for several decades and had become known to me through other lawyers I interviewed who had worked with him: 'Phil is all about fighting for justice. I mean he's just always fighting for justice, always' (Ellie), 'what really sets this firm apart is Phil … he's just always fighting for vulnerable clients' (Rihana). From his colleagues, Phil sounded to me like a sea captain who had seen his crew through some difficult times during cuts to legal aid funding and never wavered from his course. When he came into the office to meet me that morning the first thing I noticed was how quickly he walked and talked. In fact, he strode towards me and when he spoke he could cover miles of ground in minutes. I felt I had a sense of his purpose and drive within moments of meeting him.

Phil told me that he had an awareness of injustice from a young age. His parents were 'very working class' and his mother had 'a lot of issues' which made him realise 'life is a bit more complicated than most people think'. He thought because of his early life experiences he was more drawn to 'left-wing ideas' and leaving home in Scotland for University in the south of England was formative:

> There was a sense of detachment, going to what felt like a foreign country pretty young at 18 to University, where I was completely away on my own. It made, made me sort of think I suppose, a lot of that came together to say, I want to protect the vulnerable, you know, people who don't have necessarily the advantages and the um, and the support systems that others have (Phil).

When Phil talked about his time at University he revealed repeatedly the sense of distance he felt from his fellow students. He spoke about their desire to do corporate law and his own disconnection from it:

> I went to University thinking it would be a great sort of, uh, crucible of ideas and philosophies. I found it, the law, in fact, it was packed with people who were not interested in the law and just saw it as a way of getting a good job in the city, um, and financial security, and were following a path that had been sort of, pre-destined for them .... probably 75–80% of my cohort at University joined Magic Circle firms that are in London or outside London (Phil).

Similar to Ellie above he expressed real surprise that so many of his peers wanted to pursue a corporate path, as if he had not given this much thought before his journey to University. He was further surprised that they were 'not interested in the law' but concerned with 'financial security'. Phil also expressed being 'absolutely shocked' at the high number of privately educated students at law school:

> I was, I was uh, absolutely shocked by what I found there in terms of uh, at least four parts of my class at least was from private education, so I, I immediately thought, this is very weird (Phil).

There were many times during the interview where Phil would turn his narrative back to his time at law school to convey a sense of exclusion, especially so in relation to social class.[21] For example, at one point he discusses his decision to become a solicitor rather than a barrister:

> I probably would have liked to go to the Bar but I was completely put off the Bar because I was, I lacked the social confidence or commercial confidence to go to the Bar, and I didn't have any support networks ... so I decided if I was going to do the law, I'd need to be in a more collegial atmosphere because I didn't really have the confidence to do it on my own (Phil).

When I asked him a little about what he meant by lack of confidence he returned to his time at law school as a means of describing both the outward confidence he had alongside the factors that caused him to inwardly feel isolated and self-aware. Nonetheless this helped drive him forward because he wasn't going to 'go back [home] a failure' and he 'just had to toughen up and get on with it':

> I could go to University and sit in a class of 25 people and I'd be the only person who'd speak ... So part of me was quite vocal, there was another part of me that was, um, I'm in a foreign country, I've got no money really, got no experience, um, I didn't really necessarily know it at the time, but I lacked a lot of confidence (Phil).

Phil reflected on this further and told a story of being on a bus on the way to class and being mocked for his accent. He describes an acute awareness of his

[21] See, eg, Hilary Sommerlad, 'The Commercialisation of Law and the Enterprising Legal Practitioner: Continuity and Change' (2011) 18 *International Journal of the Legal Profession* 73.

difference: 'you know, I was aware I was an outsider, I was aware that people struggled too with my diction, I was aware that I didn't fit in'. He made express references here to his class background but also noted that in some ways, coming from Scotland, made it a little easier at times: 'I found that in England people like to pigeon-hole you very early on and they found it more difficult with me, because they didn't know what class I was'. Phil returns time and again to the fact that he didn't want to go home 'feeling like a failure' and this incentivised him to persevere. Phil's story resonates with that of another participant, Lena, a legal aid solicitor who qualified around the same time. Lena told me that the biggest challenge she has faced in her legal career has been her class background: 'on a personal level, it's affected my confidence at different times'. Like Phil, she describes a sense of simply not fitting in and of being around people who went to different institutions, albeit that she was unable to fully articulate it: 'it's because of my working class accent … it's very difficult because it's a middle class profession, it's people who've been to [trails off]'.

In Phil's story he went on to describe a difficult time moving to London to look for paralegal work in the hope of securing a training contract. He was 'sleeping on floors' until he finally 'got a foot in the door' in a law firm. These struggles generally seemed to make him more determined for the many fights ahead in his professional life. However, when we began to explore other areas in the interview I found it interesting that he would often return to frame them in light of his educational experience. When relating a particularly memorable case for example:

> You know, I was, I was conscious I was coming up against arguments but I was, I wanted to be fighting against top lawyers and expected to fight against top lawyers. The people that I saw at university went off to city firms, which I'm not scared of. I sat in law school classes, they weren't interested in the law. It didn't make them great lawyers, it just made them lawyers, you know, in better suits, working in better offices (Phil).

Phil's experience of social exclusion and alienation at law school had a lasting impact on his professional life. He narrates legal strategies through the lens of his experience and *maintains* a frame that clearly separates his own professional identity from that of corporate lawyers. As he puts it, the alienation he experienced made him 'toughen up and get on with it'. A particular interpretation of social alienation theory resonates with Phil's experience: although we might assume that to be alienated is problematic and evokes sympathy, it can have an almost 'heroic stature' in the alienated individual. As one social experience is dispossessed an alternative is created.[22] Indeed, for early theorists such as Rousseau and Grotius social alienation was a positive ideal, a stepping out

[22] Iain Williamson and Cedric Cullingford, 'The Uses and Misuses of 'Alienation in the Social Sciences and Education' (1997) 45 *British Journal of Educational Studies* 263, 271.

in order to frame a personally meaningful notion of civilised society. And while Hegel used the term in a contradictory fashion, Williamson and Cullingford assert that it was nonetheless 'impregnated with some sense of personal yearning for fulfilment and the implied notion of struggle between the individual and society and its institutions'.[23] Phil's story illustrates the way in which experiencing social alienation at such a formative time might galvanise progressive lawyers, permeating their values towards the formation of the professional self. For Phil, in a constructivist learning sense, this was about looking back to experiences prior to law school and building the values he took from them into his developing identity.

BRINGING US EXPERIENCE HOME

> That's when it started to wake me up. (Ankita)

The stories of participants who studied in the US form a stark contrast to Phil's experience. During my fieldwork I was very much struck by the number of study participants who also had incredibly formative experiences there. Some travelled to the US for postgraduate studies, some for yearlong courses and others for work experience related to their studies. In all, twelve participants spent time in the US that seemed to open up new ways to think about the law:

> There's something about American Universities. It's just this sort of can do attitude. Whereas I find UK Universities are a bit CV focused … always seems to be, what can we do to improve your CV? Rather than why are we actually doing this in the first place? (Ruth).

> They have these radical lawyers there you know, a movement of radical lawyers (Michael).

> So when I went to [US University] I had a vague idea of what I wanted to study and I chose – I'd never been to America – and I chose there because it felt like it would be at the centre of things … I thought there would be all kinds of exciting international people, the professors were a really interesting mix of practitioners and academics. People doing both (Ankita).

These experiences were not confined to recent decades in the study. Aidan, talked about having a formative experience America in the early 1970s when he was in his teens. He described going on a trip to a high school in the south not long after desegregation and an inspirational 'young American lawyer from Georgia' came to talk to them. Aidan remembered how he spoke about the outlawing of drugs with a 'very interesting sociological take' on 'race and social issues' that impacted upon his early understandings of race in the US and how the law

[23] ibid 265.

'impacted upon certain groups'. I was struck by a similar story told by Kathleen who had visited the US as part of her studies just a few years before Aidan. She too described the racial segregation she experienced as formative ('it was revolting … just wrong, horrible') in her desire to become a lawyer. Likewise, Kenneth, also studied in the US in the 1960s (see further discussion below) and worked on racial discrimination casework, which impacted upon his later career in the UK. For all of these participants, experiences in the US in the 1960s and 70s were illuminating in connecting the law to social issues and in providing glimpses of the types of lawyers who worked in pursuit of social change. This also aligns with the discussion in chapter two about the development of public interest law in both theory and practice during this time.[24]

These connections were made particularly clear in Ankita's story. We arranged to have our interview over several coffees one morning near her office. Ankita worked in policy and campaigning for an NGO and, even before we met, my impression of her was that she understood high-level workings of institutions and was an excellent communicator across them. This certainly proved to be the case and her commitment to understanding policy through legal frameworks is enduring. It is not difficult to trace her approach to her time in the US where she studied a policy-based subject but took law related courses and several law related practical projects:

> There were a number of professors who were people whose work was very much about the real world, so it was academia but it was making a difference, and a lot of that was at the intersection between law and politics, and it was really exciting and inspiring (Ankita).

Ankita talked in detail about her experience on this course and how she'd been 'really lucky' to get on a special programme that meant that she could do practical work, 'real world projects with real organisations', which she described as follows:

> And then when we were on the ground in Zambia, we met people from all different walks of life and backgrounds who were doing work on gender violence issues, and some of the most inspirational ones were the female lawyers, there was an association of female lawyers out there … and they were really fighting for individuals to get justice in the system, and to make the system better and it felt really tangible (Ankita).

Ankita describes a sense of respect for the lawyers she met and a belief in what they were doing. She said that she knew she had 'wanted to do something that would make a difference' and she saw how the law could help her achieve that. The legal experience gave her an understanding of both the potential of the law to make change but also the tools she herself would need to play

[24] Scott Cummings, 'The Pursuit of Legal Rights and Beyond' (2012) *UCLA Law Review* 506, 512.

a part in that process: 'I'm quite bright but I didn't really have any technical skills other than analytical skills ... that's when it started to wake me up ... that if you could use the law you might actually be able to make a difference'. Following this awakening, Ankita returned to the UK and continued to seek out people and projects to work on while doing a law conversion. Unlike Phil who described a lonely and difficult early pursuit of employment, Ankita's support network in the US was instrumental in helping to guide and support her path to legal practice:

> Jacqueline: Where was your network?
>
> Ankita: Really spread out. I had friends from the US who sort of, remained my best friends and even to this day ... and some previously as well, had worked in a range of social justice environments in different countries all over the world, and so that was a really good sounding board ... I was quite young compared to a lot of them.

Ankita twice described this network as a 'fantastic source of ideas' and also touches hereupon themes of luck and chance in getting access to opportunities ('I could not have been luckier'), similar to other participants in the study as outlined in chapter four. For example, Ankita describes getting in touch with a contact from University who is a highly regarded human rights lawyer and commented:

> So it's funny how, you end up with such a small world. This is the problem right that, in a sense, you're very privileged because you've been to [elite University] but you see people turning up in the same places ... I was incredibly lucky ....

Ankita developed strong networks of like-minded lawyers both at home and abroad: 'I'm sure we were connected because we were interested in social justice and similar minded.' Her experience in the US facilitated interactions with others pursuing work she wanted to do, and helped to support her in achieving it. She describes another friend who 'basically helped [her] understand where the good people were'. Many of the people she met during her formative time in America remained close friends and they are a continuing source of support given her work in the field of human rights. In fact, studying international human rights in the US is particularly illustrative of a means by which students gain access to a *global* network of like-minded lawyers through international programmes. It is worth noting in this context the wealth of funding, comparative to the UK, that law school clinics have in the US to facilitate these opportunities.

Another lawyer who works in a legal charity and has experience in law centres, Kimberly, outlined a personally meaningful experience of clinical legal education in the US. She stressed that the University she attended there 'invested heavily in the clinic model' and that it was 'pivotal' in her decision to choose to study there. By contrast, she thinks that UK legal education lacks a 'critical' and 'progressive' approach:

> Jacqueline: What is your impression of the UK legal education system?

> Kimberly: I think that we should push heavily for the development of more law clinics. I just believe in clinical legal education. We need to meet the enthusiasm of students for social justice because actually the economic structure for qualifying as a lawyer discourages that. I also think that in the teaching of law we can encourage that more progressive and more critical approach …

The participants who have had clinical US experience were champions of that educational approach in the stories they told. Indeed, another participant had recently returned to the UK and sought funding and support to set up a similar programme to that he had experienced in the US.

There are noticeable parallels between these more recent experiences in the US and that of another study participant who studied in America more than four decades previously. Kenneth completed a postgraduate fellowship in the early 1960s and worked together with a law professor on an early race discrimination case. He said that becoming a part of the team working on the case sparked his interest in discrimination, which later formed a considerable part of his career:

> In fact I was extremely fortunate … I worked on an extraordinary case where a progressive property developer had bought a piece of land to develop as a housing estate and it was to be a multiracial housing estate. This greatly upset the local people including their local government. And they made a compulsory purchase order on the land to stop it being a multiracial estate. So it was a key discrimination issue. I became part of the team that worked on the case and that certainly sparked my interest in discrimination (Kenneth).

This case and Kenneth's experience working on it features strongly in his narrative despite the passage of nearly 50 years. More than the case itself, the relationships Kenneth formed working on it were sustained over time. One key friendship was his roommate at the time, from whom he got the job working on the case:

> Kenneth: I've kept in touch with all these people over the years, particularly [roommate], I saw him all the time, his children stayed with us.
>
> Jacqueline: Would you say you were like-minded?
>
> Kenneth: Oh yes. Yes … He was the most, um, he was a really charismatic person. He was incredibly clever. He was second in his class and could have jobs anywhere. He wanted to stay in academia.

Kenneth was clearly impacted by his US experience in the same way that Aidan and Kathleen were around the same time, who both also mentioned the impact of their exposure to racial segregation and the law's interaction with it (this being not long after the US Supreme Court desegregation case of *Brown v Board of Education*). For Ankita, and others, more than four decades later their experiences also opened doors to networks and experiences and their time spent in America comprises an illuminating chapter in their life stories. Across the decades therefore working on cases with particularly inspirational lawyers, who became close friends, allowed participants to hold a clear picture in their minds of the connection between the theory and practice of law, seeing the law not simply in books but in action.[25] Their US awakenings had longevity and, for many, the networks they established with other progressive lawyers sustained them through the move from legal education to practice and beyond.

A FORMATIVE UK EXPERIENCE

> That's seen me through all the way. (Sue)

Apart from Ellie described above, only a small minority of those I interviewed related educational experiences in the UK that were formative and personally meaningful to the same extent as those who had studied in the US. In fact, even stories of UK clinical legal educational experience were underwhelming by comparison. Participants tended not to go into as much detail about clients or cases and memories were not related with the same emotion or passion. In fact, even for those who had been at law school relatively recently, the experience was not related with much enthusiasm or certainty in terms of its impact on their decision to pursue progressive practice:

> Jacqueline: How did you find your clinic experience in terms of guiding your decisions about what to do?
>
> Emily: I think it probably had an impact. I know other people who I was on the course with and it turned them off law. I did family and that really appealed to me. I did come out of university thinking that's what I want to do.

Another participant, Tim, described being involved in a long established clinic at a law school in the UK but expressed surprise that the culture of the law school generally was not access to justice or human rights focussed, similar to the experience I outline at the beginning of the chapter: 'I'd say overwhelmingly there was still a corporate focus … when I described wanting to work in human rights or legal aid the advice was that there was no clear path into it'.

The clear exception to this is Sue. Sue has spent more than 20 years representing clients in housing and social welfare but has always grasped opportunities for related projects and campaigns. She runs a busy housing scheme in a London court providing advice to extremely vulnerable clients facing eviction or repossession. Sue has developed a role in the public domain

[25] Jerome Frank, 'Why Not a Clinical Lawyer School?' (1933) 81(8) *University of Pennsylvania Law Review* 907; Jerome Frank, 'A Plea for Lawyer-Schools' (1947) 56 *Yale Law Journal* 1303.

giving voice to the poverty and exclusion faced by her clients. She recently received a professional 'lifetime achievement' award for her work. When I walked into her law centre off a busy high street on a cold winter evening I could not have felt more warmth. Sue has a calm manner and engaging smile and I could see immediately why she is so well liked in the law centre movement and beyond. Her small office was piled high with case files and her desk was strewn with thank you cards from grateful clients. Although clearly extremely busy, Sue explained she never liked to say no to an opportunity to share her professional experiences. She wants to correct the mistaken narratives around social exclusion as a result of the austerity agenda and to better describe the work that lawyers are doing in the fight against it. When I pressed her on why it was important to her to get these stories into the public domain she said:

> I think that it's just that society has lost the ability to … the sense of community and empathy. I think if you tell stories that will hook people in so they think 'gosh, that could happen to me, or my mum, or my sister or whatever' then I think you get them to start to think about change and about accepting that the world isn't black and white. People aren't bad or good. People on benefits aren't scroungers. You know we've had so much of that really … (Sue).

Sue had clearly developed a storied approach to her work ('if you're a lawyer and you can write then you're in the story, by being in the story you know so much and you can capture it'). She studied law and sociology in the early 1980s and her eyes lit up as she effusively related her time at law school. She described her initial decision to choose this path:

> Sue: So I did law at College and thought it would be really nice to change the world. You know, a lot of my friends lived in difficult circumstances, not me, but a lot of social housing and stuff. My parents had bought their own house. They were at the beginning of that really. And so I just had a … well my Mum had a really good sense of justice … she always said you shouldn't judge someone until you've walked a mile in their shoes … I don't know … that's just what I did. And so then I went to Warwick University and that was just amazing.
>
> Jacqueline: When was that?
>
> Sue: That was 1981–85 … it was all about how law is ever changing and you have to understand it in context. That's seen me through all the way.

I was intrigued to hear that Sue had studied at Warwick and that she described her experience as having sustained her throughout her career ('that's seen me through all the way'). Warwick law school took great pride in its 'law in context' approach and championed it when it when the law school was established in 1967.[26]

[26] Ralph Folsom and Neal Roberts, 'The Warwick Story: Being Led Down the Contextual Path of the Law' (1979) 36 *Journal of Legal Education* 166.

The 'Warwick ethos' rested on legal realism and the movement against legal formalism, which at the time was led by a group of young academics who had been influenced by time spent in the US and Africa.[27] Law was taught in light of its social, economic and political context with an emphasis on subjects relevant to those experiencing poverty and a focus on social reform.[28] While Sue attended prior to the formal establishment of clinical legal education she describes the importance of her own student 'collective' with whom she established a student led initiative:

> So yeah, law and sociology, what you had was about twenty students on the course. We were kind of a collective together. We would all go to the bigger lectures together. And in the year above me were a couple of really good people … we set up a little law centre on the bridge between the union and the university and we gave advice to students on tenancies (Sue).

There is a stark contrast between Sue's collective experience and the social alienation felt by other study participants. She constructs her experience with a connection between informal and formal learning:

> The University was powerful and progressive, we had strikes and demonstrations outside the classroom but inside the classroom I learnt that the law could be used as a tool to make change (Sue).

None of the other study participants described such radical activities at law school in the UK in the same way, although the relevant literature does of course note legal education's contribution to political activism and a move away traditional positivism.[29] Sue began to tell me about one protest, her own memory of it having recently been stimulated by a photograph she had been sent. While she was incredibly animated relaying the events, what struck me most was her own sense of surprise in hindsight at the protest ever having taken place in a University setting:

> I'm just looking for a picture, someone sent this to me from 1983. Sir Keith Joseph comes to Warwick and he's just made massive cuts to education and this is all of us trying to get to him. And there's me [laughs] I must be like twenty. That was at Warwick University! The University got fined thirty grand for that riot (Sue).

Sue passed on the photograph (Figure 1 below). It depicts well the collective sense of belonging that Sue describes and its reflection of her own fond nostalgia about her time at Warwick. While appreciating it is only a snapshot,

[27] Avrom Sherr and Julian Webb, 'Law Students, The External Market and Socialization: Do we Make Them Turn to the City?' (1989) 16 *Law and Society* 225.

[28] Zenon Bankowski and Geoff Mungham, 'Warwick University Ltd, Continued' (1974) 1 *British Journal of Law and Society* 179.

[29] Sommerlad and Hammerslev (n 5) 30.

most students in the photograph are animated, not angry or violent. They are smiling or laughing towards the camera. Although we learn from Sue that the University eventully 'got fined for that riot' they seem largely at ease with their actions, perhaps not even wary of any potential repurcussions. On the face of it, these do not appear to be students overly concerned that involvement in a University riot might blot the landscape of their future careers in corporate law.

A study of of Warwick law students in the late 1980s accords to an extent with Sue's experience. A large-scale survey revealed that most students saw the curriculum as geared towards addressing the resolution of social issues rather than solely orientating students towards 'big city firms'. Indeed, 'an overwhelming majority' wanted a clinical component in the curriculum and came to Warwick with a 'practical bias' that was maintained during their time there.[30] Most students were 'imbued with a sense of responsibility in the lawyer's 'social welfare' role'.[31] Nonetheless, the study fell short of concluding that Warwick *created* progressive lawyers as such. While there was some evidence that students were liberalised during their time at Warwick they did not necessarily connect this to their legal education. Likewise, while they valued the 'reformist' approach in the curriculum the study concluded that only a small number carried this into their future careers.

Sue is clearly one of the few who chose to take a reformist approach to her career: 'I think the law is about not looking down but looking out and seeing how you can make things better'. She valued the contextual focus on social welfare at Warwick and the formative experience of studying together with others who wanted to use the law to make change in society. The largely quantitative study above appears to dismiss the *few* radicals who emerged from Warwick in the 1980s almost as an afterthought. Sue's life experience suggests however that the values of these few were so strongly held, and their related work so profound, that their potential social impact might have been overlooked. In view of the vast expansion of legal education globally over the past two decades and the continuing pressures faced by the socio-legal academy,[32] I argue that creating opportunities for students to glimpse all possible future selves,[33] as well as 'habits of responding' to social injustice[34] are all the more important in the current climate and for the future.

[30] Sherr and Webb (n 27) 245.

[31] ibid 247.

[32] Richard Collier, '"Left Pessimists" in "Rose Coloured Glasses": Reflections on the Political Economy of Socio-Legal Studies and Legal (Academic) Well-Being' (2020) *Journal of Law and Society* 244.

[33] Francis (n 14) 197.

[34] Jacqueline Kinghan, 'Lifetimes of Commitment to Law and Social Justice' in Daniel Newman and Faith Gordon (eds), *Leading Works in Law and Social Justice* (Routledge, 2021).

Figure 1 Warwick University Protest Image (1983)

CONCLUSIONS

The narratives I have set out reveal contrasting stories of legal education, with connections across them in terms of their relationship to the pursuit of progressive legal practice. Without seeking to draw generalisations from this data, the narratives nonetheless provide insight into rarely captured perspectives of student experience. Phil, and many other study participants, experienced a sense of alienation while studying with commercially orientated students such that they set themselves apart and felt propelled towards a different path. This embracing of *otherness* is consistent with Sarat and Scheingold's framing of cause lawyers and presents ethical tensions explored in the next chapter. For participants who had formative experiences in the US and the small minority who had similar experiences in UK law schools, a contextual approach appears to have shaped their professional identity. For example, Ankita now works at the intersection of legal policy and practice in human rights and Sue takes an embedded approach representing clients in a community law centre. Importantly, they develop networks and a strong sense of identity across different network nodes. They described glimpsing, through experience, the type of lawyer they wanted to become. Notably as clinical legal education was developing in the UK in the 1970s, critics outlined tensions: that the 'helping' ideology simply masked distance and control, that clinics 'extend the hegemony of law and institutions' and that students might learn to use the law to help the socially disadvantaged 'but understand nothing about the social context within which the law operates'.[35] For Ankita and Sue especially this does not appear to have been the case, their work is expressly concerned with understanding the social context of the law and their law school experiences set them on a powerful course towards squarely confronting the difficult tensions that Twining outlines about legal education, and about law's role in society. They, like many other participants, were especially determined to find and maintain networks together with other people who held similar values in legal education and beyond. The contrasting narratives in this chapter reveal the ways in which many law students feel excluded by their educational experiences as well as the influential role of experiential learning for those few study participants who had meaningful exposure to progressive lawyering practice during their time at law school.

[35] Bankowski and Mungham (n 28) 183–84.

7

Professional Legal Ethics and the Progressive Social Self

Let's not kid ourselves. Let's not hide around niceness. I'm using the law politically. I'm using it to show working class people and campaigners that law is a vehicle of struggle. (Lena)

As outlined in chapter two, there is some controversy as to the ethical decision making of lawyers pursuing social change.[1] Ethical tensions arise, for example, where lawyers' political goals might challenge notions of independence,[2] where they arguably subvert client's interests for that of a wider cause[3] or when they speak on behalf of individuals and groups but are said to lack the legitimacy to do so.[4] Against this background, I explore in this chapter the extent to which collective identity might have a bearing upon the ways in which lawyers conceive of and understand their ethical decision-making. I adopt a wide view of legal ethics in the context of the study to include 'the ways in which the rules and norms of lawyering, individual values, and considerations of justice, clients and practice organizations, shape individual conduct'.[5] Similar to other studies that have sought to capture how particular environments might impact upon ethical choices, such as 'in-house'[6] or 'communities of practice' in discrete subject areas,[7] I consider how lawyers construct

[1] Robert Rosen, 'On the Social Significance of Cause Lawyering' (2000) 3(2) *Legal Ethics* 169; Andrew Boon, 'Cause Lawyers and the Alternate Ethical Paradigm' (2004) 7 *Legal Ethics* 250. See also, Corey Shdaimah, 'Legal Service Lawyers: When Conceptions of Lawyering and Values Clash' in Leslie Levin and Lynn Mather (eds), *Lawyers in Practice: Ethical Decision Making in Context* (University of Chicago Press, 2012).

[2] Austin Sarat, 'Between the (Presence of) Violence and the (Possibility of) Justice' in Austin Sarat and Stuart Scheingold (eds), *Cause Lawyering: Political Commitments and Professional Responsibilities* (Oxford University Press, 1998) 318.

[3] Margareth Etienne, 'The Ethics of Cause Lawyering: An Empirical Examination of Criminal Defense Lawyers as Cause Lawyers' (2005) 95 *Journal of Criminal Law and Criminology* 1195, 1209.

[4] Gerald Lopez, *Rebellious Lawyering: One Chicano's Vision of Progressive Law Practice* (Westview Press, 1992).

[5] Lynn Mather and Leslie Levin, 'Why Context Matters' in Levin and Mather (n 1) 7.

[6] Richard Moorhead et al, *Designing Ethics Indicators for Legal Service Provision* (The Legal Service Board, 2012) 4.

[7] Lynn Mather et al, *Divorce Lawyers at Work: Varieties of Professionalism in Practice* (Oxford University Press, 2001).

and relate their ethical decision making across the different network nodes of progressive legal practice. Within such networks of practice, it has been noted that 'groups of lawyers within whom practitioners interact and to whom they compare themselves and look for common expectations and standards' has the capacity to shape their conduct.[8] In view of the extent to which the theme emerged in lawyer's own stories and its relevance to the 'turning point' discussed in chapter four, I narrow the focus in this chapter to the consideration of 'who' progressive lawyers represent, for example, the state, corporate bodies or those (subjectively) considered to be the perpetrators of injustice, and their own perceptions of those choices and decisions.

In terms of lawyer regulation, in the US professional rules are arguably more lenient than for lawyers in the UK and focus more on lawyer's autonomy to accept or refuse instructions.[9] Lawyers are given an express right to refuse to take on a client's case, albeit they are encouraged not to refuse unworthy causes.[10] By contrast, self-employed barristers are bound by the cab rank rule as discussed in chapter two.[11] In England and Wales (and similarly replicated in Scotland and Northern Ireland) solicitors must also act with integrity, such that any refusal of instructions to act must be reasonable and they must not allow their independence to be compromised. At a European level these rules are reflected in core principles that state in clear terms that 'a lawyer needs to be free – politically, economically and intellectually – in pursuing his or her activities of advising and representing the client'.[12]

As outlined in chapter two, unlike conventional lawyers cause lawyers look to the context *outside* of the law to inform their decision-making, which has a bearing on their ability to regard a choice as ethical or unethical.[13] I set out in chapter four how the narratives of progressive lawyers in the study involve clear turning points away from other types of legal practice, most notably away from corporate practice towards representing victims of injustice or state power. The 'us and them' narrative that facilitates their positioning in a different professional space from *other* lawyers presents a challenge in terms of reconciliation with professional ethics and required neutrality. Progressive lawyers' narratives present a heightened collective sense of doing what is 'good' but this becomes

[8] ibid 6.

[9] Thomas Shaffer, 'Legal Ethics and the Good Client' (1986) 36 *Catholic University Law Review* 319.

[10] American Bar Association Model Rules of Professional Conduct (1983) Rule 1.2(b). These are adopted in most individual states.

[11] Bar Standards Board, Code of Conduct, Rule C28 (BSB, 2015). The rule gets its name from the rule that licensed Hackney Carriage (cab) drivers cannot refuse to carry passengers, subject to some limited exceptions. It rests in principles of access to justice and is designed in part to ensure not only that unmeritorious clients get representation but that they also might have their *choice* of representation. The cab rank rule does not apply to solicitors in England and Wales.

[12] Council of Bars and Law Societies of Europe's Charter of Core Principles, Explanatory Note (CCBE, 2008).

[13] Carrie Menkel-Meadow, 'The Causes of Cause Lawyering: Toward an Understanding of the Motivation and Commitment of Social Justice Lawyers' in Sarat and Scheingold (n 2).

ethically problematic where it involves a rejection of clients who are somehow on the 'wrong' side.[14] This chapter therefore focuses on the ways in which the representation of the progressive social self serves to embed professional ethical controversy. I explore how the 'us and them' narrative is presented in ethical decision-making and on their own perceptions of adherence to ethical rules of professional conduct. I analyse the decisions made as to case selection and representation and how participants relate those decisions to their own individual and collective values. The critical questions are whether progressive lawyers see themselves as 'set apart' from the rest of the profession in their ethical decision-making and whether they present a connection between their decision-making and their progressive politics.

The discussion of these tensions is explored through discussion of three common sets of responses to the question of whether they would ever represent the state (in this context the government, local authorities or enforcement agencies) or corporate bodies. My starting point therefore was not participants' understanding of the ethical rules themselves[15] but the collective social interactions that relate to the actual practice of the interpretation of those rules.[16] The groups of participants I outline in this chapter I term 'resolute', 'constrained' and 'conflicted' and I intend these terms to have multiple meanings. For those who are *resolute* in refusing cases they are also naturally more resolute in their politics. They express their refusal to represent the state or corporate bodies in strong and clear terms. While there might be some exceptions (for example, acting for the state where it is prosecuting corporate bodies for fraudulent activity) they remain clear in their own minds as to the political and value driven justification for their decision. For those who take a *constrained* approach there is a sense of holding back in their narratives: they tend to reveal feeling constrained as to whether to accept or refuse instructions from particular clients. They are also more likely to be more constrained in how they view their professional life as an *outlet* for their political beliefs. These participants often describe having political affiliations that they keep separate from their professional lives or are more likely to reflect on having been more active in politics in the past before qualifying as a lawyer. Finally, those who were *conflicted* tended to reveal, upon probing, conflicting accounts of their refusal of instructions from corporations or state actors. Most of the participants who fall into the conflicted category are barristers at the independent Bar (thus falling within the 'barrister-campaigner' subset), which is perhaps unsurprising in view of the cab rank rule. They at times were quite resolute and would then swing to more balanced or neutral accounts of their decision making and the interplay of their professional and political lives. These participants were also more likely to *rely* on ethical conflict of interest as a means of avoiding the issue of having to refuse instructions.

[14] Rosen (n 1) 175.

[15] Moorhead et al (n 6).

[16] Richard Moorhead et al, *In-House Lawyers' Ethics: Institutional Logics, Legal Risk and the Tournament of Influence* (Hart, 2018); Shdaimah (n 1).

I noted with interest that most participants fell within the *resolute* or *conflicted* categories and *constrained* responses all came from participants in the early or late stages of their careers. Those who had retired tended to look back over their time in practice and talked about the importance of professional neutrality and not refusing cases on political grounds, even though their narratives as a whole might also reveal some inconsistencies with this assertion. Likewise, participants in the early stages of their careers expressed an understandable unfamiliarity and uncertainty that can be characterised as constraint. None of the participants (at any stage of their career) misunderstood my questions in relation to 'who' they might act for or made any assumption that it might concern lawyer independence *from* the state.[17] And while I had assumed there might be particular approaches held by each subset of practitioners this was not the case. Some legal aid lawyers were resolute and others were constrained; some barristers were balanced and others were conflicted. What remains consistent across all areas of practice and five decades of the study is a strongly articulated collective desire to engage in representation of clients and causes that are personally meaningful; but different constructions of the relationship between this desire and its ethical consequences.

RESOLUTE POSITIONS

For progressive lawyers who are resolute in their politics, their professional lives reveal a similarly strong and unwavering commitment to representing those whom they perceive to be the victims, rather than perpetrators, of injustice. It is for this *resolute* group of participants that the law and legal practice becomes a most obvious outlet for political beliefs. In their stories, their professional and personal lives are inextricably interwoven. A clear example of this approach lies with Lena, a law centre solicitor with more than two decades of experience across many areas of social welfare law. I introduced Lena in chapter three and noted her socialist politics as a strong current running through her legal practice. Throughout her story Lena presented as someone with a particularly heightened awareness of how she is perceived and often talked about herself through the lens of how she thought other people saw her. She positioned herself with reference to other progressive lawyers in her narrative as she especially saw herself as being different from more elite progressive practitioners whom she described as the 'public interest law establishment'.[18] The lawyers she referenced in this regard tended to work together 'legal, political and other elites … seeking to

[17] David Luban, 'The Moral Complexity of Cause Lawyers Within the State' (2012) 81 *Fordham Law Review* 705.

[18] This is a point raised by several legal aid and law centre solicitors in the study. See, eg, discussion in ch 3 of Ben's objection to the labels of public law and human rights at the Bar.

influence what gets placed on courts' agendas'.[19] Following Hilbink's typology,[20] such 'grasstops' lawyers fit the elite/vanguard cause lawyer profile and Lena quite clearly sees herself as being at the other end of the spectrum within the grassroots profile:

> I do 'at the coalface' public interest law. I'll actively go and see the client in their environment. I'll meet with campaign groups … Not necessarily to get work but because I'll say this is how you can use the law – now just let me know if you want to (Lena).

Where Lena situates herself in relation to other practitioners is relevant to the ethical approach she takes as she negotiates her own approach in relation to others. For example, having described her 'at the coalface' work she goes on to describe an elite organisation that pursues strategic litigation by working in a more balanced way to 'generalise public interest law in the legal profession' and distinguishes her own work by saying she prefers to 'generalise law in campaigns'. Lena is subversive in connecting her work to campaigns and the pursuit of social change; thus she is clear that she will not act for corporations nor will she do most types of government work:

> Jacqueline: Would you ever represent the government or any arm of the state?
>
> Lena: No, god no.
>
> Jacqueline: And the reason for that?
>
> Lena: I'd sooner do another job. Yeah. I couldn't represent the government. I think the only way I could do it is if it was tax evasion against big corporations. That would probably be the only thing I could do. Against big businesses or in the environmental sphere.

Lena is resolute here ('I'd sooner do another job'). Having asked her about case selection I probed a little further and it was at this point in the interview that a shift occurred:

> Jacqueline: So Theresa May recently criticised left wing activist lawyers – would you say you're using the law politically in the way she describes?
>
> Lena: Yes, I am. Absolutely. Yeah, I'm using the law for political means [pause]. Let's not kid ourselves. There's a war going on between them and us. Of course there's a class war, and we're winning. Let's not kid ourselves. Let's not hide around niceness. I'm using the law politically. I'm using it to show working class people and campaigners that law is a vehicle of struggle.

The exchange continued with Lena becoming animated and posing a series of questions ('Do I use legal aid to help people? Yes. Is there a political motivation

[19] Effie Fokas, 'Directions in Religious Pluralism in Europe: Mobilizations in the Shadow of the European Court of Human Rights Religious Freedoms Jurisprudence' (2015) 4 *Oxford Journal of Law and Religion* 542–43.

[20] Thomas Hilbink, 'You Know the Type: Categories of Cause Lawyering' (2004) 19 *Law & Social Inquiry* 657.

on every single case? No'). Analysing the transcript I noticed that when she finished there was a silence as I struggled to think of the best way to respond. I (perhaps wrongly) moved the interview into another area having sensed some tension and this seemed to create further frustration on Lena's part. Looking back at the transcript, Lena was both reaching out and creating distance. Her assertions of 'let's not hide around niceness, let's not kid ourselves' on the one hand included me as a member of the group of lawyers she was referring to ('them and us'); and on the other hand created distance by perhaps suggesting *I* was kidding myself and hiding around niceties.

This simultaneous reaching out and creating distance was a recurrent theme in how Lena analysed her own place within progressive lawyering networks. Lena remained quite firmly resolute about her professional decision-making throughout and did not present as being conflicted about case selection and client representation. However, at multiple times in the interview she would return in her story to how others perceived her all while referencing the type of progressive lawyer she didn't want to be like:

> But where there is an opportunity to use the law politically I will use it politically but I will use it in such a way I hope anyway that I don't come across as a knight in shining armour (Lena).

When we discussed the barristers she instructs at the Bar she said that she uses those who are 'left of centre' but don't necessarily 'trade on it'. Here again she distinguished her own work from the elite public interest law 'establishment' who she thought could be 'very picky'. Lena is determined in her decision-making and throughout her narrative shows a desire to resolutely pursue certain types of work and not others; and to occupy a particular space of grassroots legal activism within the progressive lawyering movement.

Several other law centre solicitors expressed similar resolute decision-making, albeit from different positions. While Lena narrates her legal practice in opposition to other types of elite practitioners and created distance, other law centre solicitors expressed their ethical decision-making by reaching out to accepted collective ethical ideals. This was especially common for those participants who were part of the law centre movement in the 1980s and 1990s. Stefan described case selection mechanisms in the 1990s, which resonate with the controversy I outlined in chapter two challenging the independence of law centre case selection.[21]

> Jacqueline: Was there a selection mechanism on the merits?
>
> Stefan: Yeah, yeah, now what we did, which again we were all signed up for was they we won't act for landlords, we won't act for employers, we won't act for perpetrators of domestic violence – where we got into some difficulty – we won't act for perpetrators of racial or sexual harassment.

[21] Diana Leat, 'Rise and Role of the Poor Man's Lawyer' (1975) 2 *British Journal of Law and Society* 166, 177.

> Jacqueline: Can you dig into that a little bit?
>
> Stefan: Because it's all about power. Generally, those people have power and they have money ... Yes, everyone is entitled to advice and representation. But they can get that somewhere else ... I've got no problem with that. Generally, the underlying thing is that those people have more power and our job is to represent people without power.

I note that I asked Stefan whether they selected cases on merits and in legal terms this generally means objectively selecting on the strength of the case and its likelihood of success. Stefan responded however by outlining case selection based on what they perceived to be meritorious cases in terms of client status (victim/perpetrator). Law centre lawyers were 'all signed up' to this approach and at several times during the interview Stefan repeated the collective decisions they took ('yeah, it felt everybody was signed up to the same thing, which was to right injustices'). The decisions around case selection all reference the collective 'we' of the law centre rather than 'I' as a lawyer. On the face of it, the case selection mechanism arguably conflicts with the rationale behind community law centres that Stefan himself described early in the interview:

> The whole idea is we represent the local community, we're in the heart of the local community. We open our doors [sic] anyone can come in (Stefan).

By contrast, Stefan later described how if a man came in for advice on a family law problem but during the course of the interview it emerged that there was an allegation of harassment or violence against him, they wouldn't represent him. Stefan remained resolute when we discussed some of the ethical tensions of this approach. He admitted they 'sailed close to the wind' and often the details of any ethical issues weren't clear in his memory:

> I remember taking the case at some point from the SRA [Solicitors Regulation Authority] about the circumstances in which we can terminate a retainer. I can't remember the detail now. But I was aware there was kind of an issue there (Stefan).

Stefan moved several times between potential ethical tensions to outlining again how everyone in the law centre was 'on board' with the selective approach they took. Several times he turned to collective decision-making and then back to potential ethical problems all the while dismissing them: 'I did think oh hang on, what are our professional obligations? But we were all very comfortable. We were all signed up. You know you come across lawyers who say everyone deserves a defence? But none of us really felt like that.' Here again, he situates his decision-making alongside other lawyers both within and outside the network in order to negotiate his ethical choices. We returned to the issue several times. For example, when Stefan discussed managing legal aid contracts I asked:

> Jacqueline: Was there ever any conflict with the legal services contracts and the Legal Service Commission. Do you think they were aware of the criteria you were putting in place?

> Stefan: That's a good question, I'm not sure they were. Again, I can't remember. I can't remember whether we had to hide that from them or whether they knew and it was. … [trails off].

On one view, so long as the selection mechanisms allowed practising lawyers to maintain their independence and integrity there would be no ethical conflict. It would also be a clear conflict of interest for a solicitor to represent, for example, a landlord they had previously pursued a case against so having a policy in place at a law centre might minimise conflict.[22] From the 1970s these tensions were observed and, interestingly, one London law centre was clear that to counter allegations of 'class bias and political involvement' when staff where engaging in political demonstrations, for example against oppressive local landlords, they should do so 'as individuals and not use the name of the Centre'.[23] Nonetheless, while there is a clear commitment to generally representing those experiencing poverty and social exclusion the *resolute* nature of the refusal to represent certain client groups is clear in Stefan's description of his own law centre practice. Looking back over time, his hesitation and uncertainty suggests some ethical ambiguity because it seems that Stefan is now unable to clearly make sense of the case selection in strict ethical terms. What he can clearly recall however is the collective nature of those decisions and an undeniable intuitive sense that they were right.

Many other solicitors in the study, predominantly in legal aid, revealed similar approaches. When I asked Eve for example if she would ever represent the government she similarly responded resolutely with a firm 'no'. Her explanation again was in relation to what *other* lawyers do: 'there's lots of people who would do that and I'm not one of them. I want to be against the state because that's where my political activism lies'. Andrea's response was broadly similar when asked if she would represent corporate bodies, following a resolute 'no' she explained:

> Um, because I don't want to defend the indefensible. And I completely see the place of people who act in those situations. I, I'm definitely not one of those people who thinks that all those people are demons because I understand why it's important for everyone to have access to fair and good representation … (Andrea).

The framing of collective identity is again clear here as Andrea describes 'all those people' who represent corporations. She then rests her ethical decision-making next to her own values thus stressing their importance to ethicality. As with Stefan, her values and motivations seem to override any strict interpretation of ethical requirements. For Andrea, and several other participants in the study, emotion features strongly in this context: 'this is where my heart is

[22] Philip Leask, 'Law Centres in England and Wales' (1985) 7(1) *Law and Policy* 61, 62.
[23] Roy Goode, 'The Operation of a Law Centre – The UK Experience' (1975) *Legal Service Bulletin* 253, 256.

first and foremost' (Rihana); or it is connected to an expression of anger or exasperation: 'If [state actors] all put their hands up, we'd be in a much better society. But they won't! Just that, you know, I'm not motivated by fighting for the big man.' (Andrea).

Andrea returns several times in her narrative to 'fighting' for justice on behalf of clients and distinguishes herself from lawyers who 'try to be very sort of neutral about everything' which she strongly asserts is not the 'right approach'. For Andrea, her resolute decision-making closely relates to her desire to be engaged in a fight that she believes in. This engagement is similar to that of Martin, a politically active barrister in a progressive set of Chambers and one of the few barristers in the study who was resolute in their decision-making around refusal of instructions. He explained that he would never accept instructions from the government or corporate bodies and again makes reference to collective rather than individual decision-making: 'It's about for me, who has the power? Who has the resources? It's very simple. It sounds very trite to say but that is what [Chambers] exists for. It's all we exist for.'

Martin seems to take some confidence in the collective approach of what he terms the 'radical Bar'. The controversial framing of cause lawyers in the literature as being more virtuous than other lawyers[24] is exposed in Martin's observation that he takes 'a slightly more moralistic look at the cab rank rule'. By refusing instructions from corporate actors and the state Martin believes he is further engaging in the fight for justice and that his own interpretation of the ethical rules imposed on the Bar rest on stronger morals than those held by *other* lawyers. The question of course of 'whose' standard of morality lawyers should even comply remains largely unsettled.[25] In each of the sets of resolute ethical decision-making I have analysed, participants nonetheless reflect on their own approach by comparison to others and often in critical terms. This becomes even more apparent in the group of *constrained* participants.

CONSTRAINED POSITIONS

As I have outlined above, participants who presented as *constrained* in their ethical decision-making often felt constrained by their status as a lawyer in terms of expressing their politics either personally or professionally. That is not to say they were not political, they often pursued political causes tirelessly but the *expression* of that pursuit was constructed with care and often with some trepidation. The constrained participants in the study were at pains to be perceived as neutral in their approach and particularly so in comparison to *resolute* progressive practitioners.

[24] Rosen (n 1).

[25] Elizabeth Chambliss, 'Whose Ethics? The Benchmark Problem in Legal Ethics Research' in Levin and Mather (n 1) 48.

I found Kenneth, a highly esteemed human rights lawyer with five decades of legal practice behind him, to have an intriguing narrative in this regard. Like other constrained participants in the study he is careful not to *personally* attach himself to particular causes. His response to my question below also highlights well the lack of familiarity with cause lawyering theory by lawyers in the UK:

> Jacqueline: Would you ever have identified as being an activist lawyer?
>
> Kenneth: Oh yes, I think so. Yes ... but you know in America they have, in fact I even have a book which I've got somewhere here that someone gave me which is called 'cause lawyering'. Cause lawyering! [laughter].

During this light-hearted exchange I recall thinking how striking it was that Kenneth was someone *I* perceived to be a quintessential cause lawyer in light of the human rights work he had pursued over so many years; yet he did not perceive himself in that way. In fact, Kenneth seemed often at pains to communicate the type of lawyer he thought he was *not*, more than the type of lawyer he was. In the interview he was quite eager to continue the cause lawyering discussion and to differentiate his own professional work from that of other more radical lawyers:

> I think there are certain lawyers who have always been thought of as left wing, you know, radical lawyers because they have presented themselves in that way, I mean I would say Ben Birnberg[26] and Mike Mansfield[27] would be an example of that. I have always felt that was wrong (Kenneth).

The reference here to how radical lawyers have 'presented themselves' is revealing. Kenneth is not so much objecting to the radical politics per se as to the presentation of those politics in professional life. This resonates with the discussion in chapter three as to the divergent labelling of progressive legal identity, especially where the term 'activist lawyer' might be concerned. When we spent some time looking back at his own cases he returned to this point, stressing that as a lawyer you have a professional duty to 'take on a client's best interests which may not happen to coincide with your politics'. Kenneth seemed to be trying to make sense of how to reconcile his own 'activist lawyer' past and the professional duties he also held dear through a narrative that conveyed neutrality but revealed constraint. It was quite striking for example that Kenneth delved into

[26] Benedict Birnberg had a leading civil rights practice within a general practice firm he set up in 1962 (now known as Birnberg Peirce). On retiring in 1999 he described himself as 'really very conservative – with a small "c" – in a number of ways, or rather, a radically-minded conservative': Linda Tsang, 'Law: Farewell to a Non Fat Cat' (*The Independent*, 25 February 1999).

[27] Michael Mansfield was called to the Bar in 1976 and worked on a number of high profile miscarriages of justice cases. He self-identifies as a 'radical barrister' and would rest within the *resolute* group of ethical decision-makers. It has been said that Mansfield 'always prided himself on taking a different approach to his involvement in cases. Whilst his fellow barristers stuck to the prevailing orthodoxy of detached involvement with those they represent, Mansfield invests himself personally in each case': Thom Dyke, 'Memoirs of a Radical Lawyer' (*New Statesman*, 24 September 2009).

his memory to try to share examples of right-wing clients he had represented during his years in practice:

> And I have acted for Tories, I was even once consulted by, what's his name? He was a very famous right wing Tory who was absolutely charming and delightful. I didn't do anything for him in the end. But you know, I have acted for Tories [pause] .... Um, yes, I acted for a chap who was the Chairman of the [redacted Conservative organisation] in quite a major case. I in a way put the professional obligation ahead of one's personal politics. Obviously I've got my own politics but when I'm doing my job that shouldn't be a factor (Kenneth).

I noted the underlying constraint in Kenneth's sense-making of his decisions to represent certain clients in the past: 'I in a way put the professional obligation ahead of one's politics'. His constrained position is revealed further by him only remembering – through five decades of legal practice – one example of actually representing someone on the other side of his politics. Kenneth nonetheless expressed in clear terms a desire to distinguish himself from more radical, resolute lawyers.

Other participants were equally constrained in their case selection decisions. Michael, a barrister, described an approach that might arguably be in conflict with a strict interpretation of the cab rank rule but he was, like Kenneth, at pains to appear more measured than other participants in his response:

> Jacqueline: Would you ever act for the government?
>
> Michael: I'd rather not. There are cases where I can see they're on the right side either legally, morally or politically. But my practice is acting for claimants, for the victims of state power because that's where the power imbalance is.

Ankita conveyed a very similar approach saying that there's 'enormous value in understanding how government decisions are made' when asked if she would ever represent any arm of the state. She elaborated that she's a 'firm believer that standing and shouting from the outside consistently never works' because you need to 'understand your opponent'. However, her constraint around acting for the government was clear as she moved between what she described as a 'firm belief' and the fact that she didn't feel 'comfortable' doing it: 'if I'm honest with myself, although I work as hard as I could, I wouldn't feel engaged and passionate about it'. I considered at first that Ankita might be conflicted in her approach but unlike the conflicted participants she is clear in her decision not to represent the government and self-reflective about her constraint. For example, she referred to her own 'unconscious bias' where she might not be an effective advocate for the government because she wouldn't be 'passionately' fighting for them. She expressed her decision not to apply to be on a government panel because although the work would be 'interesting' she couldn't do the work 'from the other side ... that was just not something I could do'. It appeared that Ankita had thoughtfully weighed the possibilities available and made a decision about which 'side' to be on, albeit a constrained one.

Another barrister, Gail, similarly described a practice working mostly for claimants and against the government but was constrained in the sense that she also wanted to describe the importance of acting for corporations or arms of government in educating them about their human rights obligations: 'you know, I advised a bank recently about their obligations under the Equality Act. And they were just desperately anxious that they might be directly discriminating against their customers (Gail)'. This was replicated in other aspects of her narrative where she described favouring alternative dispute resolution over contested litigation:

> Um, but I think in public law the sort of, the absolutely confrontational approach to litigation doesn't always work. It's much more nuanced than that (Gail).

Another legal aid solicitor cited recent cuts to legal aid as a factor in not ruling out working for an arm of the government in future:

> Jacqueline: Would you ever work for a local authority?
>
> Rihana: I've always been against it and always thought, no, they're the other side. They're the opposition. I don't know … you could be the one who goes in there and be the one to make that change … I think if I was faced with not being able to work in legal aid practice anymore because I simply couldn't get the work then it would be a consideration. You know, I still need to live, pay my mortgage, family. But this is where my heart is first and foremost.

The 'us and them' in Rihana's narrative here relates to so frequently taking cases against local authorities ('they're the opposition'). Her suggestion that she might move to work there raises interesting questions. If Rihana chose this course as a result of pressures on legal aid practice, is it still likely she would be socially or professionally viewed as someone who subscribed to progressive values? The narratives reveal that the value judgments that progressive lawyers place upon *each other* are perhaps as stringent as those they impose upon themselves and may well perpetuate exclusivity. Indeed, as Andrea illustrates above, taking a neutral or balanced approach or working for 'the other side' is negatively perceived by more resolute practitioners and contrary to the 'fight' for justice.

One participant, Ben, conveyed perhaps the clearest constraint in his narrative. As I described in chapter three, he expressed lament at the end of our interview about having to put his communist politics to the side in order to pursue his legal career. He felt that strong political affiliations would not have been helpful to his clients throughout his career. This same sense of constraint is replicated in his ethical decision-making:

> Jacqueline: What would you say your approach is?
>
> Ben: Well I think you know [pause] I think it's about being respectful of the decisions you're trying to challenge. The organisations accepting that government lawyers are trying to do their job and they're not, you know, the sort of guardians of evil.

Ben, like Gail, described favouring negotiation if possible and took an understanding approach to the pressured job of government lawyers and to, some extent, moved slightly beyond the otherness of the 'us and them' construction to positioning himself to where he could appreciate they were 'trying to do their job'. Unlike the resolute decision makers who expressed quick criticism of the government and corporate bodies and their decisions, Ben wants to point out that they're not 'guardians of evil' and tries to have a more nuanced in his perspective, despite having a practice that is almost exclusively made up of challenging the state by way of judicial review.

CONFLICT AND CONTESTATION

The participants who fall into this category presented as being the most conflicted about their ethical decisions and the majority of the group were barristers rather than solicitors. Interactions with these participants also tended to create the most conflict in the interviews themselves with participants often becoming uncomfortable or even frustrated with the subject matter. This was clear in my encounter with Dominic towards the end of my fieldwork. Dominic is a senior barrister and when I asked him if he would ever represent the government he said in resolute terms: 'I don't represent the government because they would never instruct me.' I immediately sensed the tone of the interview changing and Dominic became a little defensive: 'Is there any reason why I wouldn't be good representing the government or police officers? Of course not. In fact I've had many cases where those on the other side say why haven't we got a lawyer like him?' Dominic continued to assert that the government doesn't instruct him because 'they never even ask'. After some further discussion he said curtly: 'the short answer is the cab rank rule something that's an issue in my professional life – no. I'm just never instructed by the government'. He was at such great pains to assert that the cab rank rule simply wasn't 'an issue' that I was intrigued and pressed a little further:

> Jacqueline: That's interesting, I do hear that a lot from some barristers. But there are others who are a bit more up front …
>
> Dominic: The whole thing is about perceived equality. You have to get yourself on government lists if you want to do the treasury work[28] and apply for treasury panel. Nah, life is too short
>
> Jacqueline: I'm not sure what you're saying. Would you want to be on the list?
>
> Dominic: Well okay then [pause] fine, if you're going to press me. You know what? I let my politics speak through the work that I do. And I've always been like that. If you're asking me a direct question about the cab-rank rule, I've got no desire to represent state agents.

[28] Treasury counsel are appointed by the Attorney General to advise on and conduct important and complex cases on behalf of the Crown Prosecution Service. There is a 'panel' of barristers routinely used by the government in this regard.

Dominic sought to rely on conflict of interest as a reason for not acting on behalf of the government. However, I was asking a hypothetical 'would you ever?' question that he found understandably difficult to answer. He went on to indicate that the reason was more about how time consuming it was to go through the process of getting instructed ('Nah, life is too short'). This still seemed inconsistent and while pressing the issue was perhaps uncomfortable for us both, it revealed important fluctuation between a resolute approach and a position that excuses the ethical tension created by that very approach. Ultimately, Dominic rests on his politics as the justification here: 'I let my politics speak through my work' and then becomes extremely firm in his desire not to represent 'state agents'. Dominic intimates that conflict of interest is the reason he is not being instructed by the government but appears conflicted in how he presents his decision-making. In the end, his own construction of the issue seemingly *puts* him in conflict with the cab rank rule.

I had a similar encounter with another barrister who has been in progressive legal practice for more than four decades. Over the course of his career Aidan has been committed to a number of high profile causes and achieved transformative results through his litigation, with many cases resulting in legislative change. The conflict in Aidan's narrative is replicated by some conflict around the role of politics in his professional life. While he is not party political, and quickly seeks to distinguish himself from other party political colleagues, he holds several causes very close and has used his legal practice as a means of remedying the injustice of those causes in clear terms. So on the one hand he is at pains to describe himself as neutral but with qualifications: 'I'm conventional but humanitarian'. When I asked him whether he would describe himself as an activist lawyer he began to stumble:

> I, well, look … against [redacted cause] yes. I think I would say um my opposition to it was very deep and, and, and you know, I thought it was wrong. I hope I never came to blows with the other side [laughs] or with the judges. But you know I felt it much more deeply (Aidan).

I listened to this section of the interview several times and was struck by how much the tone began to shift. There is a nervous laughter as he describes an awareness of how other lawyers and judges might perceive his activism. He went on in this passage to describe several other areas of activism where he was engaged in using the law as a tool for change[29] and references his own experience of a movement: 'I felt part of a movement towards the improvement of [human rights] and there were lots of like-minded people working in that direction'. Like many of the *resolute* decision makers Aidan begins to situate his response to the interaction of law and politics in his professional life with reference to other

[29] To preserve anonymity I am not replicating the specific areas of law in full but they are all broadly related to human rights.

barrister-campaigners through close interactions in the context of his Chambers community. However, he notes:

> [pause] But I've never had a very coherent political philosophy. I mean human rights has been my passion and um and I follow that but you know, colleagues of mine like [politically active barrister] have a big need to put that in a wider context. They had a wider perspective than myself. Uh, uh, there's something to be said for both attitudes (Aidan).

Aidan is keen to ensure that he is *seen* as different to radical and resolute barristers and in terms of his presentation of self this may well be the case. However, while not party political his attachment to particular causes clearly demonstrates that political choices have been made in his career; and that these choices have had a remarkable impact on the causes he has pursued. The hesitation and nervous laughter around his *positioning* reveals conflict as he finds it difficult to make sense of some of his work in the past without compromising the neutral presentation of self to which he seems so attached.

This became clear when we touched in more detail on the cab rank rule. He said quite resolutely that 'certainly, yes' he does 'believe' in the cab rank rule and like Dominic turned his response very quickly to the fact that governments don't instruct him due to conflict:

> No, I do believe in the cab rank principle. It so happens that governments don't often ask me to act for them. But I've never said no on ideological grounds. I've sometimes been too busy or conflicted in a sense that I was so involved in a series of cases that were going the other way (Aidan).

It seemed to me strange that Aidan would respond in very clear terms that he would 'never' say no to a case on ideological grounds given his passionate opposition to particular injustices, which could arguably be undone by accepting instructions on the other side of the cause to which he has been committed for so long. When we probed this further the tone of the interview shifted and he conceded there was 'one line he would draw' and that he didn't think you should have to act in a case internationally 'to the extent that you have to do something that your own society doesn't countenance'. In fact, the exception Aidan envisages is not built into the exceptions to the cab rule in plain terms.[30] A barrister can refuse instructions where accepting them would require you to do *foreign work* or act for a *foreign lawyer*, but it does not seem that this is designed to cover refusing cases on moral grounds. In fact, the rule is designed to achieve the opposite. A barrister appearing in another jurisdiction would be bound by the ethical rules of that jurisdiction and it is interesting to note that Aidan, like many other barristers in the field of human rights, has been called to the Bar by several other jurisdictions that also have the cab rank rule, or a version of it, in

[30] Bar Standards Board (n 11) Rule 30.

place. When I further asked Aidan about whether he would accept instructions generally to prosecute in a case rather than defend he said:

> I would do it, I mean you know I, I've never been asked. Well that's not entirely true, I have been asked occasionally (Aidan).

There was again some conflict here around whether had been asked or refused instructions. He was again at pains to stress any refusal would not have been on ideological grounds and that he was either 'too busy' or 'involved in cases going the other way':

> I mean I haven't got any ultimate opposition to prosecuting and I've always made it clear to the CPS I would. I did just the other day get approached but I'd already consulted with someone in Chambers about the other side of the case so I couldn't take it (Aidan).

Aidan again appears conflicted as he is quick to point out the justifications for not being able to take the case. Like Kenneth, looking back over a long career (four decades) he struggles to think of examples of when he has acted on the 'other' side a matter. This is of course common, barristers develop their careers in certain specialisms, and it has been argued this makes it easier for cause lawyers to have a human rights career at the Bar (rather than as a solicitor) given that they often achieve 'iconic status' in so doing.[31] Flood and Hviid raise the point that the cab rank rule means that barristers in theory have to accept instructions regardless of the morality of the outcome the client desires and they should not be 'unrealistically barred from choosing clients'.[32] Aidan's story reveals he has dedicated his professional life to many progressive causes and to fighting for victims and claimants throughout. While his decisions to refuse instructions might not be in strict breach of the cab rank rule (for example, he cites conflict of interest and capacity issues) his narrative as a whole reveals a strong sense of morality that has guided his career and his decisions.[33] The prevalence of that morality seemed hard at times for him to reconcile with the neutral presentation of self he so desires, and his collective identity in the space in seeks to occupy within his progressive networks.

Another barrister in the study qualified in the 1970s and who was a member of a radical set of Chambers revealed a similarly conflicted narrative. Gideon was by far the most upfront about ethical conflict in his work and, in fact, of all the participants in the study Gideon's story was most strongly characterised by conflict in different ways. Looking back, there was an acute sense of distance between him and his career and the people he had worked so closely with for so

[31] Boon (n 1) 152.

[32] John Flood and Morten Hviid, *The Cab Rank Rule: Its Meaning and Purpose in the New Legal Services Market* (Legal Services Board, 2013) 39.

[33] See, eg, Fran Webber, 'Ian Macdonald QC 1939–2019: A Tribute' (2020) 82 *Socialist Lawyer* 20.

long and also with some of the earlier ethical choices he had made. For example, looking back on his radical set of Chambers he said all the members were 'signed up to the values':

> Jacqueline: Did you have a particular approach in terms of who you represented?
>
> Gideon: Absolutely, oh yeah. A particular side.
>
> Jacqueline: Did the Bar Council ever object to that?
>
> Gideon: They didn't want to touch us. They were probably right in thinking it wouldn't last long. Can you imagine the headlines though? 'Bar Council investigates barristers who only act for the poor.' It wouldn't have looked good.

At first, his position seemed quite resolute and assured. When I pressed Gideon on which 'particular side' he took he was quite clear and his position was reminiscent of the constructions of law centre solicitors outlined in chapter three: 'you know basically we were acting for those who were the least resourced by the law substantively and procedurally'. While Gideon's position appeared resolute I knew that he had later developed a considerable practice working on behalf of local authorities and so asked him about how this developed:

> Jacqueline: You began to act for local authorities?
>
> Gideon: We were only acting for local authorities that we deemed to be acting in the interests of the tenants.
>
> Jacqueline: What would happen if you were instructed by ….
>
> Gideon: Well that was the thing. It became untenable [pause]. Look, there was a very well-known barrister in housing. He was very highly regarded for the tenants and the homeless but I knew he had a quite large paper practice acting for local authorities. It was hypocritical. These things don't hold. They don't last if you're working for a system that has certain in built things.

Gideon's conflicted position began to emerge at this point in our encounter. While he has spent so many years working on 'a particular side' he described that it became 'untenable' to maintain that position. I note with interest that in order to make his point Gideon refers to another progressive practitioner from what he described as a 'radical' set of Chambers and references *their* conflict. He understands his own choices and decisions in relation to another barrister that he thought made more objectionable choices. He concludes with turning back again to what appears to be another resolute statement that 'these things don't hold' if you're 'working in a system has certain in built things'. As such, Gideon moves back and forth between resolution and conflict in his constructions of ethical decision-making. He expresses this in terms of an idealistic vision and a realistic choice. Unlike Aidan, he doesn't relate feeling bound by the cab rank rule itself ('we broke all the rules'). The contestation here rather arises from the distance between the quite opposite resolute positions he takes that are in conflict with one another, and his own values, which he articulates as being in conflict with 'the system' itself.

CONCLUSIONS

I have outlined in this chapter three types of approaches to ethical decision-making that aim to develop our understanding of cause lawyering and legal ethics. My focus has been on how lawyers frame and construct these ethical decisions within and across their networks. Consistent with Boon's observations on the 'cold climate' for cause lawyering in the UK[34] the exploration of ethical decision-making reveals some uncomfortable positions for lawyers in the study. It is clear however, first, that participants seek to delineate, negotiate and understand their ethical choices about client representation consistently with how they construct themselves as progressive lawyers. They take their ethical cues from other lawyers within their networks and practice settings[35] or otherwise by comparison to 'other' lawyers. Where they adopt a divergent approach they often make sense of so doing with reference to other progressive lawyers. Barrister-campaigners do so mostly with reference to other barristers, although solicitors tend to relate to other practitioners within and across several network nodes including barrister-campaigners. This demonstrates the ways in which the networked identification of progressive lawyering itself provides a frame that shapes their understanding of ethical decision-making. Secondly, participants all tended to relate their decisions as being on moral terms related to power imbalance or commitment to particular human rights causes. For some, consistent with the cause lawyering literature, this is described as being a higher moral purpose than that of 'other' lawyers. Thirdly, progressive lawyers reveal three interrelated responses to ethical decision-making: *resolute*, *constrained* and *conflicted*. These responses are linked by participants to their values and to their relationships with one another, which points to their social significance.

It is clear that progressive lawyers have a heightened awareness of the relationship between politics and their professional selves. They negotiate and relate their decision making against the backdrop of the requirements of the rules on lawyer neutrality and independence, whether they described upholding them or not.[36] This was especially the case for the *conflicted* participants in the study, who tended to be self-employed barrister-campaigners, and conveyed contestation and conflict between strongly held values, on the one hand, and the requirements of neutrality inherent in professional ethical rules on the other.

[34] Boon (n 1).

[35] Lynn Mather and Leslie Levin, 'Why Context Matters' in Levin and Mather (n 1) 4.

[36] In this respect I note however that this chapter has not been concerned with whether participants *in fact* uphold or breach ethical rules but rather their constructions of so doing and how these are socially and collectively framed.

8

Sustaining Progressive Lawyering

> If there's any chance I will keep going and, you know, the best wins take the longest and … the best, I think the best lawyers don't give up. (Phil)

> This work needs to be done. But this work can only be done if you have a heart for it. You can't be a progressive lawyer if you don't have a passion for it. The hours are long, the money isn't as lucrative but it's really satisfying work. If an individual really has a passion for social justice and being able to change the law because that's we do. The changes impact not a few but many. (Dominic)

THIS CHAPTER EXPLORES the challenges to progressive practice, as perceived by participants in the study, in order to outline the ways in which their collective identity might make a difference to how their work can be sustained in future. Throughout my fieldwork participants tended to outline challenges to progressive lawyering while at the same time the means by which they thought those challenges could be overcome. A number of key themes are drawn out from my analysis across different subsets of practice, some of which are encapsulated by Dominic above who stresses that the 'work needs to be done' in the future by those who have 'a heart' and 'a passion' for it. In this chapter my focus rests in resource because participants tended to describe the future of the profession in terms of the resource needed to sustain it. These different types of resource are socially constructed and participants assume that the terms they use, whether it was passion, commitment, knowledge or funding are mutually understood and collectively accepted to be under threat. In this chapter I outline and analyse the separate but interrelated resource issues raised. These are, first, funding as a constraining feature for the future of progressive practice but also a threat to widening access to the profession. Secondly, maintaining what participants describe as passion for the work notwithstanding difficult and constrained circumstances. This passion relates to persistence in order to persevere and 'fight' on behalf of clients but also for long-term commitment to the causes of access to justice and human rights in order to make an impact. Thirdly, an urgent perceived need to pass on knowledge, which relates to sharing experience and expertise with the next generation of progressive lawyers and also to mentorship in the form of support and guidance. Finally, with respect to barrister-campaigners in the study, the theme of 'excellence' arose and is considered in this chapter in terms of how it might be balanced with the perceived importance of a commitment to human rights and progressive values. My aim in this chapter is to analyse each of these themes in turn, and to consider how they relate to issues of social mobility and access to the profession, in order to interrogate how participants collectively hope to sustain progressive lawyering networks in future.

A further overarching theme in this chapter is emotion management. The resource issues that participants relate to sustaining the future of the profession often facilitated storytelling about the risk of burnout for progressive lawyers. This was especially so for legal aid and law centre participants in the study who described the emotional labour of working directly with vulnerable client groups in response to the question of the 'qualities' needed to do the job. Research encounters often involved powerful interplay between, on the one hand, emotion management working with vulnerable clients: '… it's really depressing' (Ruth); '… it's super tough' (Eve), and on the other emotion related to anger provoked by injustice: 'I think I can feel emotional in the sense that I can feel very angry about things, very strongly about things' (Ben). Emotion management[1] is relevant to 'conscious' lawyering,[2] as well as professional resilience.[3] In this chapter I explore narratives in the study that relate to maintaining the strength of network ties that are central to Diani's conception of social movements.[4] In view of the perceived negative impact of resource constraints on the profession in future, a continuing shared belief in being able to make a difference appears key. Where this efficacy is challenged, I have observed how collective identity evolves to accommodate that challenge. Emotion has a defining role to play in this context as participants tended to reveal their perspective on sustaining group identity in ways that were primarily emotionally driven. This is especially clear in perceptions of the importance of passion and persistence to progressive legal practice but also features in narratives of funding limitations and constraints to legal service provision.

FUNDING AND BURNOUT

> I wake up early and I worry about where the money is coming from. (Rodrigo)

The austerity narrative discussed in chapter four again dominated encounters with participants on the future of the profession. This was often relayed with a pervasive sense that the future of progressive legal practice is under threat due to funding constraints. By comparison, participants from the 1970s, 1980s and

[1] Arlie Hochschild, *The Managed Heart: Commercialization of Human Feeling* (University of California Press, 1983).

[2] Gerald Lopez, *Rebellious Lawyering: One Chicano's Vision of Progressive Law Practice* (Westview Press, 1992); Gerald Lopez, 'Living and Lawyering Rebelliously' (2005) 73 *Fordham Law Review* 2041.

[3] Sharon Bolton, *Emotion Management in the Workplace* (Palgrave MacMillan, 2005).

[4] Mario Diani, 'The Concept of a Social Movement' (1992) 40(1) *Sociological Review* 13.

1990s talked wistfully of days when legal aid was more readily available. There was a 'high point' (Rodrigo) up to the early 1990s in particular when market rates and payment on account for legal aid fees facilitated much easier working practices. The availability of legal aid funding in earlier decades of the study also rested within a more positive cultural acceptance of legal aid lawyers and their work. For early law centre lawyers, similar to the neighbourhood law centre in the US which were lawyer centric and expanded, to a degree, the notion of the lawyer as statesman,[5] lawyers reflected that their work in earlier years of the study was culturally perceived as more valuable evidenced, for example, by the more expansive local authority and community support as well as adequate remuneration for services.

In discussions about the future of progressive practice participants had an acute sense of how they are perceived in wider culture and this was often linked to funding and remuneration. Progressive lawyering both processes the public sphere in which it rests while at the same time trying to assert itself upon it.[6] However, as I outlined in chapters two and five, this has led to backlash, both in government decision-making and in the public domain, which is also perceived as a continuing threat. Scathing portrayals of lawyers have pervaded the UK national public sphere since the late 1990s and have often been directed towards legal aid and left-wing lawyers.[7] Again the interplay with legal aid is pertinent given that over the past 40 years successive governments have prayed in aid of the notion of the 'fat cat legal aid lawyer' to curtail legal aid provision. For example, in 1999 the then Home Secretary Jack Straw took objection to legal challenges to anti-social and exclusion orders and responded by attacking 'so called civil liberties' lawyers at an annual conference of the Police Superintendents Association, saying they were 'hypocritical', 'well-heeled' and living in 'prosperous neighbourhoods':

> I'm pretty angry about this … [t]hese people who represent the perpetrators of crime and then get into their BMWs and drive off into areas where they are immune from much of the crime.[8]

By 2001 annual lists of the highest earning legal aid lawyers began to be published later attracting headlines such as '£15m for Just One Firm on The Legal Aid Gravy Train'.[9] During the most recent wave of legal aid cuts in 2012 these trends

[5] Louise Trubeck, 'Public Interest Law: Facing The Problems of Maturity' (2011) 33 *University of Arkansas Law Review* 432.

[6] Hank Johnston and Bert Klandermans, 'The Cultural Analysis of Social Movements' in Hank Johnston and Klandermans (eds), *Social Movements and Culture* (Routledge, 2003) 5.

[7] Richard Maiman, 'They All Have Different Policies so of Course They Have to Give Difference News' in Austin Sarat and Stuart Scheingold (eds), *The Cultural Lives of Cause Lawyers* (Cambridge University Press, 2008) 141.

[8] Jason Bennetto, 'Hypocrite lawyers are attacked by Straw' (*The Independent*, 15 September 1999).

[9] James Chapman, '£15m for Just One Firm on the Legal Aid Gravy Train: Scale of Taxpayers Bill Revealed as Coalition Vows to Save £200m' (*Daily Mail*, 4 June 2013).

continued. While the then Lord Chancellor accused lawyers of being hypocritical for bemoaning their salaries, many junior barristers and solicitors faced an uphill struggle in countering the public notion that they were well off.[10] A plea has been made for the government to change the propagated line from 'fat cats' to one of legal aid lawyers working as public servants.[11] A 2018 book written by a whistleblowing barrister entitled *Stories of Law and How it is Broken* aimed to shed light on a criminal justice system at breaking point[12] and, far from being 'fat-cats', described the unprecedented pressures faced by lawyers working within a broken system: '[I] consider what I do on a day to day basis to be not just a privilege but a civic responsibility. And it is for the same reasons that the current state of our criminal justice system should terrify us'.[13] These observations have been made frequently in many other areas of law, with the retiring President of the Family Division recently lamenting: 'Anybody who thinks we currently have a network of courts which enables access to justice is deluding themselves'.[14]

As I have outlined, for lawyers in the study working in legal aid the lack of funding is a particularly pressing issue. When I asked legal aid law firm solicitors what the greatest challenge was in their work they *all* responded with either the cuts to legal aid or the stress and frustration of working with the Legal Aid Agency: '[It]can be just so frustrating. You can get really angry with the legal aid agency' (Ellie). I explored several of these narratives in chapter four but here I highlight the circumstances of two participants who hold senior positions in legal aid firms and the challenges they describe. I have selected them because they have both been working in legal aid for several decades. They have a wide perspective based on many years recruiting new lawyers into their firms and convey a sense of responsibility for the wellbeing of their staff. Rodrigo, for example, has had a varied career working in London both as a solicitor for three decades and also campaigning around access to justice issues. He seemed upbeat in our interview and I spent several hours with him talking about the twists and turns of his career, and valuing his openness and willingness to share stories from his past. We were coming to the end of the interview and he had described recent developments in his firm's work, including the contracts they hold in areas where legal aid is still available that also facilitate judicial review

[10] Harriet Williams, 'The Myth of Fat Cat Barristers' (*New Statesman*, 18 May 2012).

[11] Martha Spurrier, 'Address to the Young Legal Aid Lawyers Association' (23 April 2015).

[12] A Public Accounts Select Committee Report published in May 2016 described the criminal justice system as 'bedevilled by long standing poor performance including delays and inefficiencies, and costs are being shunted from one part of the system to another' concluding that it was 'close to breaking point': Public Accounts Select Committee, *Efficiency in the Criminal Justice System* (HMSO, May 2016) available at https://publications.parliament.uk/pa/cm201617/cmselect/cmpubacc/72/7202.htm.

[13] The Secret Barrister, *Stories of Law and How It's Broken* (Picador, 2018) 5.

[14] James Grierson, 'Access to Justice in Family Courts Inadequate' (*The Guardian*, 27 July 2018).

challenges. The exchange below outlines well my own mistaken assumption about Rodrigo's positivity around the substance of his work, and his passion for it, being somehow linked to sustainability:

> Jacqueline: You do seem a bit more positive than some legal aid lawyers – that's just the impression I'm getting – of the current climate, and I'm wondering is it because you know, you've done well to keep good contracts, perhaps it's not quite as precarious as where others might be at?
>
> Rodrigo: I think it is precarious.
>
> Jacqueline: Do you still think it's precarious?
>
> Rodrigo: Oh, yeah [pause]
>
> Jacqueline: Even having those contracts that you've got left, it's still …?
>
> Rodrigo: Oh, yes, the, the cash flow is very, very difficult, um, and so, I mean, there are times when I've had, not quite sleepless nights, but I wake up early and I worry about where the money is coming from.

I recall this coming somewhat as a surprise given how positive and effusive Rodrigo had been about his work. Nonetheless the interview then turned to the importance of legal aid work and Rodrigo revisited what motivated him ('legal aid … that's you know, I mean that's what inspires me'). Despite the resource constraints and the twists and turns his career had taken, working in legal aid service provision had remained constant throughout the decades alongside a commitment to public services generally ('commitment to the welfare state, commitment to legal rights, to welfare benefits, to legal aid and to public services'). It was this commitment to public service that he wanted to instil in the next generation of lawyers despite how 'precarious' the future might be for legal aid.

Phil also stressed looking back over his career that he had felt 'valued in society' but noted by comparison 'it's plummeted since then' (the 1990s). He described making a 'reasonable living' before, and similar to Rodrigo, there was a stark contrast to today's legal practice where he has faced challenges. Phil drew attention to the fact that legal aid law firms are businesses that 'have to make a profit' and made a distinction several times with law centres:

> A charity gets 25–30% top up on legal aid rates from charitable donations. We don't get that. We have to … I have to pay the bills in this office without charitable donations. It's not a law centre (Phil).

Similar to my encounter with Rodrigo the natural flow of the interview seemed to slow at this point and while touching on resource pressure Phil paused and said: 'I've had to re-mortgage my house in the last two years to stop myself from going bankrupt and keep the place going.' Even against this backdrop however, just as Rodrigo pointed to the importance of a commitment to legal aid and public service, here too Phil turned to stressing the importance of 'commitment' and commented that 'fighting for the rights of clients … that's what sustains me'. When I asked Phil whether what motivated him into his career in legal aid is also what keeps him in it he said 'absolutely, 100% yes'. He stressed that he tries to select lawyers with a commitment to these same core values of the firm, commenting that it is important to 'get them to events that support that culture … you make [new lawyers] aware of it'. Phil also saw it as his job to keep more junior lawyers and trainees motivated because 'we need to be upbeat, we need to shield the rest of them … our job is to take the shit and keep smiling'. He saw the need to maintain interest in the profession in order 'to keep renewing it … to bring new blood in and to keep the standards up'.

It would seem therefore that notwithstanding the funding constraints and the anger, dismay and exasperation intimated as a result of legal aid cuts, motivating others ('new blood') into the profession and maintaining a commitment to its values is a key priority for Rodrigo and Phil. The motivation of lawyers is seen as being instrumental to upholding a collective sense of empowerment and is in itself another important resource that is needed in order to sustain the profession. Indeed, there has been concern about the lack of newly qualified solicitors coming through[15] with, for example, the youngest solicitors in some geographic areas of criminal legal aid work being in their 50s and certain areas of law being particularly difficult to recruit in and expertise is at risk of being lost, this is especially so for finding contract supervisors who oversee legal aid contracts.[16] Ruth, another legal aid law firm lawyer, had described the legal aid cuts as being 'galvanising' on the one hand but she also expressed her concern for the future because of a lack of legal aid resource in terms of funding new jobs:

> Jacqueline: So at the [Legal Action Group] conference did it feel galvanizing, like what you've described?
>
> Ruth: A little bit. But it gets harder each year. The conferences get smaller. The age groups, like I'm probably one of the youngest and I'm 35. Other than the students, which is really encouraging but the problem is where are they going to go? How are they going to get into our work?

The problem of resource was not confined to solicitors but was also expressed as a concern by barristers in the study and particularly those working in criminal law. One barrister, Aidan, commented on the 'sacrifices' that junior members of his Chambers have to make to do the work and compared it to when he started his career in the 1970s:

> I think there still a massive amount of incredibly dedicated people doing that kind of work in a much, much more difficult financial situation than we were in you know. Who really you know make sacrifices to do that sort of work. Young people in this Chambers, one has to take one's hat off you know. They're doing it in a much more difficult environment, yeah (Aidan).

[15] Owen Bowcott, 'Criminal defence solicitors may be extinct in five years' (*The Guardian*, 17 April 2018).

[16] Natalie Byrom, *The Impact of Cuts to Civil Legal Aid on Practitioners and Their Clients* (Warwick Centre for Human Rights, 2013).

Another barrister-campaigner, Dominic, resolutely said that the biggest challenge in his work was 'funding … it just depresses me' and when I pressed further and asked him whether the lack of funding affected his morale:

> Of course it does. The work remains the same and the importance of the work remains the same but you are so underpaid and the work you do is so stressful compared to your opponents you can't help but think that's so unfair (Dominic).

Several barristers described moving into other areas of work in order to maintain financial stability: 'I'm now moving into international work, I use the well-paid international work to fund the other work I do' (Dominic), 'You have to find ways to specialise' (Michael). One barrister in the study had in fact left the profession by the time of the interview. Like Dominic, she connected the low remuneration for her criminal legal aid work to a sense of not feeling valued and to low morale. She told a story about listening to Chris Grayling[17] on the radio and feeling an acute lack of respect towards barristers and for her work:

> Chris Grayling was making cuts. Our Chambers had to move, we downsized massively so I was working from home and I was listening to the news on all the time and what Chris Grayling was saying. I thought you're breaking spirits. I felt I got to the point where I was like I know what I'm doing is really valuable but you [Chris Grayling] just don't see it. Everything you were brought up with, the way Mum and Dad brought me up led to me being called to the Bar. It isn't just a qualification, it's a whole person (Jemma).

The link to identity is especially clear here. Jemma conveys that she felt personally attacked by the rhetoric around the cuts and by the low regard placed on legal aid criminal defence work in particular. She connected her work to her values, her family and her sense of self. When we discussed the possibility of moving into other areas she said it simply wasn't where her passion lay: 'I'm just not going to argue about car accidents'. She described feeling constrained by the long hours and poor pay ('It was so horrible, I was so miserable') and ultimately connected the low value placed on her work in the public sphere to her own sense of low morale and dissatisfaction. I noted with interest how Jemma's sense of self-worth changed over time: having said in her story above that *she* knew the work she was doing was valuable at the time she then described becoming ultimately worn down by the dominant narrative and perceived poor rates of pay: 'If you don't feel like you're respected for what you're doing and you're not properly remunerated then you don't value your role as well. You don't value yourself.' Jemma's story was emotionally laden both in recalling her time as a criminal barrister and her dedication to clients and then in her ultimate disappointment in leaving the profession. She described burnout ('At the Bar, you don't look after yourself emotionally and physically') and links her own sense of

[17] Secretary of State for Justice (and the first non-lawyer Lord Chancellor) from 2012 to 2015 who had oversight of the implementation of legal aid reforms under LASPO 2012.

low self-esteem to the lack of value placed on her work in wider culture, despite having developed an early passion for it so closely linked to her own values. She said she still 'thinks about cases everyday' but went on to describe a remarkable transformation since having left: 'I have an allotment now … I swim in the sea. I know myself. I actually live'.

This story is not uncommon and is in fact reminiscent of Sommerlad's study of political legal aid lawyers outlined in chapter two, which found that the new public management delivery of services led to pressure and low morale.[18] In the context of this study, Jemma's experience raises questions for a network that relies so heavily on shared belief and solidarity. Jemma no longer believed in her work because she felt acute pressure and that she was being poorly remunerated for a demanding and emotionally draining job in a wider culture that didn't value her work. Similar to Rodrigo and Phil the professional constraints had personal consequences: 'I was so miserable' (Jemma), 'I've had to re-mortgage my house in the last two years …' (Phil), 'I wake up early and I wonder where the money is coming from' (Rodrigo). Ruth, a legal aid solicitor, also commented that she could 'understand why so many people have left' the profession saying that 'it's hard enough fighting for clients' without the additional 'hurdle' of fighting for legal aid. While this is common in many public service professions[19] arguably few collectively demand at the same time the level of 'passion' and 'fight' of progressive lawyering notwithstanding difficult circumstances, as evidenced by the austerity narrative of the study. One cause lawyering study in fact demonstrates a greater likelihood of longevity for lawyers where they demonstrated mixed motives (ie, commitment to the cause while also seeking financial reward) whereas those with pure 'cause' commitments were more likely to experience burnout.[20] The interplay between the key themes of funding and passion explored in this chapter is clear: at a time of constrained resource maintaining passion for the job is both a necessity and challenge to the future of progressive lawyering.

PASSION AND PERSISTENCE

> You can't be a progressive lawyer if you don't have a passion for it … you've got to persevere. (Ruth)

The stories of research participants tended to end where they had begun. As I outlined in chapter four, participants began their stories with why they chose a

[18] Hilary Sommerlad, 'I've Lost The Plot: An Everyday Story of the Political Legal Aid Lawyer' (2001) 28(3) *Journal of Law and Society* 335, 337.

[19] Jermaine Ravalier et al, 'Public Service Stress and Burnout Over Twelve Months' (2014) 64 *Journal of Occupational Medicine* 521.

[20] Ronen Shamir and Sara Chinsky, 'Destruction of House and Construction of a Cause: Lawyers and Bedouins in the Israeli Courts' in Austin Sarat and Stuart Scheingold (eds), *Cause Lawyering: Political Commitments and Professional Responsibilities* (Oxford University Press, 1998) 227.

path to law and connected this to their own values, which were often relayed in passionate and emotionally driven language. At the end of interviews we would reflect on the future and, as I have described above, would usually finish the interview by discussing the qualities needed to sustain practice in years to come. Here too, values underpinned by emotion featured strongly and participants often turned to their own sense of caring, believing and valuing the work they do. As I set out in the research methodology in chapter three, for the majority of study participants the interview encounter formed a sense-making exercise where they seemed to appreciate the opportunity to remember why they turned to law in the first place. In this section I will first explore how participants collectively connected the need for the next generation to evidence passion for progressive lawyering to their *own* values and belief in their work rather than monetary gain. Secondly, I outline the challenge of emotion management and the risk of burnout in order to explore the tension between needing to 'really care' about progressive legal work and the risk of caring too much.

I note first that passion for the work is linked to network ties.[21] Participants often interchangeably stressed feeling a strong connection to the value of the work and also to the network of people they work with. Rodrigo articulated this as follows: 'I'd always lived on the basis that I really loved what I was doing, I'd, I'd come back from holiday and I might go into the office before I needed to just to see what was going on and, meet my friends …' Lawyers express wanting to see new entrants also connecting to their network, which tends to blur professional and personal life. Andrea also described how at the heart of the network is a sense of simply identifying and relating to one another, referencing the dominant turning point away from corporate law:

> Jacqueline: What do you think is at the heart of that network?
>
> Andrea: I think it's because we're all very like-minded people. If we wanted to make big bucks none of us would be doing legal aid. We'd be in big glass buildings.

Andrea hints here at the expectation that new entrants to the profession should be similarly motivated. Law centre lawyer Ruth described having work experience students in her office and being primarily concerned with their motivation. Here too, we see the connection between a progressive lawyer's turn from the financial incentives of corporate law and a desire to see this same turn, or an awareness of it, in others:

> When [they] ask me whether I'd recommend a career in this type of work I say every single time, I say it depends on what your motivation is. What are you motivated by? If you're motivated by money a career in social welfare law is not for you. If you're motivated by a desire to help people and actually make a difference and not to add zeros to your bank balance then it is something you should consider (Ruth).

[21] Jeffrey Goodwin and James Jasper, 'Emotions and Social Movements' in Jan Stets and Jonathan Turner, *Handbook of the Sociology of Emotions* (Springer, 2006) 611.

Many other participants across subsets of practice related a similar desire to see passion for the work alongside a lack of being motivated by financial incentives: '... you just have to really care' (Dominic), 'you have to really want it' (Ruth), '[I would say] don't do it unless you really care but don't kid yourself ... you'll have to make big sacrifices and you'll find you're not financially compensated for those sacrifices' (Phil), 'you have to be motivated not by money but by the work' (Rihana). For most participants the construction of this motivation is rooted in their own experience. Ankita described moving from private practice into the charity sector:

> Jacqueline: So you're not motivated by money?
>
> Ankita: No, God no. Joking, no. I think I went down, uh, down to a third or less when I went to [redacted NGO].

Several participants also reflected on the tension between being passionate about the job and the need to manage one's emotions. I noticed it first at the beginning of several interviews in relation to the choice of areas of practice for participants who reflectively revealed an understanding of their own strengths but also their limitations with respect to emotion management. While their own values are seen as a positive influence and strength, both on behalf of themselves and in respect of others, there are limitations where the passion for a particular type of work might in fact stretch one's 'emotional threshold' (Gail). Both Gail and Jessica describe a turning point where they realised they were not emotionally resilient enough to pursue a career in asylum and immigration law. They wanted to pursue areas where they knew they could make a positive change within the constraints of the system and immigration law felt too hopeless:

> I think I had probably imagined when I went into it that I was going to be working much more directly with very vulnerable people but I think everyone has a kind of emotional threshold. I suppose it's partly based on your sense of empathy, your sense of resilience or you know your own personal background, how far you can actually put yourself out there for people (Gail).
>
> But I basically realised I didn't have the heart for it in reality. Because [sic] for those who are genuine it's just completely heart breaking. And for those who aren't genuine it's just incredibly frustrating and angry making (Jessica).

Progressive lawyers relate the need to believe you can make a difference but also the difficulty of maintaining that belief in difficult and often traumatic circumstances. For Gail and Jessica, reaching their 'emotional threshold' gave them an awareness of the types of work to which they felt most suited. Andrea works day to day with many grieving families and when I asked her what qualities she needed to keep doing the job she said:

> I think you need to be really empathetic. I think I'm a bit of an over empathiser which at the beginning made it a really tricky balance for me doing this job and at times has been really difficult (Andrea).

When I asked Andrea how she coped and managed this she reflected back on her own motivation and belief that she can 'make a difference'. I found it interesting that she drew a comparison with other professions that demand emotional labour. She expressly said she would rather be a lawyer than a social worker 'because you're completely on their side and you're fighting for them'. For Andrea, her way of coping with the emotion of the work was to keep 'fighting for tangible benefits'. Andrea's story had been particularly focussed on the 'fight' and 'challenge' of progressive lawyering and, like Jessica and Gail, a belief in the job is the means of coping with the emotional labour of the job: 'that is where I shift my focus when it's really depressing'. Likewise, when I asked Ben what the most important factor was in sustaining his practice he said that apart from resource it was 'achieving what the client wants to achieve' and 'never losing sight of that' no matter what the circumstances. Similarly, Rihana, another legal aid solicitor, commented when talking about the emotional labour of her cases: '[I]t's frustrating, don't get me wrong. It's stressful but I think it's getting results that sustains me'.

In terms of emotion management, how lawyers in the study seem to cope with trauma alongside maintaining passion for the work appears problematic. The 'fighting for tangible benefits' approach is a coping mechanism that acts as a distraction in order to get the job done but may well intensify emotional labour. Ellie, an early career legal aid lawyer, described similarly to Andrea as being 'empathetic' and said she has 'always found it easy to relate to people'. Ellie talked about wanting to do the job well because she doesn't like to let people down and continued by telling a story about a vulnerable client:

> I had another client who has serious mental health issues and the doctors just kept assessing her as absolutely fine. Um, I remember I got off the phone with the police and in the call I said 'she was found sweeping the road with a piece of bread, how can you say she's okay?' (Ellie)

When I probed Ellie further on this case I was struck by her response. She said that she was in the office and 'started crying' when she had put the phone down and how her colleagues had reacted:

> [E]veryone in my office just ran up to me and basically gave me a verbal slap. They said you can't get this upset about clients or you're going to burn yourself out. So since then I've maybe cried like twice about clients (Ellie).

Participants doing the most emotionally intensive work related a mentality of switching off, focussing on the job and getting results such that they might even receive a well-meaning 'verbal slap' from colleagues for failing to do so. I note that this was the case predominantly with law centre and legal aid solicitors. Phil similarly commented when I asked how he disengaged from the difficult circumstances of his clients: 'you don't really, you just build up scar tissue'. Eve said it was 'super tough' managing the emotional labour of her law centre role and lamented: 'sadly, the only way to manage it is to turn your brain off to it'.

The importance of emotional resilience for social justice lawyers has been explored elsewhere[22] and also in the context of clinical legal education.[23] It is acknowledged that emotional demands of working with vulnerable clients can lead to 'surface acting' by less experienced solicitors as a coping mechanism, which can in turn lead to stress and depression.[24] There is a difficult balance to be struck between being driven and passionate about client's cases in order to get results but also disconnecting one's emotions enough to cope.[25] In light of the narratives of this study it seems pertinent to question however whether the results orientated approach, that seemingly neglects emotional labour ('turn your brain off to it'), might in fact exacerbate rather than alleviate the problem of burnout in the long term.

The sense from the narratives is nonetheless that perseverance is key notwithstanding difficult circumstances. Participants tended to describe the importance of being passionate alongside the need to persevere and be determined in the job as a factor in sustaining their work and that of new entrants to the profession. There is no doubt that working at the same time to dismantle the system and also struggling to provide legal services *within* that system can be tiring and all consuming. My impression is that today's progressive lawyers create an *expectation* of the next generation that they will persevere against the odds where that is what they have done and continue to do: 'You've just got to persevere. You've got to keep at it.' (Ruth). Participants working in legal aid and law centres in particular, who have remained in those subsets of practice, were more likely to make appeals to the passion and perseverance needed in order to sustain one's career. There is a stark contrast therefore between the collective construction of these themes and the experience of burnout, as described for example by Jemma above. Another participant, Eve, who left her law centre position to work in another subset of practice intimated that the work had been emotionally draining and demanding:

> [T]he law centres are silly because they over work their staff and then you can't do it anymore. It's really sad. Three years previously they were social justice warriors but it tires them out and then you can't do it anymore (Eve).

Eve's repetition of 'you can't do it anymore' rests in personal experience and was expressed with some regret. Her own experience relates directly to sustaining the profession, and how the work of law centres in particular, face the risk

[22] Michael Kelly, *Lives of Lawyers Revisited* (University of Michigan Press, 2007).

[23] Colin James, 'Seeing things as we are: Emotional Intelligence and Clinical Legal Education (2005) 8 *International Journal of Clinical Legal Education* 123; Chalen Westaby, 'A Qualitative Study of the Impact of Law Clinic's on Students' Perceptions of Emotional Labour Expectations' (2014) 48 *The Law Teacher* 248.

[24] Chalen Westaby, 'Feeling Like a Sponge: The Emotional Labour Produced by Solicitors in Their Interactions with Clients Seeking Asylum' (2010) 17(2) *The International Journal of the Legal Profession* 153, 154.

[25] Joy Kadowaki, 'Maintaining Professionalism: Emotional Labor Among Lawyers as Client Advisors' (2015) 22(3) *International Journal of the Legal Profession* 323.

of burnout and challenges in maintaining the passion and commitment of their staff in constrained times. While Eve, unlike Jemma, remained in progressive legal practice she reflects with an experientially informed perspective on the need to collectively find ways to help 'social justice warriors' persevere in their work for the future.

KNOWLEDGE AND EXPERIENCE

> The basic human experience that a lawyer develops is very difficult to pin down (Kenneth).
>
> How do we pass on the knowledge? We saw the law centres emerging in the 70s, I was there! And now they're disappearing. The great knowledge they had isn't being passed on. We have to think of ways to draw on it and pass it on. (Helena Kennedy, 2018).

The sense that many of the leading practitioners from the late 1960s and early 1970s were retiring, and their experience and perspectives were at risk of being lost, played an important role in the early stages of designing this study. The narratives of practitioners from early decades in the study have demonstrated especially the connection between the past and the present through their similar constructions of legal tools for social change, experiences of legal education and the challenges of ethical decision-making consistent with progressive values. It is those participants in the study who have also stressed the need to capture experience and pass it on to the next generation of progressive lawyers.

I was struck by Kenneth's story in particular because of an issue related to experience that was clearly concerning him at the time of interview and relates to the value of social interactions. Kenneth was in progressive legal practice for more than five decades and when we sat together in his study at home and he raised an issue that troubled him almost as soon as we had sat down to begin the interview. Even before I asked a question, he animatedly described his scepticism at some recent work in the field of digital delivery of legal services and digital courts. He was at pains to point out that he did not object to digital technology per se ('I'm not a Luddite you see') but felt that with proposed reforms there was a distinct lack of choice for clients: 'we are forcing the public to mass computerization … the public don't want to do it, they want human advisors'. Kenneth seemed familiar with work in this area[26] but in his view it did little to capture the nuance of what is needed to effectively deliver legal advice to vulnerable clients. He reflected several times, 'my concern is how to capture experience' about the work of him and his peers. When describing his career in the early 1970s

[26] Roger Smith and Alan Paterson, *Face to Face Legal Services and Their Alternatives: Global Lessons from the Digital Revolution* (The Nuffield Foundation, 2014).

Kenneth returned to the issue of 'experience' again by raising the work of a leading proponent of digital legal service delivery and commenting by comparison he didn't have 'that experience, you just don't see any of that ... not a thing'. Kenneth made a number of further distinctions that highlight again the 'us and them' construction of progressive lawyering collective identity rooted:

> He worked for a large law firm, he doesn't claim ever to have worked in a legal aid firm or even been inside a Citizens Advice Bureau. He has a chapter on access to justice but when it comes down to it he doesn't have any suggestions for us, the non-commercial side, about how it's going to be done (Kenneth).

Kenneth described how his legal representation over the years had always been based on ensuring that service provision to the poor and vulnerable should be of the same level as those of wealthy and fee-paying clients. In his view the work on digital legal service delivery treats those clients as a 'lower level of people ... it's odd, it's very odd. It's very perfunctory'. After so many years working in legal aid Kenneth felt regret that the future of legal services was being based on corporate law firm innovation: '[T]he whole thing is geared to [redacted corporate law firm] and all those sort of people.' His own social identification is clear with the reference to 'those sort of people' who he does not relate to being the lawyers, or clients, that his own experience is designed to inform or whose interests he wants to protect and maintain in future. Kenneth returned to the issue of capturing experience many times in the interview in one form or another. When we talked about sustaining the profession at the end of the interview he stressed again:

> The issue that troubles me most in a way is the way in which the basic human experience that the lawyer develops, which is very difficult to pin down in any sort of pedagogical way but the thing that worries me most is that there are quite a lot of lawyers who have built up over many years a sort of general way of doing things, knowing how things operate (Kenneth).

At this point Kenneth again turned again to digital service delivery: 'It's going back to this thing about online. What does the human do that the machine doesn't?'. I sensed frustration and perhaps even feelings of exclusion for Kenneth because, now retired after many years in practice, the new reforms didn't 'acknowledge' the skills he had built up over the years. Referring again to 'human experience' and digital reform he said: 'And um, somehow or other we haven't evaluated that, we don't give it weight in decision making and in policy, we haven't even acknowledged it.' Kenneth repeatedly refers to experience here with the pronoun 'it' however the extent to which he turns back to that experience in his narrative personalises it, connecting questions around the future of effective legal service delivery to his own past and to a concern about the future.

It is clear therefore that Kenneth perceives that for lawyers to be able to sustain their progressive work with individuals experiencing vulnerability in society, more attention needs to be given to the 'human' element of that work. For Kenneth, the relationships across and within networks between lawyers, and their clients, is key. As the discussion in this chapter illustrates, my analysis of the narratives around sustaining the profession for legal aid and law centre lawyers in particular highlight emotional labour and human experience, thus collectively relating to what Kenneth describes. While working with vulnerable clients is demanding it is accepted as a necessary and important part of the job so that clients are supported: '[Y]ou have to always let them know that someone is there and is ready to speak on their behalf … that we're on their side' (Rihana). Kenneth identifies a policy failure to assess how the digital delivery of legal services will support those with, for example, physical or mental ill health or language barriers and whether it will be effective. As Clements comments in this context, digital processes fail 'when confronted by the complex, messy problems of the clustered variety'.[27] Clements views this very 'compartmentalism' and 'fragmentation' of legal services delivery as a prime example of a systemic failure to view legal problems holistically and recognise their interconnectedness.[28] While, he acknowledges, it is not difficult to see why 'chatbots, smart apps and other IT widgets' are an attraction to public bodies and charities delivering services they hold 'little or no promise' for resolving complex, clustered problems.[29]

It is unsurprising that Kenneth would feel a great sense of wanting to pass his expertise to the next generation and to utilise the many years of building up knowledge about 'how things operate'. His story is however illustrative of a more general set of narratives that touch upon the perceived importance of being on 'the frontline' (Phil) or at 'the coalface' (Lena) contrasted with the sheer frustration of that work not being recognised as valuable in the public sphere and by key decision-makers in, for example, legal policy making and management. For Kenneth, a realisation that his job might be replaced by technology ('the basic thrust of all this work is … destroying the legal profession … putting lawyers out of work') is troubling such that it was a recurrent theme of our encounter. Like other participants, Kenneth constructs what it might take to *sustain* the profession in terms of what he perceives to be a *challenge to* the profession. Similar to the challenges of resource and emotional labour described above, participants have a tendency to reflect on what it might take to fight and persevere to carry out their work in future notwithstanding difficulties and challenges. While their responses to challenges differ to a degree they remain within close range.

Digital technology featured both as a challenge *and* as a means of facilitating networks of practice for others in the study. Importantly, Phil raised digital developments as a means of sustaining legal aid practice when it is under threat in order to stay competitive. When I asked him directly about his approach in

[27] Luke Clements, *Clustered Injustice and the Level Playing Field* (Legal Action Group, 2020) 43.
[28] ibid 42.
[29] ibid 123.

trying to keep his firm afloat he outlined a list that started and ended with 'good IT' as a means of building up 'systems and networks':

> Good IT. You know, all the usual stuff. Um, trying to pay better, select better, train better, get a good ethos going, yeah, um, having people in first thing in the morning at half eight, having a regime that was ambitious compared to the competition … lawyers need to be ready to go to court at 9:15 with information on overnight cases, you know, everyone has got a BlackBerry who is on call, you know, our regime is messages first thing in the morning, the case information is coming through. You, you build up systems and networks (Phil).

Phil directly links the use of digital technology (in different forms) in his story to facilitating interaction between lawyers so they can share information and do their jobs well and be 'ambitious compared to the competition'. He also describes the importance of good training and getting 'an ethos going' through mentorship.

Mentorship was also a prevalent theme among study participants, and relates to the 'human element' Kenneth identifies, featuring across the decades with newly qualified participants describing inspirational figures in their recent past: 'I thought I want to be like her … She just seems really passionate about it. She has dedicated her life to trying to help people' (Ellie); 'it was so exciting to me … seeing [redacted barrister] on her feet, [it] was just like, she cared, this is not just a case' (Ankita). Practitioners from the early years also related fondly those lawyers who were influential in their own career direction and development with clear memories despite the passage of time of five decades: 'I did training with him and he was a magnificent teacher … he taught me my duty as a lawyer, he always said you've got to find a way in the grey where we walk … he was superb' (Kathleen). Quigley highlights in his 'Letter to a Law Student Interested in Social Justice' the importance of the history of social justice lawyering:

> [T]here is a rich history of social justice advocacy by lawyers whose lives rise above the limited horizons of the culture of lawyers … it is our job to learn the history … become familiar with these mentors of ours and understand the challenges they faced to become advocates of justice.[30]

As the extract from Helena Kennedy at the beginning of this section outlines, finding ways to pass on the knowledge and mentor the next generation with the voice of experience at a time of challenge and change is important for study participants. This is perhaps especially so given the emotional labour and risk of burnout explored above. However, there seems to be some uncertainty about continuing integration of digital technology in a way that facilitates, rather than hinders, interaction with others across networks and how it might effectively be a resource to draw upon in future.

[30] William Quigley, 'Letter to a Law Student Interested in Social Justice' (2007) 1 *DePaul Journal for Social Justice* 7, 13.

BARRISTERS AND EXCELLENCE

> You've got to have a commitment to excellence (Gideon).

I highlight in this section a divergent theme that arose in encounters with barrister participants in the study. While no participants from other subsets of practice mentioned excellence as a determining factor several senior barristers in the study referred to it first as a quality needed to do the job in future. The Bar has long been described as an elite profession[31] and the means by which they recruit new entrants into the profession maintains and reinforces intellectual elitism by specifically requiring evidence of intellect, to exacting standards, upon interview. One participant, Gideon, in fact stressed the need for 'excellence' and a 'commitment to excellence' as a sole requirement needed for sustaining the 'left-wing Bar'. He considered this at length and it seemed at odds with other assertions Gideon made earlier in the interview about the importance of left wing values and having a 'cause'. He clarified:

> I do think that. A combination is … absolutely … Well, okay, you're drawing this out of me very well. I think my central theme is that what makes a great barrister is a combination of a commitment of excellence applied to either a subject or a cause. But you need both (Gideon).

Gideon maintained his 'central theme' and described several examples of barristers who he thought demonstrated the commitment to excellence and to a cause, including examples of barristers who got 'carried away by their own excellence, they lacked the commitment'. Reading over the transcript I saw that Gideon had used the word 'excellence' some 15 times over a 12-minute section of our interview. He expressed great concern that the left simply wasn't excellent enough ('I'm not aware of a tradition on the left that says you can only join us if you're absolutely first rate') and expressed a fear that the commitment to values, while necessary, might compromise excellence: 'I think if you ask for a commitment to human rights it just allows you to take on people who aren't that good'. Gideon made it very clear that to sustain the left wing bar for the future 'a principled stance of excellence' was a critical consideration. This perspective was shared by Adil, another barrister-campaigner, who reflected on it in relation to the 'shrinking' Bar in terms of availability of work.

There is an important interplay between 'intellect' and 'commitment' for barristers on the left. Content analysis of the websites of progressive sets of barristers Chambers confirms the assumption of 'excellence' being required with one leading set determining that tenants should be of 'wholly exceptional

[31] David Lemmings, *Professors of Law: Barristers and English Legal Culture in the Eighteenth Century* (OUP, 2000).

ability'. Another barrister campaigner, Aidan, also described 'intellectual capacity' as the first quality he thought important for barristers but added that you also have to 'demonstrate a commitment to human rights and an ability to make a career at the bar'. I asked Aidan to give me some examples of what might constitute these latter qualities to which he said:

> They're hard to define but certainly it's an enthusiasm, a never say die spirit, an ability to project yourself and to you know, encapsulate an issue and very often dogged perseverance … (Aidan).

Aidan commented that for some of the 'best barristers' in his Chambers their perseverance was their 'unique' quality. I note that Aidan related this 'perseverance' differently from solicitors who describe the perseverance needed to work in legal aid or in law centres, and from barristers working exclusively in criminal legal aid. Aidan referred to 'a never say die spirit that is incredibly important in our areas of law' and to 'vision'. He commented that vision is all about 'having an ability to see an issue and open it up, how one might take a case to advance a cause'. As such, Aidan weaves together intellect in terms of seeing a legal issue with perseverance for advancing a cause. Unlike participants who relate perseverance to not giving up despite a lack of resource or emotional exhaustion, for Aidan it is about persevering on an issue until you get the result for your cause that you desire or need. While he is not as explicit as Gideon, the underlying requirement of intellect similarly remains alongside 'vision' and he perceives it as important for selecting new pupils and for sustaining a commitment to human rights at the Bar.

Aidan also touched upon an important issue, which is the social mobility aspect of being required to demonstrate a 'commitment' to human rights. In terms of being successful in getting an interview for pupillage in Chambers he commented that this 'tends to mean that people score heavily if they've been off in the world doing work for NGOs' but identified a 'problem' where someone from 'a poor background [who] just says what I want to do is be a lawyer and I just want to get on with it and earn money?' Aidan did not offer solutions to what he described as a potential 'disadvantage' and I asked about this by way of follow up he commented: '[L]ook, many of us who have ended up in this sort of work would not have gotten in under the current criteria'. He referred here to his 'archetypal Oxbridge background' and the fact that, at a young age, he simply wouldn't have demonstrated the commitment that so many new entrants to the progressive Bar must now show. This raises questions from a collective perspective given that there seems to be an expectation of commitment to the cause and while there is some appreciation that prospective barristers from different class backgrounds may not be able to afford to demonstrate their commitment, in a highly competitive field where that commitment is nonetheless still required few solutions were offered as to how to overcome this challenge.

SOCIAL MOBILITY AND ACCESS

> I think it's very, very difficult now (Lena).

A common theme that arose across the subsets of practice for participants who qualified in the preceding decades of the study was their sense that they would simply not be able to access the profession today. Aidan's comment 'many of us who have ended up in this sort of work would not have gotten in' relates one such observation because he sensed he would not be able to demonstrate the commitment now required. However, more pressing observations came from those participants from other class backgrounds who had been in receipt of grants and, in the case of two solicitors, housing benefit during their education and training. They expressed that entering the profession now would be, in their view, impossible and had concerns about the impact of these constraints on widening access.

Lena for example commented, 'I think it's very, very difficult now … with tuition fees … I think it would have been very hard for me to justify going to University with that debt piling up'. She said she would have had to pursue employment to pay off the debt but observed that 'by getting a job, from my background, I think the chances are I would have ended up staying in employment [rather than qualifying as a lawyer]'. Ben commented similarly based on his own experience:

> Jacqueline: What would you say to students who might want to pursue this area of practice?
>
> Ben: I think the big worry that I have, having told you what my history was, of getting a two year maintenance grant and housing benefit, I physically don't know how people can afford to do it any more … Um, I'm just not sure what strategies people can have to come into it without being bankrupt as a result.

He said that as an employer they were 'looking at what they could do to assist people' but that as a legal aid firm, rather than a corporate City law firm who can afford to cover the vocational stage of legal training, it was 'very difficult'.

There seemed to be a real sense of disbelief about the challenges facing new entrants to the profession but at the same time a lack of coherent strategy as to how to overcome it. Faced with so many other resource constraints it seemed especially difficult for legal aid firms in particular to find solutions to the problem. During the second half of my fieldwork I noted a rise in participants mentioning the Justice First Fellowship scheme that funds training contracts for lawyers in law centres and legal aid firms. Established in 2014, it grew in numbers (at the time of writing there are fifty fellowship posts) and reputation as my fieldwork progressed. It has been described as 'giving hope' to those who had otherwise given up on finding a way to qualify as social welfare lawyers. Matthew Smerdon, the CEO of the Legal Education Foundation, commented a familiar sense of urgency in the early years of the programme: '[T]here just simply won't be lawyers qualifying in the numbers that they used to. Where is the next generation of specialist lawyers going to come from?'.[32] I interviewed several newly qualified practitioners and trainees who had been in receipt of fellowships. They all collectively expressed in strong terms that they simply couldn't have qualified without the fellowship support and some had been close to giving up on progressive legal work entirely due to a lack of jobs and funding. One fellow, Tim, described being offered a training contract in a firm he was working at throughout his studies but that didn't represent his values: 'I still applied for a training contract there because I was desperate. But I couldn't take it and I handed in my notice'. He received a fellowship to train in a charity commenting, 'in every way that matters I've found it fulfilling'. Another Justice First Fellow, Annie, said she was 'just so desperate to get a training contract' in a law centre or legal aid law firm but stressed the difficult prospect of working as a paralegal for many years 'on £18,000 living in London and having to commute from zone 6' to be in a competitive position for a training post when it arose. She said she was 'feeling deflated' and had almost 'given up' because of the lack of training opportunities and because it 'wasn't a very empowering process'. Annie's tone changed entirely when she described hearing about the fellowship: 'I just jumped at it … the work looked so interesting, strategic litigation as well … and I was just really interested'. Each of the participants in receipt of fellowships described the opportunity similarly.

In terms of sustaining the profession I noted with interest how the fact of the fellowships seemed to be offering hope and lifting morale not only to fellows and other potential entrants to the profession but to participants working in legal aid firms and law centres who wanted the 'new blood' as Phil described above, but had no other means of funding those posts. My impression was that the very fact of the fellowships was changing the culture within otherwise resource constrained environments. For example, Ruth, a legal aid solicitor, connected her own experience of having been in receipt of a funded training contract from the Legal Services Commission (now the Legal Aid Agency) to the difficulty for those without resource to access training. She expressed lament they were no longer available but immediately mentioned the Justice First Fellowships as an alternative ('LEF seems to have stepped in to replace the LSC') and said they hoped to apply as a law firm to be able to take a fellowship trainee in the near future. For several other law centre lawyers a similar collective sense of relief was conveyed in relation to the fellowship programme. However, it remains to be seen the extent to which the programme will be able to sustain progressive lawyering into the future as the training posts are only for two years after which period fellows have to either find other ways to fund their positions or move elsewhere. To date, fellows have however mostly found positions in related types of work or secured funding to remain in the law centres in which they have trained.[33]

[32] Emma Howard 'Going into Legal Aid Work is Career Suicide' (*The Guardian*, 6 January 2016).
[33] Fiona Bawdon, 'Legal Life Changers Spread their Wings' (*New Law Journal*, 27 July 2018).

While the programme goes some way in alleviating a considerable challenge to the future of the profession, participants highlight other problems that have yet to be overcome. The fellowship programme only funds the training contract itself and not higher or vocational education, which both carry significant fees. As Lena and Ben point out, the problem of University fees and the lack of welfare support compared to the past is acute, with the most financially insecure being deterred or unable to pursue progressive legal practice in future.

CONCLUSIONS

In this chapter I have discussed a number of resource challenges relevant to the future of progressive lawyering. They are particularly relevant because they are collectively perceived and constructed as being valuable, while at the same time under threat, by participants in the study. As outlined in chapters four and six, the collective identity of progressive lawyers is contingent upon shared values such that the resources of passion and perseverance are deemed critical for sustaining their practice notwithstanding other resource deficiencies, especially that of funding. The themes raised here are interdependent and it is clear that the austerity narrative again provides a frame for the presentation of other narratives on sustaining progressive lawyering. Resource pressures and other problems within the justice system bear relevance to constructions of esteem, low morale and managing the risk of burnout. For lawyers, the ability to actually do the job well and achieve results appears to be the means by which they also cope with the pressures and stresses created by such emotionally demanding work. The focus on 'tangible results' also strongly relates to collective empowerment: lawyers construct a need to collectively believe the work they do matters in order to sustain their work in future, which perhaps goes some way in explaining the renewed focus on strategic and systemic impact explored in chapter five.

The links between personal experience and the collective construction of how to overcome challenges to sustaining the profession can be traced across the network nodes of the study. For example, participants who perceive themselves to have especially persevered seem more likely to *expect* perseverance from the next generation and participants who are at risk of having their skills made redundant due to the passage of time are more likely to stress the urgency of capturing knowledge and experience. Finally, alongside these emerging interdependent themes of *funding*, *passion*, *perseverance* and *knowledge* remains the problem of widening access to the profession. Experiences of exclusion are prevalent, however, a collective, strategic response to the lack of diversity in the profession has not been articulated and appears critical to growing and sustaining a conscious movement of progressive lawyers for the future.

9

Lawyers, Networks and the Future of Progressive Lawyering: 'This Work Needs to be Done'

> Most lawyers just want to earn a living and leave politics to others … most lawyers frankly do not give a damn.[1]

Lawyers in this study make personal choices that construct and sustain their identities as progressive lawyers. Their stories help us to better understand the connection between their professional and personal lives and the networks within which they work. In this concluding chapter, the key themes developed throughout the book are brought together. First, how processes of differentiating, constructing and presenting collective identity across the network nodes of the study serve to suggest that a progressive lawyering movement exists in the UK. These findings are presented along Diani's conception of social movements set out in chapter two comprising: (i) networks of informal interaction; (ii) shared beliefs and solidarity; and (iii) collective action on conflictual issues. Secondly, this conception of lawyering is connected to resource challenges in future. Finally, possible ways of overcoming those challenges with a particular focus on the role of legal education are considered.

Since the conclusion of the fieldwork for this book a landmark case challenging the Prime Minister's advice to the Queen to prorogue Parliament in relation to Brexit reached its way to the Supreme Court.[2] The new leader of the opposition, Keir Starmer QC, relied on his status as a progressive lawyer in his Labour Party leadership campaign.[3] The Ministry of Justice have conducted a review

[1] Richard Abel, *English Lawyers: Between Market and State* (Oxford University Press, 2003) 470. Reproduced by permission of Oxford University Press.

[2] *R (on the application of Miller) v The Prime Minister*; *Cherry and others v Advocate General for Scotland* [2019] UKSC 41.

[3] '[Keir Starmer] was there … helping the families of strikers who'd had their benefits cut off by the Tory government, he gave free legal advice to the poll tax protesters … [he] stood up for protesters when the full force of the state was against them … I don't think anyone really expected someone who had dedicated his career to defending workers, trade unions and activists to become Director of Public Prosecutions. Keir never forgot where he came from, as DPP he stood up to the powerful, he had the courage to prosecute MPs for cheating on their expenses …' Keir Starmer Labour Leadership campaign video available at www.keirstarmer.com.

of the impact of LASPO, resulting in a new Legal Support Action Plan and the reinstatement of legal aid in some limited areas;[4] and separate inquiries have been established by the All-Party Parliamentary Group on Legal Aid and the Justice Committee addressing, in part, issues of retention in the legal aid sector.[5] Outside of England and Wales, where cuts have not been so extensive to date, legal aid reforms have also been considered.[6] A justice system already creaking as a result of court closures and funding cuts is now experiencing unprecedented strain as a result of the backlog created by the Covid-19 pandemic.[7] Many legal aid lawyers report extreme stress as a result of changes to working patterns as a result of lockdown.[8] At the same time, legal tools have played an important role in challenging the lawfulness of Covid-19 related policy on issues including educational provision, testing in care homes and the procurement of Personal Protective Equipment (PPE). Against this background, reminiscent of the 'backlash' set out in chapter two, the UK Government has announced a review into the scope of judicial review powers.[9] To add to the uncertainty, whether the Human Rights Act 1998 will remain, as well as how ongoing commitments under the EU Charter of Fundamental Rights will be framed, are both unclear as we move into a post Brexit constitutional landscape. Rather than speculate as to what access to justice might look like for lawyers working in future, I suggest in this final chapter how lawyers' networks of practice might be sustained notwithstanding uncertainty and change in the light of the study findings.

CONCEPTUALISING A PROGRESSIVE LAWYERING MOVEMENT

Networks of Interaction

My ethnographic participant-observation facilitated early identification of network nodes that underpinned the research. The interactions of barrister-campaigners, law centre lawyers, NGO lawyers, legal aid lawyers and law clinic

[4] For example, for separated migrant children in immigration cases and reinstating face-to-face legal advice in discrimination, debt and special educational needs cases. See *Post Implementation Review of LASPO, parts 1 and 2* (Ministry of Justice, 2019); *Legal Support: The Way Ahead, an action plan to deliver better support to people experiencing legal problems* (Ministry of Justice, February 2019).

[5] See, eg, Young Legal Aid Lawyers, *Submission to the Justice Committee Inquiry on the Future of Legal Aid* (YLAL, 2 November 2020), available at www.younglegalaidlawyers.org/sites/default/files/Justice%20Committee%20Consultation%20Response_0.pdf.

[6] Scottish Government, *Rethinking Legal Aid: An Independent Strategic Review* (Scottish Government, 2018).

[7] Sue James et al, *Justice Matters: Essays from the Pandemic* (Legal Action Group, 2020).

[8] Nick Hilborne, 'Legal Aid Lawyers Under Severe Pressure because of Covid' (*Legal Futures*, 18 November 2020).

[9] The Public Law Project, *Statement on the Independent Review of Administrative Law Process* (October 2020), available at https://publiclawproject.org.uk/wp-content/uploads/2020/10/PLP-Statement-on-the-Independent-Review-of-the-Administrative-Law-Process.pdf.

lawyers are represented in their movements across network nodes and their intra-network identification of lawyers 'like us' within them. Progressive lawyers are members of a plurality of professional sub-groups (ie, Haldane Society of Socialist Lawyers, Young Legal Aid Lawyers, Legal Aid Practitioners Group, Scottish Human Rights Consortium) and other organisations (ie, Liberty, Amnesty, JUSTICE, the Law Centres Network) that are interconnected within a wider structure 'generated and reproduced through action'.[10] In chapter four, participants collectively described personally meaningful interactions across these networks in their pathways to legal practice. Analysis shows common rites of passage within and through organisations where lawyers gain experience and a sense of place, maintained through both formal and informal professional ties. Despite contestation as to labelling, their collective identity within the network nodes is clear: 'we're all very like-minded people' (Andrea), 'we were a collective in every sense of the word' (Stefan), 'there's a real camaraderie' (Gail), 'we're all driven by the same things' (Martin). In their relationships and interactions they present as holding one another in mutual high regard and their sense of place is often emotively expressed: 'this is where my heart is first and foremost' (Rihana). Across these nodes lawyers recognise one another as being within or outside the wider progressive lawyering network and, most notably, frame that recognition in their collective turning points away from corporate law and through a frame of 'us and them' conceptions of legal professional identity: 'the thought of spending my life with them wasn't too good' (Rodrigo); 'shuffling other people's money in the City, that's just not for us is it?' (Martin).

Participants also describe experiences of legal education where they look for opportunities that provide access to early networks, which have sustained them in their careers: 'that's seen me through all the way' (Melissa), '[they've] remained my best friends and even to this day' (Ankita), 'I've never looked back' (Dominic). Importantly, Diani focuses on a looser 'network of informal interactions between individuals, groups and/or organisations' with the boundaries of a social movement being defined not so much by organisation, or even action, but by 'the specific collective identity shared by actors involved in the interaction'.[11] The constructions of shared experiences, attitudes and commitments in participants' narratives and in my wider ethnographic encounters demonstrate that progressive lawyers come to think of themselves as being part of a broader movement. Their image of progressive lawyering identity, based on their interactions with one another, is compatible with their image of themselves and they differentiate themselves from 'other' lawyers within and across their own networks.

The theme of informal networks of interaction was prevalent in chapter six where I conducted in-depth narrative analysis of formative experiences of

[10] Mario Diani, 'Networks and Participation' in David Snow et al (eds), *The Blackwell Companion to Social Movements* (Blackwell, 2004) 339, 339.

[11] Mario Diani, 'The Concept of a Social Movement' (1992) 40(1) *Sociological Review* 8–9.

legal education. These stories diverged dependent upon social alienation: 'I was absolutely shocked by what I found there' (Phil), and the extent to which opportunities for experiential learning were available: '[I]t made me think about how I could make a difference and why it was important that I should' (Isabelle). It is notable given that cause lawyering theory and recognition of more radical lawyering identities is more widespread in the US that participants who had educational experience there described it as being personally meaningful: 'I worked on an extraordinary case' (Kenneth), 'it was really exciting and inspiring' (Ankita), 'they have these radical lawyers there you know … a movement of radical lawyers' (Martin). For these participants, and a minority who had similar formative experiences in the UK, social justice orientated experiential opportunities provided access to early networks which have sustained them in their careers: 'that's seen me through all the way' (Melissa), '[they've] remained my best friends and even to this day'" (Ankita), 'I've never looked back' (Dominic). For others who did not have such experience the sense of wanting to distinguish themselves from more commercially orientated students sets them apart and propelled them towards different paths. Across these divergent narratives of legal education, participants describe a process of searching for networks where they could interact with others in the pursuit of similar goals. They exist and persist outside of traditional organisational boundaries and rest in relationships often formed through shared experience.

Shared Beliefs and Solidarity

The study demonstrates that the shared beliefs across the network nodes are predominantly connected to participants' personal histories and early political consciousness: 'My fifteenth birthday present was membership of the Labour party' (Martin), 'My parents saw the left as being the voice of social justice' (Ankita). The presentation of individual values which exist across a wide spectrum are otherwise collectively shared and rest upon a commitment to using the law for social change, to 'challenge power' (Eve) in various forms and make a 'wider impact' (Ben). In chapter four I outlined constructions of participants' decisions to become lawyers connected to left political values and a desire to 'do the right thing and make a contribution' (Andrea). As such, a public 'story of self' for participants provides a way for them to portray their shared motivating values and experiences and solidarity with one another.[12] They reach out across the network so their 'story of self' becomes a 'story of us' and attempt to overcome difference, especially divergent class backgrounds, by appealing to a shared purpose. Participants describe in various ways a motivating desire to

[12] Marshall Ganz, *What is Public Narrative: Self, Us & Now* (Working Paper, 2009) 2, available at https://dash.harvard.edu/handle/1/30760283.

make a social contribution, and perhaps especially so through their presentations of a lack of any financial incentive in their work. They differentiate and delineate themselves as not wanting to be like 'other' lawyers on this basis: 'I didn't want to be like her, I didn't want to have the kind of practice which was very much, rich people' (Rodrigo). This shared construction of purpose remains notwithstanding contestation as to labelling of their work in different fields of legal aid, social welfare and human rights. In their stories participants describe wanting to get 'tangible results' (Martin) across these areas and link these to an ethical approach that focuses on representing the disempowered in society.

Progressive lawyers' ethicality is an important feature of their shared beliefs and solidarity. In chapter two I set out the controversy that surrounds the ethics of cause lawyering where lawyers choose to 'take sides' and arguably subvert the norms of lawyer neutrality by doing so. It has been argued that cause lawyers perceive themselves to be bound by higher moral standards which serves to suggest that 'other' lawyers are on the 'wrong' side.[13] The analysis in chapter seven does not resolve these controversies but rather seeks to shed light upon them: 'I take a slightly more moralistic look at the cab rank rule' (Martin). Boon noted that cause lawyers in the UK 'maintain cause affiliations while deliberating not parading them'.[14] My analysis of ethical decision making in chapter seven reveals the uncomfortable encounters that rest, for some participants, in maintaining but not presenting one's affiliation to a cause. I interrogated the way in which progressive lawyers present their ethical decisions not to represent the state, state actors or those they perceive to be otherwise disproportionately empowered in society. The strength of network ties is apparent by virtue of the ease with which lawyers conceive of their own decisions, and their presentation of them, through the decisions of other progressive lawyers: 'radical lawyers have presented themselves in that way … I have always felt that was wrong' (Kenneth), 'I don't want to defend the indefensible … I completely see the place of those people who act in those situations' (Andrea), '… my colleagues have a big need to put that in a wider [political] context' (Aidan). This delineation provides a frame for understanding their own ethicality and also serves to strengthen their constructions of collective identity by reaching within and across the network nodes in order to make sense of their decisions. I identify that participants take three different positions that also connect to the presentation of their political values and describe them as *resolute, constrained* or *conflicted*. These positions provide new insight into the relationship between the character, context and capacities of progressive lawyers' ethical decisions. Notwithstanding these different positions, participants reveal their wider shared beliefs and solidarity through a common construction of ethical decisions on moral terms related to power imbalance in society and a related collective commitment otherwise to access to justice.

[13] Robert Rosen, 'On the Social Significance of Cause Lawyering' (2000) 3(2) *Legal Ethics* 169.
[14] Andrew Boon, 'Cause Lawyers and the Alternate Ethical Paradigm' (2004) 7 *Legal Ethics* 250.

Consistent with Etienne's study[15] of criminal cause lawyers, I also develop through chapters five and six an analysis of shared ideology linked to scepticism of government action: 'If [state actors] all put their hands up, we'd be in a much better society. But they won't! Just that, you know, I'm not motivated by fighting for the big man.' (Andrea). The performance of this scepticism is embedded in network interactions. Participants in the study frequently position the state as the empowered 'other' in the same way that corporate law firms serve this function: 'I've got no desire to represent state agents' (Dominic), 'My practice is acting for claimants, for the victims of state power because that's where the power imbalance is' (Michael). This was also apparent at the beginning of my narrative interview encounters, where participants were quick to construct their decision to pursue a career in the law to their left values regardless of any direct question about this connection and to otherwise relate, or reach out, with shared understandings of left political affiliations (broadly construed). Participants maintain solidarity by taking sides in a moral and political struggle and embed their individual values, and choices, within their wider collective identity.[16]

Collective Action on Conflictual Issues

I have sought to demonstrate throughout the difference that collective identity makes to progressive legal practice, with a focus on day-to-day decision-making and the tools lawyers choose to use to achieve change. Participants take action where it is consistent with their values but also when they think it might be effective (ie, using a legal tool because they perceive that it will potentially be successful). As we have seen (in chapter five), there is historic divergence in narrative constructions of law centre practice as being either high volume and reactive on the one hand, or strategic and proactive on the other. These differences are replicated in the cause lawyering spectrum outlined in chapter two with grassroots practitioners at one end and elite/vanguard at the other.[17] However, whether through individual casework or strategic litigation, participants are connected by their desire to positively impact large numbers of people in their work. This is especially clear when more senior lawyers look back over the decades of their careers regardless of which tools they chose to use to achieve that aim: '[W]e would actually brainstorm about how one could attack the system' (Aidan), 'My best highlights were, the cases, and I think literally hundreds … thousands of cases, which were evictions …' (Stefan).

[15] Margareth Etienne, 'The Ethics of Cause Lawyering: An Empirical Examination of Criminal Defense Lawyers as Cause Lawyers' (2005) 95 *Journal of Criminal Law and Criminology* 1195, 1209.

[16] Austin Sarat and Stuart Scheingold, *Something to Believe In: Politics, Professionalism and Cause Lawyering* (Stanford University Press, 2004) 5.

[17] Thomas Hilbink, 'You Know the Type: Categories of Cause Lawyering' (2004) 19 *Law & Social Inquiry* 657.

My analysis demonstrates that, more recently, collective action around austerity reforms has facilitated a growing awareness of more proactive approaches and interplay across the cause lawyering spectrum, as evidenced by interactions within and across the network nodes of the study. These interactions in the current context are reminiscent of the factors that relate to individual desire and motivation to participate in social movements more generally:

> [A]lthough the relative importance and causal order of the factors is disputed, collective action is more likely when people have shared interests, feel relatively deprived, are angry, believe they can make a difference, and strongly identify with relevant social groups.[18]

Writing in 2011, Francis pointed to the fact that 'we cannot ignore the location of much of the UK's progressive lawyering within state-managed structures'.[19] In a short space of time, this context has dramatically changed in England and Wales. The most recent directory of legal aid in fact shows only 14 welfare benefits advice agencies and reduced services in most other areas:[20] 'It's just devastated our clients to be honest. And it's frustrating as a lawyer …' (Ruth), '… it has been horrible, since 2013. It has been horrible …' (Rihana), 'it's just there are holes that people fall down and they can't get back up again. And it's just too hard you know?' (Melissa). This has allowed more collaborative and creative sites of progressive lawyering to develop in England and Wales and shared interest in these approaches nationwide. Law centres in particular have sought alternative funding in order to pursue strategic casework and many legal aid law firms are re-structuring to facilitate private work in other areas, arguably freeing them from historic constraints. The combined effect of the Lobbying Act, LASPO 2012 and restrictions on judicial review has further incentivised lawyers towards collective and strategic action:[21] 'I think it's made law much more political … it's brought home to the legal profession the importance of rights of access to the courts … people feel it more keenly' (Gail). Progressive lawyering networks are engaged in cultural politics because they construct an 'oppositional identity' against austerity driven measures.[22] I have found that the perceived historic distance between day-to-day casework and strategic litigation is therefore less acute in law centres and small charities: 'in terms of how effective we can be it's important that we do strategic work' (Kimberley), 'I just want to stay in strategic litigation now …' (Tim). Civil society organisations think in different ways about how to advocate for their service users and, at the same

[18] Craig McGarty et al, 'New technologies, new identities and the growth of mass opposition in the Arab Spring' (2013) 35(6) *Political Psychology* 725, 726.

[19] Andrew Francis, *The Edge of Law: Emergent and Divergent Models of Legal Professionalism* (Routledge, 2011) 109.

[20] Legal Aid Agency, Standard Civil Legal Aid Contractors List (LAA, 2018).

[21] Harriet Samuels, 'Public Interest Litigation and the Civil Society Factor' (2018) *Legal Studies* 1, 5.

[22] Kate Nash, 'The Cultural Turn in Social Theory: Towards a Theory of Cultural Politics (2001) 35(1) *Sociology* 77, 86.

time, progressive lawyers across network nodes demonstrate the shared beliefs and solidarity necessary to pursue collective action for social change and to counter the negative impacts of austerity.[23] Throughout the fieldwork, participants were alive to this concern (the 'austerity narrative') no matter which subset of practice, or period of time, and it framed their storytelling and also wider ethnographic encounters.

In conclusion, the cause lawyering literature has long pointed to the value of collaboration and to the importance of networks for creating opportunities for lawyers to benefit from alliances.[24] Following Diani's conception, this research demonstrates how progressive lawyers define themselves as part of a broader social movement, based upon their collective identity and a shared desire to pursue legal action in the pursuit of social change. They are also perceived as such by their opponents, including the state, as demonstrated by the curbing of their activities and negative framing in the public sphere.[25] Their articulated opposition to the potential overreach of state power serves to reinforce their identity as they collectively perceive themselves as being set apart from 'other' lawyers.

A PROGRESSIVE LAWYERING FUTURE

I explore in this final section three interrelated concerns around sustaining progressive legal practice. The first is social mobility and access to the legal profession. The second is resource, with a focus on burnout and emotion management for lawyers, especially those working in legal aid and law centres. The final concern is linked to a limitation I have identified in my research, which is the extent to which it is able to capture nationwide disparities and complexities in progressive legal practice. I set out how these concerns are interrelated, to some extent, by the role of legal education in helping overcome them.

The theme of class has featured strongly in the study. As I noted in chapter four, issues of race and gender discrimination arose but tended to be explored in an intersectional sense through the lens of social class.[26] I revealed how participants from working class backgrounds where more likely to relate: (i) an experience of working hard to enter the profession; (ii) a formative

[23] Joe Lepper, 'Life after the Lobbying Act' (2015) *The Charity Times*. See also Jacqueline Kinghan and Lisa Vanahala, *Supporting Systems Changers Through the Use of Collaborative Legal Approaches* (The Public Law Project, 2020).

[24] Stephen Meili, 'Latin American Cause Lawyering Networks' in Austin Sarat and Stuart Scheingold (eds), *Cause Lawyering and the State in a Global Era* (Oxford University Press, 2001).

[25] Samuels (n 21); Liana Buchanan, 'Community Lawyers and Systemic Change' in Asher Flynn and Jacqueline Hodgson, *Access to Justice and Legal Aid: Comparative Perspectives on Unmet Legal Need* (Hart, 2017) 141.

[26] Jennifer Tomlinson et al, 'Privileges and Penalties in the legal profession: an intersectional analysis of career progression' (2019) 70(3) *The British Journal of Sociology* 1043.

personal experience related to injustice; and/or (iii) work experiences (often non law related) that led to a career in law. By stark contrast, participants from privileged backgrounds were likely to describe a legal career as one of a number of available options or a path they 'stumbled' onto. An issue that preoccupied participants from the 1970s, 1980s and 1990s – who at the time had received maintenance grants and did not pay University fees – was the realisation that the path they took simply wouldn't be available to others in the same position now: 'I physically don't know how people can afford to do it anymore … I'm just not sure what strategies people can have to come into it without being bankrupt as a result' (Ben). I observed more widely a sense of desperation in this context and that the 'brain drain' and advice deserts in legal aid practice would be further exacerbated by the heavy financial burden required to study and train as a lawyer. Many participants noted that widening access to the profession is particularly difficult when students who cannot afford University fees, or unpaid work experience are disproportionately impacted by barriers.[27] This context has only been made more acute given the disproportionate adverse impacts created by the Covid-19 pandemic: 43 per cent of members of Young Legal Aid Lawyers reported in April 2020 that they were extremely or quite worried about their job security and 67.5 per cent reporting their volume of work had 'significantly decreased' or 'been decimated'.[28] This rests alongside research pointing to the 'stress, unhappiness and discomfort' experienced by millennials in the profession more widely.[29]

The Justice First Fellowships go some way in alleviating these problems and provide a pathway to practice in charities, law centres and legal aid law firms who would otherwise be unable to fund training positions. However, many students entering the profession come with high levels of debt and a comprehensive solution is needed that will require high level institutional support. One such model, which operates successfully in the US, is a system of student loan repayments operated by Universities for students pursuing careers in public interest rather than corporate law.[30] A wider commitment by law schools to integrated programmes of clinical legal education would also assist in helping students gain work experience: 'I just believe in clinical legal education. We need to meet the enthusiasm of students for social justice because actually the economic structure for qualifying as a lawyer discourages that (Kimberley)'. This could include funded 'externship' models where students have exposure to lawyering across

[27] *Young Legal Aid Lawyers: Social Mobility in a Time of Austerity* (Young Legal Aid Lawyers, 2018).

[28] *Young Legal Aid Lawyers Covid-19 Report* (Young Legal Aid Lawyers, 2020) 14–16.

[29] Lydia Bleasdale and Andrew Francis, 'Great expectations: millennial lawyers and the structures of contemporary legal practice' (2020) 40(3) *Legal Studies* 376.

[30] The repayments are often funded by alumni donations. See, eg, Georgetown Law School Loan Repayment Assistance Program, available at www.law.georgetown.edu/admissions-aid/financial-aid/loan-repayment-assistance-program/.

the network nodes of progressive practice and can see the links between them.[31] Here too, lies the possibility of engagement with conscious lawyering linked to emerging collective legal consciousness.[32] It is important to make a commitment to understanding the experiences of law students and early career lawyers, especially in relation to pertinent issues such as socio-economic disadvantage and race discrimination,[33] and consciously integrating processes and pedagogy alive to them. Further integration of the voices and experience of progressive lawyers in the UK into legal education, both in the past and present, will also go some way in ensuring that the resources of *passion, perseverance, knowledge* and *experience* might be located and sustained for the future. Finally, the study demonstrates the importance of a renewed focus on identifying *early* networks for students from widening participation backgrounds because of their capacity to provide the formation of networks and collective identity.[34]

The second concern rests in the resource issues related by study participants analysed in chapter eight. I often observed the interplay between lawyers' preoccupation with the challenges to the progressive lawyering movement in future and the ways in which those challenges might be overcome. For example, how participants highlighted the need for passion for the work while relating their own passionate opposition and anger at the injustice of the impact of austerity reforms on vulnerable and disadvantaged groups. Participants who perceived themselves to have especially persevered were more likely to expect perseverance from the next generation of progressive lawyers. Dominic stresses that the 'work needs to be done' but only by those who have a 'heart' for it. The ability to do the job well and achieve results for clients also appears to be the way in which lawyers cope with such emotionally demanding work and the risk of burnout, however, this risks being counter-productive in the long term.[35] The different types of required resource that participants identify are socially constructed and are all mutually perceived to be under threat such that lawyers interact across their networks to explore ways in which they might be sustained for the future.

The desire for change is in itself a resource to be drawn upon. The austerity narrative of the book is one in which other narratives are framed and creates

[31] Jacqueline Kinghan and Rachel Knowles, 'Striking a Balance in Clinical Legal Education: Reimagining the Role of the teaching Practitioner in Casework Partnerships' in Linden Thomas et al (eds), *Reimagining Clinical Legal Education* (Hart, 2018).

[32] Gerald Lopez, *Rebellious Lawyering: One Chicano's Vision of Progressive Law Practice* (Westview Press, 1992); Anthony Alfieri, 'Rebellious Pedagogy and Practice' (2016) 23(1) *Clinical Law Review* 5.

[33] Alexandra Wilson, *In Black and White: A Young Barrister's Story of Race and Class in a Broken Justice System* (Endeavour, 2020).

[34] Diani (n 10) 351; Andrew Francis, 'Legal Education, Social Mobility, and Employability: Possible Selves, Curriculum Intervention and the Role of Legal Work Experience' (2015) (42) *Journal of Law and Society* 173, 186.

[35] Chalen Westaby, 'Feeling Like a Sponge: The Emotional Labour Produced by Solicitors in Their Interactions with Clients Seeking Asylum' (2010) 17(2) *The International Journal of the Legal Profession* 153, 154.

a legal consciousness that further incentivises progressive legal practice. Some socio-legal studies have identified socially constructed cultures of quiet conservatism that inhibit collective legal consciousness at critical times.[36] Arguably, collective action on austerity measures has galvanised lawyers to think strategically about how to challenge the status quo and work collaboratively to tackle systemic issues. McEvoy and Rebouche highlight the importance of 'critical junctures' for cause lawyers working to achieve change because they help pinpoint defining moments that provide insight into how collective organisations 'see, act and think of themselves'.[37] In the same way, the access to justice crisis forms a critical juncture. It provides a lens through which lawyers look back on their careers over many decades, revealing how early career progressive lawyers see themselves and socially construct their continuing pursuit of social change notwithstanding resource constraints.

The continuing crisis has however also taken its toll for many participants in the study. I observed that alongside the strong desire to 'challenge' and 'fight' the system, narratives in the study revealed that for many progressive lawyers in practice the cuts have been such a burden on their professional and personal lives that, while not yet defeated, they are worn down: 'I wake up early and I worry about where the money is coming from' (Rodrigo). Working at the same time to 'dismantle the system' and also struggling to provide legal services *within* that system can be tiring and all consuming. This was apparent for several lawyers in the study who were involved in judicial review challenges to aspects of legal aid reforms. One participant summed up their involvement in an ultimately successful case in emotional terms: 'Yeah, it's like, it's like a truck has knocked you over some time ago and you finally just got up'. Jemma described well the collision between her own sense of self and the perception of her work: 'I felt I got to the point where I was like I know what I'm doing is really valuable but you [Chris Grayling] just don't see it'. Similar to lawyers in Sommerlad's study Jemma found it difficult to reconcile the value she perceived in her work, and in herself, and the negative perception in the public sphere.[38]

The themes of emotion and burnout are therefore prevalent yet, despite some important developments in the field, still feature relatively rarely in the teaching and training of law students.[39] This is surprising given the relevance of emotion

[36] Keiran McEvoy, 'What did the Lawyers Do During the War?' (2011) 74(3) *Modern Law Review* 350.

[37] Kieran McEvoy and Rachel Rebouche, 'Mobilizing the Professions: Lawyers, Politics and the Collective Legal Conscience' in John Morison et al (eds), *Judges, Transition and Human Rights* (Oxford University Press, 2007) 277.

[38] Hilary Sommerlad, 'I've Lost The Plot: An Everyday Story of the Political Legal Aid Lawyer (2001) 28(3) *Journal of Law and Society* 335, 337; Andrew Boon, 'From public service to service industry: the impact of socialisation and work on motivation and values of lawyers' (2005) 12 *International Journal of the Legal Profession* 229.

[39] See, eg, Richard Collier, 'Wellbeing in the legal profession: reflections on recent developments (or, what do we talk about when we talk about wellbeing?' (2016) 23 *International Journal of the*

to legal practice, and to the law. Sajo highlights the role that emotion plays in shaping constitutional regimes and asserts that while traditionally scholars separated reason from passion and the legal order from emotional experience, in fact 'constitutional sentiments' exist such that constitutional order is driven to reflect 'the public sentiments of the day and, at least to some extent, basic moral emotions'.[40] Emotion is also an important feature of lawyers' networked interactions with one another: scholarship on law and emotion has in fact stressed in particular the potential of the 'growing interdisciplinary interest in *collective* decision making and emotional dynamics of groups'.[41] Attending to emotion therefore, and in particular to emotion management should be a key priority for legal educators, and especially those working in areas of social welfare and human rights.[42]

The final concerning feature for the future of progressive legal practice arises from a limitation of the study. While I experienced, and observed, a collective identity for progressive lawyers in my fieldwork in the devolved nations, the socio-political contexts differ. Despite progressive legislative frameworks, it has been said that the Scottish courts present a conservatism towards human rights arguments[43] distinct from England and Wales and the Northern Ireland maintains legacy issues from the Troubles as well as uncertainty in the Northern Irish Assembly. It has been said that we need a more 'sophisticated notion of professionalism' in which to better understand the actions and reactions of cause lawyers and this could not be more true of the UK-wide landscape of progressive legal practice.[44] A more detailed study, for example, of separate network nodes (such as within law centres or at the Bar) but across each of the separate devolved nations in the UK, analysing the prevalence of different legal tools and human rights based approaches, would assist in capturing the distinctions and similarities of practitioners in different legal cultures and their perceptions of the use of law for social change. A deeper understanding of which tools lawyers

Legal Profession 41; Kennon Sheldon and Lawrence Krieger, 'Does legal education have undermining effects on law students? Evaluating changes in motivation, values and wellbeing' (2004) 22 *Behavioural Sciences and the Law* 261; Wendy Larcombe and Katherine Fethers, 'Schooling the blues: an investigation of factors associated with psychological distress among law students' (2013) 36 *UNSWLJ* 390; Emma Jones, *Emotions in the Law School: Transforming Legal Education Through the Passions* (Routledge, 2019).

[40] Andras Sajo *Constitutional Sentiments* (Yale University Press, 2011); Andras Sajo, 'Emotions in Constitutional Institutions' (2016) 8(1) *Emotion Review* 44, 44.

[41] Susan Bandes and Jeremy Blumenthal, 'Emotion and the Law' (2012) 8 *Annual Review of Law and Social Science* 161, 161.

[42] Neil Graffin, 'The emotional impacts of working as an asylum lawyer' (2019) 38(1) *Refugee Survey Quarterly* 30.

[43] Anna Poole, 'Human Rights in Great Britain' (2016) 21(3) *Judicial Review* 162. See also Mhairi Snowden, *Discussion Paper: Overcoming barriers to public interest litigation in Scotland* (Human Rights Consortium Scotland, 2018), available at https://hrcscotland.org/wp-content/uploads/2018/11/final-overcoming-barriers-to-pil-in-scotlnd-web-version.pdf.

[44] McEvoy and Rebouche (n 37) 277.

use, and why, across the devolved nations is also critical in order for progressive lawyers to learn from one another in times of uncertainty and constitutional change.

We're All Pushing for Something

This book has demonstrated a collective identity within the progressive lawyering movement that will help sustain it into the future as they push towards change. Lawyers' motivations are intrinsically linked to their collective sense of identity and purpose:

> Jacqueline: What motivates you then day to day?
>
> Ankita: Making a difference. It's completely cheesy and anytime anyone has ever told me that I'm a cock-eyed optimist or an idealist and I have no sense of the real world, I just say, well look what's actually happened, you know, look at the changes people have made over the centuries … it's that kind of social justice movement.
>
> Jacqueline: And do you see yourself as being part of a movement?
>
> Ankita: Yes, very much so … I love feeling that I've got colleagues and that we're pushing for the same thing. Everyday I'm excited about the community I work in. There's all kind of people who, I find them really inspiring and I enjoy the atmosphere, we're all pushing for something.

I described in the preface a memory of a rainy weekend morning where I turned to law for something 'to become'. Identity is always interactively being co-created as lawyers' lives – and their clients and causes – change and evolve. Narratives can only ever reveal stories that are still in progress. Ankita draws upon the 'changes people have made over the centuries' because together progressive lawyers reach both back and forward, and towards one another, in their storytelling and in their collective pursuit of social change. Lawyers are all, no matter what stage of their careers, still 'becoming' as they negotiate who they are both within and across their networks. It is hoped that the identification of collective identity within the progressive lawyering movement in the UK will allow us to better understand lawyers changing lives as they adapt, progress and continually move forward in changing times.

Appendix One: Table of Narrative Interviews

No	Name [Pseudonym]	Type of Organisation [at time of interview]	Previous Relevant Positions	Solicitor/ Barrister	Decade of Legal Professional Qualification	Progressive Work Campaigns – C Research/Policy Work – P Strategic Litigation – SL Legal Aid – LA	Geographic Area
1	Adil	Charity	Law Centre	Barrister	2010–2020	LA SL	London/ South West
2	Aidan	Chambers	Charity	Barrister	1970–1980	LA C	London
3	Andrea	Legal Aid Law Firm	–	Solicitor	2000–2010	LA SL	London
4	Ankita	Charity/NGO	Chambers NGO	Barrister	2000–2010	LA P SL C	London
5	Annie	Law Centre	Charity	Solicitor	2010–2020	LA P C	London
6	Ben	Legal Aid Law Firm	Charity	Solicitor	1990–2000	SL LA P	London

(continued)

No	Name [Pseudonym]	Type of Organisation [at time of interview]	Previous Relevant Positions	Solicitor/ Barrister	Decade of Legal Professional Qualification	Progressive Work Campaigns – C Research/Policy Work – P Strategic Litigation – SL Legal Aid – LA	Geographic Area
7	Dominic	Chambers	Law Centre CAB	Barrister	1980–1990	LA C	London
8	Ellie	Legal Aid Law Firm	–	Solicitor	2010–2020	LA C	London
9	Emily	Law Centre	Legal Aid Law Firm	Solicitor	2000–2010	LA P	Regional (North)
10	Eve	Legal Aid Law Firm	Law Centre	Solicitor	2010–2020	LA P C	Scotland
11	Gail	Chambers/ Charity	NGO Campaigns	Barrister	2000–2010	C P SL	London
12	Gareth	Legal Aid Law Firm	–	Solicitor	2000–2010	LA SL	N Ireland
13	Gideon	Chambers	Law Centre	Barrister	1970–1980	LA P	London
14	Jemma	–	Chambers	Barrister	2000–2010	LA	Regional (Midlands)
15	Jessica	Charity/Law School Clinic	Legal Aid Law Firm	Solicitor	2000–2010	C P SL	London

16	Kathleen	Legal Aid Law Firm	Law Centre	Solicitor	1960–1970	LA P	London
17	Katy	Charity	–	Solicitor	2010–2020	LA P	N Ireland
18	Kenneth	Legal Aid Law Firm	Law Centre	Solicitor	1960–1970	LA SL P	London
19	Khadija	Legal Aid Law Firm	–	Solicitor	2010–2020	LA C	Regional (North)
20	Kimberley	Charity	Law Centre	Solicitor	2000–2010	LA SL P C	Scotland
21	Lee	Legal Aid Law Firm	Law Centre/ Charity	Caseworker	1990–2000	P LA	London
22	Lena	Law Centre	Legal Aid Law Firm CAB	Solicitor	2000–2010	LA C SL	Regional
23	Marian	–	Charity	Barrister	2000–2010	P LA C	Regional (North)
24	Marie	Charity	–	Barrister	1990–2000	LA C	London

(continued)

No	Name [Pseudonym]	Type of Organisation [at time of interview]	Previous Relevant Positions	Solicitor/ Barrister	Decade of Legal Professional Qualification	Progressive Work Campaigns – C Research/Policy Work – P Strategic Litigation – SL Legal Aid – LA	Geographic Area
25	Martin	Chambers	Law Centre	Barrister	2000–2010	SL C LA	London
26	Melissa	Law Centre	Legal Aid Law Firm	Solicitor	1980–1990	LA P C	London
27	Michael	Chambers	Chambers (other)	Barrister	2000–2010	SL LA	London
28	Phil	Legal Aid Law Firm	Legal Aid	Solicitor	1990–2000	LA C SL	London
29	Rihana	Legal Aid Law Firm/ Law Centre Volunteer	Law Centre	Solicitor	2000–2010	LA SL	London
30	Rodrigo	Legal Aid Law Firm	Legal Aid Campaigns	Solicitor	1970–1980	LA P C	London
31	Ruth	Legal Aid Law Firm	CAB	Solicitor	2010–2020	LA C	Regional (Midlands)

32	Stefan	Law School Clinic Legal Aid	Law Centre	Solicitor	1990–2000	P LA	London
33	Tim	Charity	Legal Aid Law Firm	Solicitor	2010–2020	LA SL	London
34	Wendy	Law School Clinic	Charity	–	2000–2010	LA SL P	London
35	Zachary	Law School Clinic	Charity	–	1980–1990	P LA	Scotland

Appendix Two: Narrative Interview Question Guide

Interview Themes:

Motivation
Family/Influences
Legal Education
Memorable Cases
Legal Aid (Past & Present)
Critical Events
Strategic Litigation
Campaigning
Professional Ethics
Organisational Culture
Future of Practice
Challenges

Interview Phases: Initiation, Main Narration, Follow-Up Questions, Concluding Talk.[1]

1. Can you tell me about when you decided to become a lawyer? [initiation phase]
2. What, or who, would you say was the strongest influence on your decision to become a lawyer? [initiation phase/main narration]
3. Is there anything else in your background or your values that you think significantly informs the type of lawyer you are? [main narration]
4. What would you say to your younger self now about starting out as a lawyer? What would you do differently?
5. In the early years of legal practice, what motivated you in your work?
6. What is your predominant area of legal practice? Was it always that area of law?
7. Can you tell me a story about a significantly memorable case in your early career? (Why is it memorable and meaningful to you?) [main narration]
8. What obstacles did you face in the early years of practice? [main narration]
9. Since you started working as a lawyer how has the job changed? [main narration]
10. What is your perspective on changes to legal aid provision? [follow-up]
11. What is your perspective on the proposed abolition of the Human Rights Act? [follow-up]

[1] Adapted from Sandra Jovchelovitch and Martin Bauer, Narrative Interviewing in Martin Bauer and George Gaskill (eds), *Qualitative Researching with Text, Image and Sound: A Practical Handbook* (Sage, 2000) 57–74.

12. What organisations (membership bodies, professional organisations, campaign groups), if any, were or are you involved with? [follow-up]
13. Have those networks, or any one individual, helped you in terms of your career progression? Which of your contemporaries most inspires you in your work? [follow-up]
14. What qualities do you think are most important for a lawyer? Do you think you have those qualities?
15. (Looking back) what would you say is the biggest challenge for you in your professional life? [main narration]
16. Do you conduct/are you instructed to conduct strategic litigation? Were you ever engaged in strategic litigation? Did you lead the strategy? Why did you pursue the strategy you did? Did you perceive any ethical tensions? Did you achieve your clients' goals using litigation alone? [follow-up]
17. Do you campaign on any issues relevant to your casework? Can you tell me about a particularly successful campaign? How did you get involved in the issue? [follow-up]
18. What do you think is the most important factor in sustaining your practice/the profession in future? What would you say to law students wanting to pursue this sort of work? What stories do you tell them about your work? [follow up/main narration]
19. Do you think there is a particular culture in your Chambers/charity/firm towards social justice or access to justice issues? [follow-up/concluding talk]
20. Why do you continue to do this job? What motivates you now? [concluding talk]

Bibliography

UK GOVERNMENT AND REGULATORY BODIES

Bar Standards Board, Code of Conduct, Rule C15, 2015.

Bar Standards Board, Code of Conduct, Rule C28, 2015.

Committee on Legal Aid and Legal Advice in England and Wales, *Report of the Committee on Legal Aid and Legal Advice in England and Wales*, 1945.

Frazer, L, 'Justice Update – Statement made on 12 July 2018, Statement UIN HCWS853', UK Parliament, 12 July 2018.

The Judiciary of England and Wales, *Report on Litigants in Person*, Judicial Working Group, 2013.

Ministry of Justice, *Legal Support: The Way Ahead, An Action Plan to Deliver Better Support to People Experiencing Legal Problems*, February 2019.

Ministry of Justice, *Post-Implementation Review of LASPO, Parts 1 and 2*, 2019.

Public Accounts Select Committee, *Efficiency in the Criminal Justice System*, May 2016.

Sakkberg, Y and Politowski, B, *Briefing Paper Number 7603, 9 June 2016 – Civil Legal Aid: England & Wales, Scotland and Northern Ireland Compared*, House of Commons Library, June 2016.

Scottish Government, *Rethinking Legal Aid: An Independent Strategic Review*, 2018.

Solicitors Regulation Authority, *Principles*, 2011.

Solicitors Regulation Authority, *Standards and Regulations*, 2011.

UK Government Legal Aid Agency, 'Standard Civil Legal Aid Contractors List', 2018.

UK Government, *Legal Aid, Sentencing and Punishment of Offenders Act 2012, Sch 1*, 2012.

BOOKS

Abel, R, *English Lawyers between Market and State: The Politics of Professionalism* (Oxford, Oxford University Press, 2003).

Alleyne, B, *Narrative Networks: Storied Approaches in a Digital Age* (New York, Sage, 2015).

Alvesson, M and Skoldberg, K, *Reflexive Methodology: New Vistas for Qualitative Research* (New York, Sage, 2009).

Andrews, M, *Lifetimes of Commitment: Ageing, Politics, Psychology* (Cambridge, Cambridge University Press, 1991).

Atkinson, P, Coffey, A, Delamont, S, Lofland, J and Lofland L (eds), *Handbook of Ethnography* (New York, Sage, 2001).

Barnett, S and Barnett, H, *Towards Social Reform* (London, T Fisher Unwin, 1909).

Bennett, W and Feldman, M, *Reconstructing Reality in the Courtroom: Justice and Judgment in American Culture* (New Brunswick, Rutgers University Press, 1981).

Bolton, S, *Emotion Management in the Workplace* (London, Palgrave MacMillan, 2005).

Bourdieu, P, *Distinctions: A Social Critique of the Judgement of Taste*, translated by Richard Nice (Cambridge, Harvard University Press, 1984).

Brookfield, S, *Understanding and Facilitating Adult Learning* (Maidenhead, Open University, 1986).

Brooks, P and Gewirtz, P (eds), *Law's Stories: Narrative and Rhetoric in Law* (New Haven, Yale University Press, 1998).

Chen, A and Cummings, S, *Public Interest Lawyering: A Contemporary Perspective* (Alphen aan den Rijn, Walters Kluwer Law & Business, 2013).

Clandinin, D and Connelly, F, *Narrative Inquiry: Experience and Story in Qualitative Research* (San Francisco, Josey-Bass, 2000).

Clements, L, *Clustered Injustice and the Level Playing Field* (London, Legal Action Group, 2020).

Denzin, N, *Interpretative Biography* (New York, Sage, 1989).

Diani, M, and McAdam, D (eds), *Social Movements and Networks: Relational Approaches to Collective Action* (Oxford, Oxford University Press, 2003).

Egerton, R, *Legal Aid* (New York, Oxford University Press 1945).

Emmel, N, *Sampling and Choosing Cases in Qualitative Research: A Realist Approach* (New York, Sage, 2013).

Fetterman, D, *Ethnography: Step by Step* (New York, Sage, 1998).

Francis, A, *The Edge of Law: Emergent and Divergent Models of Legal Professionalism* (Abingdon, Routledge, 2011).

Garner, B (ed), *Black's Law Dictionary*, 11th edn (Toronto, Thomson Reuters, 2011).

Garth, B, *Neighbourhood Law Firms for the Poor: A Comparative Study of Recent Developments in Legal Aid and the Legal Profession* (Alphen aan den Rijn, Sijthoff and Noordhoff, 1980).

Genn, H, *Paths to Justice* (Oxford, Oxford University Press, 1998).

Giddings, J, *Promoting Justice Through Clinical Legal Education* (Victoria, Justice Press, 2013).

Goffmann, E, *The Presentation of Self in Everyday Life* (New York, Random House, 1956).

Halliday, T, Karpik, L and Freeley, M (eds), *Fighting for Political Freedom: Comparative Studies of the Legal Complex and Political Liberalism* (Oxford, Hart Publishing, 2007).

Handler, J, *Social Movements and the Legal System: A Theory of Law Reform and Social Change* (New York, Academic Press, 1978).

Harlow, C and Rawlings, R, *Pressure Through Law* (Abingdon, Routledge, 1992).

Hochschild, A, *The Managed Heart: Commercialization of Human Feeling* (Berkeley, University of California Press, 1983).

Hynes S, and Robins, J, *The Justice Gap* (London, Legal Action Group, 2009).

James, S, Mullings, S, Groves, M and Brennan, J, *Justice Matters: Essays from the Pandemic* (London, Legal Action Group, 2020).

Jenkins, J, 'Sociopolitical Movements' in S Long (ed), *The Handbook of Political Behaviour* (New York. Plenum Press, 1981).

Jones, E, *Emotions in the Law School: Transforming Legal Education Through the Passions* (Abingdon, Routledge, 2019).

Kadushin, C, *Understanding Social Networks: Theories, Concepts and Findings* (Oxford, Oxford University Press, 2012).

Kairys, D (ed), *The Politics of Law: A Progressive Critique* (New York, Basic Books, 1998).

Kelly, M, *Lives of Lawyers Revisited: Transformation and Resilience in the Organizations of Practice* (Ann Arbor, University of Michigan Press, 2007).

Kennedy, H, *Just Law: The Changing Face of Justice – and Why it Matters to Us All* (New York, Random House, 2011).

Kerrigan, K and Murray, V, *A Student Guide to Clinical Legal Education and Pro Bono* (London, Palgrave, 2010).

King, J, *Judging Social Rights* (Cambridge, Cambridge University Press, 2014).

Kronman, A, *The Lost Lawyer: Failing Ideals and the Legal Profession*, 6th edn (Cambridge, Harvard University Press, 2001).

Lee, M and Abbot, C, *Environmental Groups and Legal Expertise: Shaping the Brexit Process* (London, UCL Press, 2021).

Lemmings, D, *Professors of Law: Barristers and English Legal Culture in the Eighteenth Century* (Oxford, Oxford University Press, 2000).

Lofland, J, *Social Movement Organizations: Guide to Research on Insurgent Realities* (New York, Aldine de Gruyter, 1996).

Lopez, G, *Rebellious Lawyering: One Chicano's Vision of Progressive Law Practice* (Boulder, Westview Press, 1992).

Luban, D, *Lawyers and Justice: An Ethical Study* (Princeton, Princeton University Press, 1988).
Lyotard, J, *The Postmodern Condition: A Report on Knowledge* (Manchester, Manchester University Press, 1984).
Mansfield, M, *Memoirs of a Radical Lawyer* (London, Bloomsbury, 2009).
Mather, L, McEwan, C and Maiman, R, *Divorce Lawyers at Work: Varieties of Professionalism in Practice* (Oxford, Oxford University Press, 2001).
Maynard-Moody, S and Musheno, M, *Cops, Teachers and Counselors: Stories from the Front Lines of Public Service* (Ann Arbor, University of Michigan Press, 2003).
Maxwell, J, *Qualitative Research Design: An Interactive Approach* (New York, Sage, 2013).
McCann, M, *Rights at Work: Pay Equity Reform and the Politics of Legal Mobilization* (Chicago, Chicago University Press, 1994).
McCann, M, *Taking Reform Seriously: Perspectives on Public Interest Liberalism* (Ithaca, Cornell University Press, 1986).
McLean, P, *Culture in Networks* (Cambridge, Polity Press, 2017).
Minnow, M and Bellow, G (eds), *Law Stories* (Ann Arbor, University of Michigan Press, 1998).
Moorhead, R, Vaughan, S and Godinho, C, *In-House Lawyers' Ethics: Institutional Logics, Legal Risk and the Tournament of Influence* (Oxford, Hart Publishing, 2018).
Nash, K, *The Political Sociology of Human Rights* (Cambridge, Cambridge University Press, 2015).
Newman, D, *Legal Aid Lawyers and the Quest for Justice* (Oxford, Hart Publishing, 2013).
Prabhat, D, *Unleashing the Force of Law: Legal Mobilization, National Security and Basic Freedoms* (London, Palgrave Macmillan, 2016).
Prosser, T, *Test Cases for the Poor: Legal Techniques in the Politics of Social Welfare* (London, Child Poverty Action Group, 1983).
Reed-Danahay, D, *Auto/ethnography: Rewriting the Self and the Social* (New York, Routledge, 1997).
Robertson, G, *The Justice Game* (New York, Vintage, 1999).
Rosenberg, G, *The Hollow Hope: Can Courts Bring About Social Change?* (Chicago, Chicago University Press, 2008).
Sajo, A, *Constitutional Sentiments* (New Haven, Yale University Press, 2011).
Sarat, A and Scheingold, S, *Cause Lawyers and Social Movements* (Palo Alto, Stanford University Press, 2006).
Sarat, A and Scheingold, S (eds), *Cause Lawyering: Political Commitments and Professional Responsibilities* (Oxford, Oxford University Press, 1998).
Sarat, A and Scheingold, S, *Something to Believe In: Politics, Professionalism and Cause Lawyering* (Palo Alto, Stanford University Press, 2004).
Scheingold, S, *The Politics of Rights: Lawyers, Public Policy and Political Change* (Ann Arbor, University of Michigan Press, 2004).
Schon, D, *The Reflective Practitioner: How Professionals Think in Action* (London, Temple Smith, 1983).
The Secret Barrister, *The Secret Barrister: Stories of Law and How It's Broken* (London, Picador, 2018).
Shacklock, G and Smyth, J (eds), *Being Reflexive in Critical Educational and Social Research* (Brighton, Falmer, 1998).
Shklar, J, *Legalism: Law, Moralism and Political Trials* (Cambridge, Harvard University Press, 1964).
Stephens, M, *Community Law Centres: A Critical Appraisal* (Aldershot, Avebury, 1990).
Twining, W, *Blackstone's Tower: The English Law School* (London, Sweet and Maxwell, 1994).
Vanhala, L, *Making Rights a Reality: Disability Rights Activists and Legal Mobilization* (Cambridge, Cambridge University Press, 2011).
Wilson, A, *In Black and White: A Young Barrister's Story of Race and Class in a Broken Justice System* (London, Endeavour, 2020).
Wilson, R, *The Global Evolution of Clinical Legal Education* (Cambridge, Cambridge University Press, 2017).
Zander, M, *The Hamlyn Lectures: The State of Justice* (London, Sweet and Maxwell, 1999).
Zirakzadeh, C, *Social Movements in Politics: A Comparative Study* (London, Longman, 1997).

CHAPTERS IN EDITED VOLUMES

Adams, T and Jones, S, 'Autoethnography is queer' in N Denzin, Y Lincoln, and L Smith (eds), *Handbook of Critical and Indigenous Methodologies* (New York, Sage, 2008).

Bellow, G, 'Lawyers for a Political Movement: California Rural Legal Assistance' in P Heymann and L Liebman (eds), *The Social Responsibilities of Lawyers: Case Studies* (Westbury, NY Foundation Press, 1988).

Birch, M, 'Re/constructing Research Narratives: Self and Sociological Identity in Alternative Settings' in R Edwards and J Ribbens (eds), *Feminist Dilemmas in Qualitative Research: Public Knowledge and Private Lives* (New York, Sage, 1998).

Boon, A, 'Cause Lawyers in a Cold Climate: The Impact of Globalization in the United Kingdom' in A Sarat and S Scheingold (eds), *Cause Lawyering and the State in a Global Era* (Oxford, Oxford University Press, 2001).

Bruner, J, 'The Narrative Creation of Self' in L Angus and J McLeod (eds), *The Handbook of Narrative and Psychotherapy* (New York, Sage, 2004).

Buchanan, L, 'Community Lawyers, Law Reform and Systemic Change: Is the End in Sight?' in A Flynn and J Hodgson (eds), *Access to Justice and Legal Aid: Comparative Perspectives on Unmet Legal Need* (Oxford, Hart Publishing, 2017).

Cappelletti, M and Garth, B, 'Access to Justice and the Welfare State: An Introduction' in M Cappelletti, M Seccombe, and J Weisner (eds), *Access to Justice and the Welfare State* (Springer, 1981).

Chambliss, E, 'Whose Ethics? The Benchmark Problem in Legal Ethics Research' in L Levin and L Mather (eds), *Lawyers in Practice: Ethical Decision Making in Context* (Chicago, University of Chicago Press, 2012).

Clandinin, D and Rosiek, J, 'Mapping a Landscape of Narrative Inquiry: Borderland Spaces and Tensions' in D Clandinin (ed), *Handbook of Narrative Inquiry: Mapping a Methodology* (New York, Sage, 2006).

Diani, M, 'Networks and Participation' in D Snow, S Soule and H Kriesi (eds), *The Blackwell Companion to Social Movements* (Blackwell, 2004).

Diani, M, 'Networks and Social Movements: A Research Programme' in M Diani and D McAdam (eds), *Social Movement Analysis: The Network Perspective* (Oxford, Oxford University Press, 2003).

Diani, M, 'Social Movements and Networks' in the *Blackwell Encyclopaedia of Sociology* (Hoboken, Wiley and Sons, 2015).

Ellis, C and Bochner, A, 'Autoethnography, Personal Narrative, Reflexivity' in N Denzin and Y Lincoln (eds), *Handbook of Qualitative Research* (New York, Sage, 2000).

Epp, C, 'Law as an Instrument of Social Reform' in G Caldeira, R Keleman and K Whittington (eds), *The Oxford Handbook of Law and Politics* (Oxford, Oxford University Press, 2008).

Flood, J 'Socio-legal Ethnography' in R Banaker and M Travers (eds), *Theory and Method in Socio-Legal Research* (Oxford, Hart Publishing, 2005).

Friedman, D and McAdam, D, 'Collective Identity and Activism: Networks, Choices and the Life of a Social Movement' in A Morris and C M Mueller (eds), *Frontiers in Social Movement Theory* (New Haven, Yale University Press, 1992).

Goodwin, J and Jasper, J, 'Emotions and Social Movements' in J Stets and J Turner (eds), *Handbook of the Sociology of Emotions* (New York, Springer, 2006).

Greene, A, 'The Human Rights Act in a Culture of Control' in C-M Smyth and R Lang (eds), *The Future of Human Rights in the UK* (Cambridge, Cambridge Scholars Press, 2017).

Johnston, H and Klandermans, B, 'The Cultural Analysis of Social Movements' in H Johnston and Klandermans (eds), *Social Movements and Culture* (Abingdon, Routledge, 2003).

Kilwein, J, 'Still Trying: Lawyering for the Poor and Disadvantaged in Pittsburgh, Pennsylvania' in A Sarat and S Scheingold (eds), *Cause Lawyering: Political Commitments and Professional Responsibilities* (Oxford, Oxford University Press, 1998).

Kinghan, J and Knowles, R, 'Striking a Balance in Clinical Legal Education: Reimagining the Role of the Teaching Practitioner in Casework Partnerships' in L Thomas, S Vaughan, B Malkani and T Lynch (eds), *Reimagining Clinical Legal Education* (Oxford, Hart Publishing, 2018).

Kinghan, J, 'Lifetimes of Commitment to Law and Social Justice' in D Newman and F Gordon (eds), *Leading Works in Law and Social Justice* (Abingdon, Routledge, 2021).

Kinghan, J, 'Teaching Access to Justice: Cause Lawyering and Strategic Litigation in Clinical Context' in C Ashford and P McKeown (eds), *Social Justice and Legal Education* (Cambridge, Cambridge Scholars Press, 2018).

Kunitz, S and Markee, N, 'Understanding the Fuzzy Borders of Context in Conversation Analysis and Ethnography' in S Wortham, D Kim, and S May (eds), *Discourse and Education. Encyclopedia of Language and Education*, 3rd edn (New York, Springer, 2016).

Maiman, R, 'They All Have Different Policies So of Course They Have to Give Difference News' in A Sarat and S Scheingold (eds), *The Cultural Lives of Cause Lawyers* (Cambridge, Cambridge University Press, 2008).

Mather, L and Levin, L, 'Why Context Matters' in L Levin and L Mather (eds), *Lawyers in Practice: Ethical Decision Making in Context* (Chicago, University of Chicago Press, 2012).

McCann M, and Silverstein, H, 'Rethinking Law's "Allurements": A Relational Analysis of Social Movement Lawyers in the US' in A Sarat and S Scheingold (eds), *Cause Lawyering: Political Commitments and Professional Responsibilities* (Oxford, Oxford University Press, 1998).

McEvoy, K and Rebouche, R, 'Mobilizing the Professions: Lawyers, Politics and the Collective Legal Conscience' in J Morison et al (eds), *Judges, Transition and Human Rights* (Oxford, Oxford University Press, 2007).

Meili, S, 'Latin American Cause Lawyering Networks' in A Sarat and S Scheingold (eds), *Cause Lawyering and the State in a Global Era* (Oxford, Oxford University Press, 2001).

Menkel-Meadow, C, 'The Causes of Cause Lawyering: Toward an Understanding of the Motivation and Commitment of Social Justice Lawyers' in A Sarat and S Scheingold (eds), *Cause Lawyers: Political Commitments and Professional Responsibilities* (Oxford, Oxford University Press, 1998).

Organ, J and Sigafoos, J, 'What if There is Nowhere to Get Advice?' in A Flynn and J Hodgson (eds), *Access to Justice and Legal Aid: Comparative Perspectives on Unmet Legal Need* (Oxford, Hart Publishing, 2017).

Sarat, A and Scheingold, S, 'Bringing Cultural Analysis to the Study of Cause Lawyers: An Introduction' in A Sarat and S Scheingold (eds), *The Cultural Lives of Cause Lawyers* (Cambridge, Cambridge University Press, 2008).

Sarat, A and Scheingold, S, 'State Transformation, Globalization and the Possibilities of Cause Lawyering' in A Sarat and S Scheingold (eds), *Cause Lawyering and the State in a Global Era* (Oxford, Oxford University Press, 2001).

Sarat, A, 'Between the (Presence of) Violence and the (Possibility of) Justice' in A Sarat and S Scheingold (eds), *Cause Lawyering: Political Commitments and Professional Responsibilities* (Oxford, Oxford University Press, 1998).

Schiff, B, McKim, A and Patron, S, 'Life and Narrative: A Brief Primer' in B Schiff, A McKim, and S Patron (eds), *Life and Narrative: The Risks and Responsibilities of Storying Experience* (Oxford, Oxford University Press, 2017).

Shamir, R and Chinsky, S, 'Destruction of House and Construction of a Cause: Lawyers and Bedouins in the Israeli Courts' in A Sarat and S Scheingold (eds), *Cause Lawyering: Political Commitments and Professional Responsibilities* (Oxford, Oxford University Press, 1998).

Shdaimah, C, 'Legal Service Lawyers: When Conceptions of Lawyering and Values Clash' in L Levin and L Mather (eds), *Lawyers in Practice: Ethical Decision Making in Context* (Chicago, University of Chicago Press, 2012).

Sommerlad, H and Hammerslev, O, 'Lawyers in a New Geopolitical Conjuncture: Continuity and Change' in R Abel, O Hammersley, H Sommerlad and U Schults (eds), *Lawyers in 21st-Century Societies: Volume 1 National Reports* (Oxford, Hart Publishing, 2020).

Soule, S 'Diffusion Processes Within and Across Movements' in D Snow, S Soule and H Kriesi (eds), *The Blackwell Companion to Social Movements* (Oxford, Blackwell, 2004).

Tajfel, H and Turner, J, 'A Integrative Theory of Intergroup Conflict' in W Austin and S Worchel (eds), *The Psychology of Intergroup Relations* (Monterey, Brooks/Cole, 1979).

Thorne, A and McLean, K, 'Telling Traumatic Events in Adolescence: A Study of Master Narrative Positioning' in R Fivush and C Haden (eds), *Connecting Culture and Memory: The Development of an Autobiographical Self* (Mahwah, Lawrence Erlbaum, 2003).

Tomlinson, J, 'Crowdfunding and the Changing Dynamics of Public Interest Judicial Review' in J Tomlinson, *Justice in the Digital State: Assessing the Next Revolution in Digital Justice* (Bristol, Policy Press, 2019).

Trubek, L and Kransberger, M, 'Critical Lawyers: Social Justice and the Structures of Private Practice' in A Sarat and S Scheingold (eds), *Cause Lawyers: Political Commitments and Professional Responsibilities* (Oxford, Oxford University Press, 1998).

Van der Waal, K, 'Getting Going: Organizing Ethnographic Fieldwork' in S Ybema, D Yanow, H Wels and F Kamsteeg (eds), *Organizational Ethnography: Studying the Complexity of Everyday Life* (New York, Sage, 2009).

ARTICLES

Abel, R, 'Law Without Politics: Legal Aid Under Advanced Capitalism' (1985) 32 *UCLA Law Review* 474–642.

Abel, R, 'Lawyers and the Power to Change' (1985) 7(1) *Law and Policy* 5–18.

Abel, R, 'The Paradoxes of Pro Bono' (2010) 78(5) *Fordham Law Review* 2443–50.

Acheta, A, 'Community Lawyering Review Essay' (1993) 81 *California Law Review* 1363–99.

Adams, K, Hean, S, Sturgis, P and Clark, J, 'Investigating the Factors Influencing the Professional Identity of First-Year Health and Social Care Students' (2006) 5(2) *Learning in Health and Social Care* 55–68.

Agar, M and Hobbs, J, 'Interpreting Discourse: Coherence and the Analysis of Ethnographic Interviews' (1982) 5(1) *Discourse Processes* 1–32.

Alfieri, A, 'Rebellious Pedagogy and Practice' (2016) 23(1) *Clinical Law Review* 5–36.

Alston, P, 'The Populist Challenge to Human Rights' (2017) 9(1) *Journal of Human Rights Practice* 1–15.

Amsterdam, A, 'Telling Stories and Stories About Them' (1994) 1(1) *Clinical Law Review* 9–40.

Anim-Addo, J and Gunaratnam, Y, 'Secrets and Lies: Narrative Methods at the Limits of Research' (2012) 5(3) *Journal of Writing in Creative Practice* 387.

Baker, S and Biglaiser, G, 'A Model of Cause Lawyering' (2014) 43(1) *Journal of Legal Studies* 37–63.

Bandes, S and Blumenthal, J, 'Emotion and the Law' (2012) 8 *Annual Review of Law and Social Science* 161–81.

Bankowski, Z and Mungham, G 'Warwick University Ltd, Continued' (1974) 1(2) *British Journal of Law and Society* 179–84.

Barnhardt, B and Ginns, P, 'An Alienation-Based Framework for Student Experience in Higher Education: New Interpretations of Past Observations in Student Learning Theory' (2014) 68 *Higher Education* 789–805.

Bellow, G, 'Steady Work: A Practitioner's Reflections on Political Lawyering' (1996) 31(2) *Harvard Civil Rights-Civil Liberties Review* 297–309.

Benford, R and Snow, D, 'Framing Processes and Social Movements: An Overview and Assessment' (2000) 26 *Annual Review of Sociology* 611–39.

Bens, J and Vetters, L, 'Ethnographic Legal Studies: Reconnecting Anthropological and Sociological Traditions' (2018) 50(3) *The Journal of Legal Pluralism and Unofficial Law* 239–54.

Bindman, G, 'What Made Me a Legal Aid Lawyer' (2002) 29(3) *Journal of Law and Society* 510–20.

Bleasdale, L and Francis, A, 'Great Expectations: Millennial Lawyers and The Structures of Contemporary Legal Practice' (2020) 40(3) *Legal Studies* 376–96.

Bloom, A, 'Practice Style and Successful Legal Mobilisation' (2008) 71 *Law and Contemporary Problems* 1–16.

Boon, A, 'Cause Lawyers and the Alternate Ethical Paradigm' (2004) 7(2) *Legal Ethics* 250–68.

Boon, A, 'From Public Service to Service Industry: The Impact of Socialisation and Work on Motivation and Values of Lawyers' (2005) 12(2) *International Journal of the Legal Profession* 229–60.

Bouwen, P and McCown, M, 'Lobbying versus Litigation: Political and Legal Strategies of Interest in the European Union' (2007) 14(3) *Journal of European Public Policy* 422–43.

Brooks, S and Tokarz, K, 'Conversations on "Community Lawyering": Conversations on the Newest (Oldest) Wave in Clinical Legal Education' (2008) 28 *Washington University Journal of Law and Policy* 359–402.

Brown, A, 'A Narrative Approach to Collective Identities' (2006) 43(4) *Journal of Management Studies* 731–53.

Cahn, E and Cahn, J, 'Power to the People or the Profession? The Public Interest in Public Interest Law' (1970) 79(5) *Yale Law Journal* 1005–48.

Cahn, E and Cahn, J, 'The War on Poverty: A Civilian Perspective' (1964) 73(8) *Yale Law Journal* 1317–52.

Calavita, K and Seron, C, 'Postmodernism and Protest: Recovering the Sociological Imagination' (1992) *Law and Society Review* 765, 765–72.

Campbell, C and Wiles, P, 'Study of Law in Society in Britain' (1976) 10(4) *Law and Society Review* 547–78.

Campbell, E, 'Should I Share My Journal Entry with You? A Critical Exploration of Relational Ethics in Autoethnography' (2017) 6(4) *Departures in Critical Qualitative Research* 4–22.

Collier, R, '"Left Pessimists" in "Rose Coloured Glasses"? Reflections on the Political Economy of Socio-Legal Studies and Legal (Academic) Well-Being' (2020) 47 (S2) *Journal of Law and Society* 244–61.

Collier, R, 'Wellbeing in the Legal Profession: Reflections on Recent Developments (or, What Do We Talk About When We Talk About Wellbeing?' (2016) 23(1) *International Journal of the Legal Profession* 41–60.

Cummings, S and NeJaime, D, 'Lawyering for Marriage Equality' (2010) 57 *UCLA Law Review* 1235–1331.

Cummings, S, 'Movement Lawyering' (2017) 5 *University of Illinois Law Review* 1645–1732.

Cummings, S, 'The Politics of Pro Bono' (2004) 52(1) *UCLA Law Review* 1–49.

Cummings, S, 'The Pursuit of Legal Rights and Beyond' (2012) 59(3) *UCLA Law Review* 506–49.

Dailey, E, 'Implementation of Judgments: Practical Insights from Civil Society' (2020) 12(1) *Journal of Human Rights Practice* 224–29.

Diani, M, 'The Concept of a Social Movement' (1992) 40(1) *Sociological Review* 1–25.

Duncan, N, 'Editorial', (2007) 41(3) *Law Teacher* 1–3.

Elson, A, 'The Rushcliffe Report' (1946) 13(2) *The University of Chicago Law Review* 131–44.

Etienne, M, 'The Ethics of Cause Lawyering: An Empirical Examination of Criminal Defense Lawyers as Cause Lawyers' (2005) 95(4) *Journal of Criminal Law and Criminology* 1195–1260.

Ewick, P and Silbey, S, 'Subversive Stories and Hegemonic Tales: Towards a Sociology of Narrative (1995) 29(2) *Law & Society Review* 197–226.

Farrell, J, 'Social Media for Social Change Lawyers: An Australian Housing Rights Lawyer's Experience' (2013) 20(2) *International Journal of the Legal Profession* 209–21.

Fokas, E, 'Directions in Religious Pluralism in Europe: Mobilizations in the Shadow of the European Court of Human Rights Religious Freedoms Jurisprudence' (2015) 4(1) *Oxford Journal of Law and Religion* 54–74.

Folsom, R and Roberts, N, 'The Warwick Story: Being Led Down the Contextual Path of the Law' (1979) 36(1-2) *Journal of Legal Education* 166–83.

Francis, A and Sommerlad, H, 'Access to Legal Work Experience and its Role in the (Re)production of Legal Professional Identity' (2009) 16(1) *International Journal of the Legal Profession* 63–86.

Francis, A, 'Legal Education, Social Mobility, and Employability: Possible Selves, Curriculum Intervention and the Role of Legal Work Experience' (2015) 42(2) *Journal of Law and Society* 173–201.

Frank, J, 'A Plea for Lawyer-Schools' (1947) 56(8) *Yale Law Journal* 1303–44.

Frank, J, 'Why Not a Clinical Lawyer School?' (1933) 81(8) *University of Pennsylvania Law Review* 907–23.

Ganz, M, *What is Public Narrative: Self, Us & Now*, Working Paper, 2009.

Gearty, C, 'British Torture, Then and Now: The Role of Judges' (2020) 84(1) *Modern Law Review* 118–54.

Gold, R, 'Roles in Sociological Field Observation' (1958) 36(3) *Social Forces* 217–23.

Goode, R, 'The Operation of a Law Centre – The UK Experience' (1975) 1(10) *Legal Service Bulletin* 253–57.

Goriely, G, 'Rushcliffe Fifty Years On: The Changing Role of Civil Legal Aid Within the Welfare State' (1994) 21(4) *Journal of Law and Society* 545–66.

Goriely, T, 'Law for the Poor: The Relationship between Advice Agencies and Solicitors in The Development of Poverty Law' (1996) 3:1-2 *International Journal of the Legal Profession* 215–48.

Grace, C and LeFevre, P, 'Draining the Swamp' (1985) 7(1) *Law & Policy* 97–112.

Graffin, N, 'The Emotional Impacts of Working as an Asylum Lawyer' (2019) 38(1) *Refugee Survey Quarterly* 30–54.

Hagan, J, Levi, R and Ferrales, G, 'Swaying the Hand of Justice: The Internal and External Dynamics of Regime Change at the International Criminal Tribunal of the Former Yugoslavia' (2006) 31(3) *Law and Social Inquiry* 585–616.

Halliday, S, 'After Hegemony? The Varieties of Legal Consciousness Research' (2019) 28(6) *Social and Legal Studies* 859–78.

Halliday, T, 'Politics and Civic Professionalism: Legal Elites and Cause Lawyers' (1999) 24(4) *Law and Social Inquiry* 1013–60.

Hansen, O, 'A Future for Legal Aid?' (1992) 19(1) *Journal of Law and Society* 85–100.

Hilbink, T, 'You Know the Type: Categories of Cause Lawyering' (2004) 29 (3) *Law & Social Inquiry* 657–98.

Hilson, C 'New Social Movements: The Role of Legal Opportunity', (2002) 9(2) *Journal of European Public Policy* 238–55.

Hunter, K, 'Narrative Literature and the Clinical Exercise of Practical Reason' (1996) 21(3) *The Journal of Medicine and Philosophy* 303–20.

James, C, 'Seeing Things as We Are: Emotional Intelligence and Clinical Legal Education (2005) 8 *International Journal of Clinical Legal Education* 123–49.

Kadowaki, J, 'Maintaining Professionalism: Emotional Labor Among Lawyers as Client Advisors' (2015) 22(3) *International Journal of the Legal Profession* 323–45.

Kennedy, D, 'Legal Education and the Reproduction of Hierarchy' (1982) 32 *Journal of Legal Education* 591–615.

Kennedy, D, 'The Responsibilities of Lawyers for the Justice of Their Causes' (1987) 18 *Texas Tech University Law Review* 1157–63.

Klarman, M, 'Brown and Laurence (*and* Goodridge)' (2005) 104(3) *Michigan Law Review* 431–89.

Larcombe, W and Fethers, K, 'Schooling the Blues: An Investigation Of Factors Associated With Psychological Distress Among Law Students' (2013) 36(2) *UNSW Law Journal*, 390–436.

Leask, P, 'Law Centres in England and Wales' (1985) 7(1) *Law and Policy* 61–76.

Leat, D, 'The Rise and Rôle of the Poor Man's Lawyer' (1975) 2(2) *British Journal of Law and Society* 166–81.

Liu, S and Halliday, T, 'Political Liberalism and Political Embeddedness: Understanding Politics in the Work of Chinese Criminal Defense Lawyers' (2011) 45(4) *Law & Society Review* 831–66.

Lopez, G, 'Living and Lawyering Rebelliously' (2005) 73 *Fordham Law Review* 2041–54.

Lowenstein, D and Waggoner, W, 'Neighborhood Law Offices: The New Wave in Legal Services for the Poor' (1967) 80(4) *Harvard Law Review* 805–50.

Luban, D, 'The Moral Complexity of Cause Lawyers Within the State' (2012) 81 *Fordham Law Review* 705–14.

Manderson, D and Turner, S, 'Coffee House: Habitus and Performance Among Law Students' (2006) 31(3) *Law and Social Inquiry* 649–76.

Mathew, T, 'Legal Aid and Legal Advice in England and Wales, The Rushcliffe Committee Report' (1946) 7(1) *The Howard Journal of Criminal Justice* 39–44.

McEvoy, K, 'Cause Lawyering, Political Violence, and Professionalism in Conflict' (2019) 46(4) *Journal of Law and Society* 529–58.

McEvoy, K, 'What Did the Lawyers Do During the War?' (2011) 74(3) *Modern Law Review* 350–84.

McGarty, C, Thomas, E, Lala, G, Smith, L and Bliuc, A, 'New Technologies, New Identities and the Growth of Mass Opposition in the Arab Spring' (2014) 35(6) *Political Psychology* 725–40.

McLaughlin, J, 'Risky Professional Boundaries: Articulations of the Personal Self by Antenatal Screening Professionals' (2003) 17(4) *Journal of Health Organization Management* 264–79.

Meyerson, D and Scully, M, 'Tempered Radicalism and the Politics of Ambivalence and Change' (1995) 6(5) *Organization Science* 585–600.

Miles, J, Balmer, N and Smith, M, 'When Exceptional is the Rule: Mental Health, Family Problems and the Reform of Legal Aid in England and Wales' (2012) 24(3) *Child and Family Law Quarterly* 320–32.

Minow, M and Spelman, E, 'In Context' (1990) 63(6) *Southern California Law Review*, 1597–1652.

Minow, M, 'Political Lawyering: An Introduction' (1996) 31(2) *Harvard Civil Rights-Civil Liberties Law Review* 287–96.

Misselbrook, S, 'Political Litigation and the Politics of Litigation' (2016) 22 *Auckland University Law Review* 341.

Moorhead, R, Sherr, A and Paterson, A, 'Contesting Professionalism: Legal Aid and Non Lawyers in England and Wales' (2003) 37(4) *Law & Society Review* 765–808.

Moorhead, R, 'Third Way Regulation? Community Legal Service Partnerships' (2001) 64(4) *Modern Law Review* 543–62.

Murgatroyd, S and Rees, W, 'The Radical Estate? A Response to Bankowski and Mungham's Critique of Curriculum Developments in Legal Education' (1977) 11(3) *The Law Teacher* 151–61.

Nash, K 'The 'Cultural Turn' in Social Theory: Towards a Theory of Cultural Politics (2001) 35(1) *Sociology* 77–92.

Nason, S and Sunkin, M, 'The Regionalisation of Judicial Review: Constitutional Authority, Access to Justice and Specialisation of Services in Public Law' (2013) 76(2) *Modern Law Review* 223–53.

Nicolson, D, 'Education, Education, Education: Legal, Moral, and Clinical' (2008) 42(2) *Law Teacher* 145–72.

Niemi, P, 'Medical Students' Professional Identity: Self-Reflection in the Pre-Clinical Years' (1997) 31(6) *Medical Education* 408–15.

Paik, A, Southworth, A and Heinz, J, 'Lawyers of the Right: Networks and Organization' (2007) 32(4) *Law and Social Inquiry* 883–917.

Papacharissi, Z, 'Without You I'm Nothing: Performances of Self on Twitter' (2012) 6 *International Journal of Communication* 1989–2006.

Passy, F and Giugni, M, 'Life-Spheres, Networks, and Sustained Participation in Social Movements: A Phenomenological Approach to Political Commitment' (2000) 15(1) *Sociological Forum* 117–44.

Patterson, M and Monroe, K, 'Narrative in Political Science' (1998) 1 *Annual Review of Political Science* 315–31.

Pleasence, P and Balmer, N, 'The Audacity of Justice: Recession, Redundancy, Rights and Legal Aid' (2010) 9(4) *Social Policy and Society* 475–488.

Polletta, F, Chen, P, Gardner, B and Motes, A, 'The Sociology of Storytelling' (2011) 37 *Annual Sociological Review* 109–30.

Poole, A, 'Human Rights in Great Britain' (2016) 21(3) *Judicial Review* 162–73.

Quigley, W, 'Letter to a Law Student Interested in Social Justice' (2007) 1(1) *DePaul Journal for Social Justice* 7–22.

Ramsden, M and Gledhill, C, 'Defining Strategic Litigation' (2019) 38(4) *Civil Justice Quarterly* 407–38.

Ravalier, J, McVicar, A and Munn-Giddings, C, 'Public Service Stress and Burnout Over Twelve Months' (2014) 64(7) *Journal of Occupational Medicine* 521–23.

Richards, D, 'Elite Interviewing: Approaches and Pitfalls' (1996) 16(3) *Politics* 199–204.

Rhode, D, 'Access to Justice: Connecting Principles to Practice' (2004) 17 *Georgetown Journal of Legal Ethics* 369–422.
Rhode, D, 'Public Interest Law: The Movement at Midlife' (2008) 60(6) *Stanford Law Review* 2027–84.
Rosen, R, 'On the Social Significance of Critical Lawyering' (2000) 3(2) *Legal Ethics* 169–78.
Sajo, A, 'Emotions in Constitutional Institutions' (2016) 8(1) *Emotion Review* 44–49.
Samuels, H, 'Feminist Activism, Third Party Interventions and the Courts' (2005) 13 *Feminist Legal Studies* 15–42.
Samuels, H, 'Public Interest Litigation and the Civil Society Factor' (2018) 38(4) *Legal Studies* 1–14.
Saunders, S, Kitzinger, J and Kintzinger, C, 'Anonymising interview data: challenges and compromise in practice' (2015) 15(5) *Qualitative Research* 616–32.
Scheingold, S and Bloom, A, 'Transgressive Cause Lawyering: Practice Sites and the Politicization of the Professional' (1998) 5(2-3) *International Journal of the Legal Profession* 209–53.
Schneyer, T, 'Moral Philosophy's Standard Conception of Legal Ethics' (1984) *Wisconsin Law Review* 1529–73.
Seeman, M, 'Alienation Studies' (1975) 1 *Annual Review of Sociology* 91–123.
Seeman, M, 'On the Meaning of Alienation' (1959) 24(6) *American Sociological Review* 783–91.
Selleck, C, 'Ethnographic Chats: A Best of Both Method for Ethnography' (2017) 30 *SKY Journal of Linguistics* 151–62.
Shaffer, T, 'Legal Ethics and the Good Client' (1986) 36 *Catholic University Law Review* 319–30.
Sheldon, K and Krieger, L, 'Does Legal Education Have Undermining Effects on Law Students? Evaluating Changes in Motivation, Values and Wellbeing' (2004) 22 *Behavioural Sciences and the Law* 261–86.
Sherr, A and Webb, J, 'Law Students, the External Market and Socialization: Do We Make Them Turn to the City?' (1989) 16(2) *Law and Society* 225–49.
Smith, R, 'Clinics in a Cold Climate: Community Law Centres in England and Wales' (1997) 35(3) *Osgoode Hall Law Journal* 895–924.
Smith, R, 'Human Rights and Access to Justice' (2007) 14(3) *The International Journal of the Legal Profession* 261–280.
Smith, R, 'Learning from the Abolitionists, The First Social Movement' (2012) 345(7888) *British Medical Journal* 56–58.
Smith, R, 'Legal Aid on an Ebbing Tide' (1996) 23(4) *Journal of Law and Society* 570–79.
Somers, M, 'The Narrative Constitution of Identity: A Relational and Network Approach' (1994) 23(5) *Theory and Society* 605–49.
Sommerlad, H and Sanderson, P, 'Social Justice on the Margins: The Future of the Not For Profit Legal Sector as Providers of Legal Advice in England and Wales' (2013) 35(3) *Journal of Social Welfare and Family Law* 305–27.
Sommerlad, H, 'The Commercialisation of Law and the Enterprising Legal Practitioner: Continuity and Change' (2011) 18(1) *International Journal of the Legal Profession* 73–108.
Sommerlad, H, 'I've Lost The Plot: An Everyday Story of the Political Legal Aid Lawyer' (2001) 28(3) *Journal of Law and Society* 335–60.
Sommerlad, H, 'Managerialism and the Legal Profession: A New Professional Paradigm' (1995) 2:2-3 *International Journal of the Legal Profession* 159–85.
Sommerlad, H, 'Reflections on the Reconfiguration of Access to Justice' (2008) 15(3) *International Journal of the Legal Profession* 179–93.
Sommerlad, H, 'Some Reflections on Citizenship, Access to Justice and the Reform of Legal Aid' (2004) 31(3) *Journal of Law and Society* 345–68.
Southworth, A, 'Lawyers and the "Myth of Rights" in Civil Rights and Poverty Practice' (1999) 8 *Boston University Public Interest Law Journal* 469–511.
Southworth, A, 'What is Public Interest Law? Empirical Perspectives on an Old Question' (2013) 62(2) *De Paul Law Review* 493–518.
Straw, A, 'Future Proofing: Running Human Rights Arguments Under the Common Law' (2015) 20(4) *Judicial Review* 193–200.

Tomlinson, J, 'Crowdfunding Public Interest Judicial Reviews: A Risky New Resource and the Case for a Practical Ethics' (2019) *Public Law* 166–85.

Tomlinson, J, Valizade, D, Muzio, D, Charlwood A and Aulakh S, 'Privileges and Penalties in the Legal Profession: An Intersectional Analysis of Career Progression' (2019) 70(3) *The British Journal of Sociology* 1043–66.

Tremblay, P, 'Acting "A Very Moral Type of God": Triage Among Poor Clients' (1999) 67(5) *Fordham Law Review* 2475–2532.

Trubeck, L, 'Public Interest Law: Facing the Problems of Maturity' (2011) 33 *University of Arkansas Law Review* 417–33.

Twining, W, 'Remembering 1972: The Oxford Centre in the Context of Developments in Higher Education and the Discipline of Law' (1995) 22(1) *Journal of Law and Society* 35–49.

Vanhala, L, 'Is Legal Mobilization for the Birds? Legal Opportunity Structures and Environmental Non-Governmental Organisations in the United Kingdom, France, Finland and Italy' (2017) 51(3) *Comparative Political Studies* 380–412.

Vanhala, L, Lambe, S and Knowles, R, '"Let Us Learn": Legal Mobilization for the Rights of Young Migrants to Access Student Loans in the UK' (2018) 10(3) *Journal of Human Rights Practice* 439–60.

Vaughan, S, Thomas, L and Young, A, 'Symbolism over Substance? Large Law Firms and Corporate Social Responsibility' (2015) 18(2) *Legal Ethics* 138–63.

Wardle, L, 'The Use and Abuse of "Cause Lawyering": The Bad Example of Roe v Wade' (2014) 35 *University of La Verne Law Review* 217–42.

Webber, F, 'Ian Macdonald QC 1939–2019: A Tribute' (2020) 84 *Socialist Lawyer* 20–23.

Westaby, C, 'Feeling Like a Sponge: The Emotional Labour Produced by Solicitors in Their Interactions with Clients Seeking Asylum' (2010) 17(2) *The International Journal of the Legal Profession* 153–74.

Westaby, C, 'A Qualitative Study of the Impact of Law Clinic's on Students' Perceptions of Emotional Labour Expectations' (2014) 48(3) *The Law Teacher* 248–80.

Wexler, S, 'Practicing Law for Poor People' (1970) 79 *Yale Law Journal* 1049–67.

Williamson, I and Cullingford, C, 'The Uses and Misuses of 'Alienation in the Social Sciences and Education' (1997) 45(3) *British Journal of Educational Studies* 263–75.

Wilson, R, 'The Role of Practice in Legal Education,' Working Paper, 2010.

White, L, Nickles, P and Cole, L, 'Creating Models for Progressive Lawyering in the 21st Century' (2001) 9(2) *Journal of Law and Policy* 297–334.

NEWSPAPERS, MAGAZINES, BLOGS, AND OTHER MEDIA

ActForTheAct, 'ActForTheAct Poster Campaign', Crowdfunder, 2015.

Bawdon, F, 'In Praise of Activist Human Rights Lawyers,' *Legal Voice*, 18 October 2016.

Bawdon, F, 'Legal Life Changers Spread their Wings,' *New Law Journal*, 27 July 2018.

Bennetto, J, 'Hypocrite lawyers are Attacked by Straw,' *The Independent*, 15 September 1999.

Bowcott, O, 'Cash Strapped Law Centre Turn Clients Away as Legal Aid Cuts Bite,' *The Guardian*, 18 September 2013.

Bowcott, O, 'Criminal Defence Solicitors May Be Extinct in Five Years,' *The Guardian*, 17 April 2018.

Bowcott, O, 'Thousands Left Homeless by Shortage of Legal Aid Lawyers, Say Charities,' *The Guardian*, 18 December 2016.

British Film Institute Archive, *North Kensington Law Centre Documentary*, BBC, 1973.

Bulman, M, 'Misleading and Dangerous: Home Office Condemned for Describing Solicitors Representing Migrants as Activist Lawyers,' *The Independent*, 29 August 2020.

Chapman, J, '£15m for Just One Firm on the Legal Aid Gravy Train: Scale of Taxpayers Bill Revealed as Coalition Vows to Save £200m,' *Daily Mail*, 4 June 2013.

Cross, M, 'Legal Aid's Founding Text Turns 70,' *The Law Society Gazette*, 28 May 2015.
Doughty Street Chambers, 'Using the Law as A Tool for Social Change,' 17 May 2018.
Downey, S, 'Legal Aid Agency Faces 100-firm Challenge over Criminal Contract Cuts Amid Whistleblower's Call for an External Investigation,' *Legal Business*, 8 November 2015.
Dyke, T, 'Memoirs of a Radical Lawyer,' *New Statesman*, 24 September 2009.
Fouzder, M, 'Legal Aid Cuts Creating New Advice Deserts,' *The Law Society Gazette*, 18 April 2016.
Fouzder, M, 'Judicial Review Panel Set for Evidence Deluge,' *Law Society Gazette*, 26 October 2020.
Grayling, C, 'The Judicial Review System is not a Promotional Tool for Countless Left-Wing Campaigners,' *The Daily Mail*, 11 September 2013.
Grierson, G, 'Access to Justice in Family Courts Inadequate,' *The Guardian*, 27 July 2018.
Hilborne, N, 'Legal Aid Lawyers Under Severe Pressure Because of Covid,' *Legal Futures*, 18 November 2020.
Howard, E, 'Going into Legal Aid Work is Career Suicide,' *The Guardian*, 6 January 2016.
Hussain, A, 'Legal Twitterati outrage over Home Office's activist lawyer tweet,' *Legal Cheek*, 27 August 2020.
James, S, 'At the Bar: Be Suspicious of People in Authority,' *Legal Action Group*, June 2020.
Johnson, D, 'Imagine Any MP Today Supporting Legal Aid Lawyers Being Paid 85 Per Cent of Assessed Standard Costs,' Legal Action Group, September 2020.
Lepper, J, 'Life After the Lobbying Act,' *The Charity Times*, 2015.
Lewis, O, 'Radical Lawyers, Law Centres and an Uncertain Future,' *The Justice Gap*, 28 March 2013.
Macdonald, M, 'Jobseekers Put to Test in Chambers Challenge: Trainee Barristers Seeking Entry to One of Britain's Most Radical Practices Face A Rigorous Examination,' *The Independent*, 19 April 1989.
Morgan, J, 'Are Practical Law Degrees the Future?' *The Times*, 24 May 2012.
Nason, S, 'Justice Outside London? An Update on 'Regional' Judicial Review,' *Constitutional Law Blog*, 16 November 2016.
Rowson, J, 'What is a Progressive?,' Open Democracy, 11 June 2015.
Tsang, L 'Law: Farewell to a Non Fat Cat,' *The Independent*, 25 February 1999.
Wagner, A, 'It's Not "Activist Lawyers" This Government Hates But the Laws Themselves,' *New Statesman*, 28 August 2020.
Williams, H, 'The Myth of Fat Cat Barristers,' *New Statesman*, 18 May 2012.
Winter, A, 'There is a Financial Case For Reversing Legal Aid Cuts – as Well as a Human One,' *Inside Housing*, 12 February 2020.
Yates, P, 'Excellence in Pro Bono: Freshfields' Work for Third-Party Interventions Picked up by Law Society Excellence Award,' *Law Society Gazette*, 4 November 2020.

LEGAL REPORTS, REVIEWS, AND GUIDES

American Bar Association, *American Bar Association Model Rules of Professional Conduct Rule 1.2(b)*, 1983.
Amnesty International, *Cuts That Hurt: The Impact of Legal Cuts in England on Access to Justice*, 2017.
The Bar Council, *Justice: A Precious Asset, Bar Council Party Conference Briefing 2015*, 2015.
Baker, L and Lewis, M, *Detained Fast Track Litigation Case Study: Detention Action Using the Law for Social Change*, Institute for Voluntary Action Research, 2017.
The Bingham Centre for the Rule of Law, Public Law Project, and JUSTICE, *Judicial Review and The Rule of Law: An Introduction to the Criminal Justice and Courts Act 2015, Part 4 – Summary for Charities and Not-for-Profit Organisations*, 2015.
Bondy, V, Platt, L and Sunkin, M, *The Value and Effects of Judicial Review: The Nature of Claims, Their Consequences and Outcomes,* The Public Law Project, 2015.
Boon, A, *Legal Ethics at the Initial Stage: A Model Curriculum*, The Law Society, 2010.

Byrom, N, *The Impact of Cuts to Civil Legal Aid on Practitioners and Their Clients*, The Warwick Centre for Human Rights, 2013.

Child Rights International Network, *Children's Rights: A Guide to Strategic Litigation*, 2014.

Council of Bars and Law Societies of Europe, *Council of Bars and Law Societies of Europe's Charter of Core Principles Explanatory Note*, 2008.

Ekins, R and Gee, G, *Judicial Power: 50 Problematic Cases*, Policy Exchange and Judicial Power Project, 2016.

Equality and Human Rights Commission, *Access to Legal Aid for Discrimination Cases*, June 2019.

The Fabian Society, *The Right to Justice: The Final Report of the Bach Commission*, 2017.

Flood, J and Hviid, M, *The Cab Rank Rule: Its Meaning and Purpose in the New Legal Services Market*, Legal Services Board, 2013.

Hynes, S, *LASPO Review: Revealing the Damage*, Legal Action Group, February 2019.

JUSTICE, *To Assist the Court: Third Party Interventions in the Public Interest*, JUSTICE and Freshfields Bruckhaus Deringer, 2016.

Kinghan, J and Vanhala, L, *Supporting Systems Changers Through the Use of Collaborative Legal Approaches*, The Public Law Project, 2020.

Kirby, P, *Leading People: The Educational Background of the UK Professional Elite*, The Sutton Trust, 2016.

Lambe, S and Gallagher, C, *How To Be Strategic About Strategic Litigation*, The Public Law Project, 2013.

Law Centres Network, *Law Centres Network Challenges Government on Legal Aid to Prevent Homelessness*, 18 May 2018.

The Law Society, *The Law Society of England and Wales Pro Bono Manual: A Practical Guide and Toolkit for Lawyers*, The Law Society, 2010.

The Law Society of England and Wales, *Annual Report*, 1973.

The Law Society of Northern Ireland, *Legal Aid Lobbying Pack*, 2015.

LawWorks, *The LawWorks Clinics Network Reports*, 2015.

Legal Action Group, *Justice Committee Announces Inquiry into the Future of Legal Aid*, September 2020.

Low-Beer, Ravi, Hickman, J, Lukes, A, Pickup, A, Marshall, E and Tomlinson, J, *Public Law and Clinical Legal Environments*, The Public Law Project, 2018.

Minnoch, C and Teather, R, *The Time has Come to Bring the Legal Aid Sector's Sustainability Issues into the Public Domain*, Legal Action Group, July 2020.

Moorhead, R, Hinchly, V, Parker, C, Kershaw, D and Holm S, *Designing Ethics Indicators for Legal Service Provision*, The Legal Service Board, 2012.

Organ, J and Sigafoos, J, *The Impact of LASPO on Routes to Access to Justice*, The Equality and Human Rights Commission, 2018.

Pickup, A, *Top Legal Aid and Access to Justice Cases of Recent Years*, The Public Law Project, 2018.

Pleasance, P, Buck, A, Balmer, N, O'Grady, A, Genn, H, and Smith, M, *Causes of Action: Civil Law and Social Justice*, Legal Services Commission, 2006.

The Public Law Project, *Public Law in Clinical Legal Environments*, 2018.

The Public Law Project, *Statement on the Independent Review of Administrative Law Process*, October 2020.

Smith, D, Ashton, K and Bridges L, *Third Party Interventions in Judicial Review: An Action Research Study*, The Public Law Project, 2001.

Smith, R and Paterson, A, *Face to Face Legal Services and Their Alternatives: Global Lessons from the Digital Revolution*, The Nuffield Foundation, 2014.

Smith, R, *Experience in England and Wales: Test Case Strategies, Public Interest Litigation, The Human Rights Act and Legal NGOs*, Essex Human Rights Centre, 2013.

Snowden, M, *Discussion Paper: Overcoming barriers to public interest litigation in Scotland*, Human Rights Consortium Scotland, 2018.

Society of Labour Lawyers, *Justice for All: Society of Labour Lawyers Report*, Fabian Society, 1968.

Wilson, R and Rasmusen, J, *Promoting Justice: A Practical Guide to Strategic Human Rights Lawyering*, International Human Rights Law Group, 2001.

Vanhala, L and Kinghan, J, *Using the Law for Social Change, A Landscape Review*, The Baring Foundation, 2018.
Vanhala, L and Kinghan, J, *Using the Law to Address Unfair Systems: A Case Study of the Personal Independence Payments Legal Challenge*, The Baring Foundation, 2019.
Vanhala, L, *Framework for Better Use of Law by Voluntary Sector Organisations*, The Baring Foundation, 2016.
Vanhala, L, *Successful Use of Strategic Litigation on Issues Related to Discrimination and Disadvantage*, The Baring Foundation, 2016.
Young Legal Aid Lawyers, *Submission to the Justice Committee Inquiry on the Future of Legal Aid*, November 2020.
Young Legal Aid Lawyers, *Young Legal Aid Lawyers Covid-19 Report*, 2020.
Young Legal Aid Lawyers, *Young Legal Aid Lawyers: Social Mobility in a Time of Austerity*, 2018.

LEGAL CASES

ABC (AP) v Principal Reporter and Another [2020] UKSC 26.
In the Matter of an Application by the Northern Ireland Human Rights Commission for Judicial Review (Northern Ireland) [2018] UKSC 27.
IS v Director of Legal Aid Casework & Anor [2015] EWHC Admin 1965.
Joseph Knight, a Negro of Africa v. John Wedderburn of Ballindean (1778, unreported).
Law Centres Federation Limited v The Lord Chancellor [2018] EWHC Admin 1588.
R (Ben Hoare Bell Solicitors & Others) v Lord Chancellor [2015] EWHC Admin 523, [2015] 1 WLR 4175.
R (Howard League for Penal Reform and another) v Lord Chancellor (Equality and Human Rights Commission Intervening) [2017] EWCA Civ 244, [2017] 4 WLR 292.
R (Howard League for Penal Reform and Prisoners Advice Service) v the Lord Chancellor [2014] EWHC Admin 709.
R (Public Law Project) v Lord Chancellor [2015] EWCA Civ 1193, [2016] UKSC 39, [2016] AC 1531.
R (on the application of HC) v Secretary of State for the Home Department & Another [2013] EWHC Admin 982.
R (on the application of Miller) v The Prime Minister; Cherry and others v Advocate General for Scotland [2019] UKSC 41.
R (on the application of Prudential PLC) v Special Commissioner of Income Tax [2013] UKSC 1.
R (on the application of SG and others (previously JS and others)) v Secretary of State for Work and Pensions [2015] UKSC 16.
R (UNISON) v Lord Chancellor (Equality and Human Rights Commission and another intervening) (Nos 1 and 2) [2017] UKSC 51, [2017] 3 WLR 409.
R *(UNISON) v Lord Chancellor* [2017] UKSC 51.
RF v Secretary of State for Work and Pensions [2017] EWHC Admin 3375.
R v Khan [1996] 1 WLR 962.
Somerset v Stewart in England (1772) 98 ER 499.

MISCELLANEOUS

Georgetown Law School, 'Georgetown Law School Loan Repayment Assistance Program,' 2020.
Hill, H (@henrietta_hill), Twitter post, 19 January 2019.
Kilroy, C, 'Strategic Litigation: What is it? When and How to Use It,' Speech to the IPLA Conference, Doughty Street Chambers, 19 November 2019.
Kinghan, J, Fieldwork interview with Professor Sandy Fredman, 11 December 2017.
The Legal Education Foundation, 'Justice First Fellowship: Overview," 2020.

Lord Carloway, 'Constitutional Principle and the Rule of Law,' Lord Rodger Memorial Lecture for the Judiciary of Scotland, 29 October 2020.

Patrick, A (@Angela_Patrick), Twitter post, 19 January 2018.

Pinto, A, 'Bar Council Condemns Misleading Communication by Government,' *Bar Council Press Release*, 27 August 2020.

Spurrier, M, 'Address to the Young Legal Aid Lawyers Association,' 23 April 2015.

Spurrier, M, 'Keynote Address', Legal Aid Practitioners Group Conference, 16 October 2016.

Spurrier, M, 'Using the Law as A Tool for Social Change', Public Event held at Doughty Street Chambers, 17 May 2018.

Wagner, A (@AdamWagner1), Twitter post, 21 January 2018.

Wesley, A (@tired_lawyer), Twitter post, 21 January 2018.

Index

Lightning Source UK Ltd.
Milton Keynes UK
UKHW021401280721
387870UK00002B/73

9 781509 938094